The American Assembly, *Columbia University*
and
Council on Foreign Relations, Inc.

THE CHINA FACTOR:
SINO-AMERICAN RELATIONS
AND THE GLOBAL SCENE

Prentice-Hall, Inc., *Englewood Cliffs, New Jersey* A SPECTRUM BOOK

DS
779.27
C488

Library of Congress Cataloging in Publication Data
Main entry under title:

THE CHINA FACTOR

(A Spectrum Book)
At head of title: The American Assembly, Columbia
University and Council on Foreign Relations, Inc.
Includes bibliographical references and index.
 1. China—Foreign relations—1976-   —Con-
gresses.   2. China—Foreign relations—United
States—Congresses.   3. United States—Foreign
relations—China—Congresses.   I. Solomon, Richard
H., 1937-   .   II. American Assembly.   III. Coun-
cil on Foreign Relations.
DS779.27.C488   327.51   81-10660
                                    AACR2

ISBN 0-13-132704-6
ISBN 0-13-132696-1 {PBK.}

Editorial/production supervision by Betty Neville
Manufacturing buyer: Barbara A. Frick

10 9 8 7 6 5 4 3 2 1

This Spectrum Book can be made available to businesses and organizations at a special discount when ordered in large quantities. For more
information, contact:

> Prentice-Hall, Inc.
> General Book Marketing
> Special Sales Division
> Englewood Cliffs, New Jersey 07632

PRENTICE-HALL INTERNATIONAL, INC. (*London*)
PRENTICE-HALL OF AUSTRALIA PTY. LIMITED (*Sydney*)
PRENTICE-HALL OF CANADA, LTD. (*Toronto*)
PRENTICE-HALL OF INDIA PRIVATE LIMITED (*New Delhi*)
PRENTICE-HALL OF JAPAN, INC. (*Tokyo*)
PRENTICE-HALL OF SOUTHEAST ASIA PTE. LTD. (*Singapore*)
WHITEHALL BOOKS LIMITED (*Wellington, New Zealand*)

3632

Table of Contents

ROMANIZATION OF CHINESE NAMES

In 1979 the Chinese government adopted a phonetic or *pinyin* system of Romanized spelling of Chinese names to replace the Wade-Giles system long used in the West. We have used this new system for all names in this volume except the most familiar place names such as Peking and Canton.

Pinyin	*Wade-Giles*
Beijing	Peking
Baoshan	Pao-shan
Chungching	Chungking
Deng Xiaoping	Teng Hsiao-p'ing
Fujian Province	Fukien Province
Geng Biao	Keng Piao
Gulf of Bohai	Gulf of Pohai
Hua Guofeng	Hua Kuo-feng
Huang Hua	Huang Hua
Jiang Qing	Chiang Ch'ing
Kwangzhou	Canton
Liu Shaoqi	Liu Shao-ch'i
Lin Biao	Lin Piao
Mao Zedong	Mao Tse-tung
Mao Hanying	Mao Han-ying
Peng Dehuai	P'eng Teh-huai
Qing Dynasty	Ch'ing Dynasty
Wang Youping	Wang Yu-p'ing
Zhou Enlai	Chou En-lai
Zhang Caiqian	Chang Tsai-jian
Zhao Ziyang	Chao Tzu-yang

Preface

During the decade of the 1970s the United States and the People's Republic of China resumed an association which had lapsed for over twenty years and established normal diplomatic relations. In the first few years of this new relationship, many actions, whose consequences for other aspects of the international scene need to be thoroughly examined, have been set in motion by both nations.

Both the Council on Foreign Relations and The American Assembly believed it was important that the United States should pause in the course of developing its relations with the People's Republic of China to explore in greater detail where those relations might be leading us, the impact on our national interests in other parts of the world, and the options open to us as we pursue the normalization process.

Accordingly, the Council and the Assembly undertook jointly to sponsor a project which would treat these issues in greater depth. Dr. Richard H. Solomon, head of the Social Science Department at the Rand Corporation, was retained as director and editor of this undertaking. Under his editorial supervision, background papers on various interrelated issues were prepared. From March 19 to 22, 1981, a group of distinguished Americans met at Arden House in Harriman, New York to discuss the papers and the general subject of Chinese-American relations.

Those background papers have been compiled for the present volume, which is published as a stimulus to further thinking and discussion about this subject among informed and concerned citizens. We hope that this book will serve to evoke a broader national consensus for policies with respect to all dimensions of what we have called "The China Factor."

Funding for this project was provided by the Ford Foundation, the Henry R. Luce Foundation, and the Rockefeller Foundation, for whose timely assistance we are most grateful. The opinions expressed in this volume are those of the individual authors and not necessarily those of the sponsors nor of the Council on Foreign

Relations or The American Assembly, which do not take stands on
the issues they present for public discussion.

Winston Lord   William H. Sullivan
President   *President*
Council on Foreign Relations   The American Assembly

Richard H. Solomon

1

The China Factor
in America's Foreign Relations

Perceptions and Policy Choices

"The Week That Changed the World"?

On February 21, 1972 President Richard M. Nixon and
a delegation of thirteen American officials, including Secretary
of State William Rogers and National Security Adviser Henry
Kissinger, arrived in Peking for a week of talks with Communist Party Chairman Mao Zedong [1] and Premier Zhou Enlai.
Accompanied by a press pool of eighty-seven journalists, television commentators, and broadcast technicians, the President
and his party conducted seven days of private discussions with

[1] See the section Romanization of Chinese Names, which immediately follows
the Table of Contents.

RICHARD H. SOLOMON *directs The Rand Corporation's research program on
International Security Policy issues, and also heads the Social Science Department. From 1966 to 1971 he was professor of political science at the
University of Michigan. He subsequently served as senior staff member for
Asian Affairs on the National Security Council, from 1971 to 1976. In this
capacity he participated in the normalization of U.S.–PRC relations, making nine official trips to China. His publications include* Mao's Revolution
and the Chinese Political Culture, A Revolution Is Not a Dinner Party,
and Asian Security in the 1980s.

the leaders of the People's Republic of China (PRC)—"Communist China," or "Red China," as it still was referred to in many circles. Satellite ground stations in Peking and Shanghai beamed television coverage of the President's visits to the Great Wall, Ming Tombs, and the Forbidden City to a world-wide audience estimated to be in the hundreds of millions. As the American people turned on their television sets for the morning news, they saw live evening scenes of official banquets and revolutionary Peking opera in the Great Hall of the People.

At the end of the week a joint communiqué was issued in Shanghai (see Appendix 1) that at once spelled out continuing differences between China and the United States and established the basis for normalizing bilateral relations between them. Guidelines were established for gradually defusing the issue of Taiwan and developing trade and cultural contacts between the two countries; and both sides expressed the intention to oppose any state seeking to establish "hegemony" in the Asia-Pacific region. In the elation of the hour, President Nixon asserted that this was "a week that changed the world"; an effort by the leaders of the world's most populous nation and the most wealthy to "bridge a gulf of almost 12,000 miles and twenty-two years of noncommunication and hostility" that had riven the Asian political landscape since the Korean War.

Six years later another American President, Jimmy Carter, completed the formal process of normalizing Sino-American relations. Mao Zedong and Zhou Enlai had passed away, but a new Communist Party Chairman, Hua Guofeng, announced with President Carter, on December 15, 1978, the intention to establish diplomatic relations between the United States and the PRC by the first of the new year. America's official relations with the government of the Republic of China on Taiwan were severed on January 1, 1979 and replaced with an unofficial "Institute" to maintain contact with the island's authorities and people. The residual U.S. military presence on the island was gradually withdrawn amidst Chinese expressions of a desire to achieve a peaceful "reunification" between the island and the mainland (rather than Taiwan's "liberation"). The Carter administration and the U.S. Congress, in the Taiwan Relations Act (see Appendix 4), affirmed America's interest in a peaceful resolution of Taiwan's future and the intention to continue to sell defensive armaments to the island to enable it to maintain a "sufficient self-defense capability."

In mid-January 1979, China's leading political figure of the hour, Vice Premier Deng Xiaoping, visited Washington to celebrate completion of the process of normalizing U.S.–PRC relations. During his stay Deng warned of the dangers of Soviet "hegemony" and hinted darkly that China would have to "teach a lesson" to Moscow's ally Hanoi for its recent invasion of Kampuchea (Cambodia). Within a month of Deng's return to Peking, the PRC initiated a month-long border war against Vietnam; and two weeks after the fighting subsided, Peking abrogated the Sino-Soviet Treaty of Alliance and Friendship of 1950, although—as William Hyland explores in chapter 5— PRC leaders also initiated a dialogue with Moscow designed to explore ways of reducing Sino-Soviet tensions.

In August 1979, Vice President Mondale reciprocated Deng Xiaoping's visit with a trip to Peking. In a speech to Peking University students, the Vice President expressed the view that "any nation which seeks to weaken or isolate China in world affairs assumes a stance counter to American interests." Not long thereafter, in January 1980, Secretary of Defense Harold Brown visited Peking amidst concerns about the just-initiated Soviet invasion of Afghanistan. He explored possibilities for security cooperation between the two countries. The Carter administration's prohibition on sales of military hardware to China was modified to permit transfers of nonlethal technology and defense materiel such as transport aircraft and communications equipment.

Thus by 1980, America's relations with the People's Republic of China had advanced on a broad front. Commercial exchanges, which were nonexistent a decade earlier, had grown to nearly $5 billion per year. (Trade with Taiwan, by this time, had surpassed $11 billion.) More than one thousand delegations from the PRC, totalling over five thousand people, had come to the United States in 1980 alone to meet official counterparts, inspect factories and farms, and visit research institutions and universities. More than sixty thousand Americans visited the PRC in 1980. And over five thousand students from China were now enrolled in scientific and technical programs in American schools and universities—alongside more than fifteen thousand students from Taiwan. Senior Chinese and American officials were conducting regular consultations on a broad range of foreign policy issues; and the first steps had been taken toward low-level collaboration on defense matters.

Yet as the year progressed, notes of uncertainty were introduced into the future development of U.S.–PRC relations. In May, Republican presidential candidate Ronald Reagan criticized the Carter administration's arrangements for normalizing relations with Peking. Reagan said he was considering the restoration of official dealings with Taiwan, perhaps by establishing a liaison office in Taipei with much the same character as the missions Peking and Washington had maintained before full normalization. In August, candidate Reagan sent his vice presidential running mate, George Bush, to Peking to explain his position on China policy. Bush was subject to pressure tactics during his visit, and on his departure PRC media warned against any U.S. administration adopting a "two Chinas" policy. Upon Bush's return, Reagan reiterated that he would not pretend that America's relations with Taiwan were unofficial. He stressed his support for a policy of selling defensive weaponry to Taiwan, as provided for by the Taiwan Relations Act passed by Congress shortly after the normalization of U.S.–PRC relations.

Peking's media attacked candidate Reagan, asserting that he intended to "turn back the clock" on relations with China. By year's end, however, the now-elected Reagan told *Time* magazine that the future course of his administration's China policy would "take a great deal of study." When asked whether he would sell lethal weaponry to the PRC, Reagan commented that China "is a country whose government subscribes to an ideology based on a belief in destroying governments like ours." He stressed an interest in developing friendly relations with the PRC, but said he did not want to proceed so fast in the defense field that "some day weapons we might have provided will be shooting at us." Within five months of Reagan's inauguration, however, the President had sent his secretary of state, Alexander Haig, to China to confirm the U.S.–PRC strategic relationship. Haig announced in Peking that the Reagan administration was prepared to heighten defense cooperation by considering sales of offensive weaponry to the PRC. Press leaks at the time revealed that the U.S. and China were already jointly monitoring Soviet missile tests—a contribution to SALT verification. And Secretary Haig indicated that he foresaw active Sino-American collaboration on such foreign policy problems as the Soviet interventions in Afghanistan and Indochina.

Issues in the Development of U.S.–PRC Relations

Was President Nixon's visit to China in 1972 "a week that changed the world"? There is no doubt that the process of normalizing Sino-American relations captured the imagination of the world and the American people—from the mass media hoopla which surrounded "ping-pong diplomacy" in the spring of 1971 and the intrigue of Henry Kissinger's secret visit to Peking in July which initiated the official dialogue, through public fascination with acupuncture and panda bears, to prospects for trade with a country representing nearly a quarter of humankind. Yet China has long been larger than life in the American imagination.

The dramatic and unexpected transformation in America's relations with the People's Republic of China during the 1970s, from enmity to cooperation, also had a powerful impact on world-wide perceptions of international relations: the "Nixon shock" effect on the Japanese; the consternation of Communist leaderships in North Korea and North Vietnam which were still embroiled in conflicts with the United States; and the concerns in Moscow about the sudden coalescence of an "anti-Soviet" entente of China, the United States, Japan, and America's allies in Southeast Asia and Europe which would encircle the USSR on three frontiers.

Despite the powerful impact on attitudes and perceptions brought about by these developments, however, a decade after the onset of normalization we are only beginning to acquire some perspective on the real significance of America's new relationship with China. This volume is designed to provide the assessments of a group of well-informed and seasoned participant-analysts of international affairs of the impact of the Sino-American rapprochement on the global scene. With the perspective of ten years of efforts to normalize U.S.–PRC relations, and China's own strivings since the early 1970s to reestablish a position for itself in the international community, the following chapters evaluate the significance of the China factor in world affairs: its effect on the Sino–Soviet–U.S. strategic balance; on the politics of the "Third World" of developing countries; on the East Asian region; on Europe, both East and West; and on the international economy. The objective of these assessments is to reach some judgments about the meaning of the U.S.–PRC relationship for America's international relations and national security planning, to weigh the China factor as one element in U.S. foreign policy.

Four themes or issue areas emerge from chapters that follow this introductory overview which underscore the uncertainties and problems that will shape the future development of U.S.–PRC relations.

China is smaller in life than in our imaginations. The distant and esoteric China that has long excited American imaginations—either as an enduring empire of cultural treasures, a potential market of hundreds of millions of customers, or a hostile and threatening revolutionary power—is seen at close range to be burdened with its past and the realities of an agricultural economy. China now seems far more limited in its international outreach than in decades past when we knew it through the distant chanting of strident revolutionary slogans, when it sought to be a model of global social revolution and the leader of the "newly emerging forces" of the Third World.

This is hardly to say that China is an irrelevant factor on the world scene, but only that its impact is more modest than we might have imagined in past days of confrontation. Our objective in this volume is to evaluate the real significance of the PRC's international role and domestic development potential, and to see what opportunities (or risks) exist in Sino-American cooperation on matters of foreign policy, national security, and economic and social development.

Normal Sino-American relations are still fragile. Despite the profound transformation of the 1970s in relations between the United States and the People's Republic of China, there are a variety of factors which limit, or could upset, the further development of the U.S.–PRC tie. China's political scene continues to roil in the aftermath of the purging of the radical

"Gang of Four" in 1976. Under certain circumstances the opening to the U.S. initiated by Richard Nixon and Mao Zedong, and promoted by Deng Xiaoping and Jimmy Carter, could become a matter of controversy in Peking's political factionalism. If normalization seems to hold uncertain benefits for China's security needs or economic development plans, or if the numerous students now being educated abroad return to China with perspectives that are threatening to groups within the leadership, there could be serious debate about the wisdom of current policies which "tilt" China toward the U.S., Japan, and the countries of Western Europe.

On the American side of the equation, uncertainties within our leadership about the significance of the China factor in U.S. foreign and national security policies could induce drift into the relationship; and American businessmen, put off by the long delays and policy instabilities which are now seen to be a part of conducting commercial relations with the PRC (as is detailed by Dwight Perkins in chapter 4), could conclude that the China trade is too costly and uncertain to be worth the effort.

Taiwan remains a potentially explosive issue for both China and the United States. Future American arms sales to the island could generate a strong political reaction in Peking, especially if unbalanced by U.S. efforts to help China strengthen its defenses. And Peking's abandonment of current policies of moderation and restraint toward Taiwan could elicit a strong political reaction from the United States, especially from a Reagan administration concerned about upholding the credibility of America's support for allies and friends. Moreover, political instability on the island, precipitated by a succession struggle to the current leadership of Premier Chiang Ching-kuo, or a strong movement for Taiwanese independence, could force policy changes in Peking and Washington which would seriously strain the U.S.–PRC relationship.

There is uncertainty about the China factor in U.S. foreign policy. Despite the broad base of public support in the United States for normal bilateral relations with the PRC, the China factor has yet to become an integral part of American foreign policy. Should the United States build a political entente composed of China, Japan, and its allies in NATO and ASEAN (the Association of Southeast Asian Nations) to counter the expansionist impulses of the Soviet Union? Should the China relationship take precedence in our dealings with Asia; or are America's traditional alliance relationships with Japan, South Korea, the Philippines, Thailand, Australia, and New Zealand still central to our role in the region? Does a friendly China enable the United States to divert its resources and attention to highly threatened regions such as the Persian Gulf or Western Europe? And does China's status as a developing country give the U.S. greater "outreach" in the Third World?

The consensus of the contributors to this volume is that while a cooperative U.S.–PRC relationship is an important supplement to a more flexible American foreign policy, we cannot abrogate to the Chinese responsibility for the pursuit of U.S. interests in Asia or elsewhere. China is still a regional power of modest influence; and our allies look to the United States to play the primary role in maintaining a strategic balance against the Soviet Union and in minimizing the impact of the Sino-Soviet rivalry on Asia and other regions. The challenge to the U.S. in the 1980s is to integrate the China factor into our foreign relations without compromising the interests of other allied and friendly states.

There is a lack of direction to U.S.–PRC security cooperation. Parallel with the uncertainties surrounding the China factor in American foreign policy, there is deep division of opinion on the issue of how the China relationship affects America's national security and defense interests. In part this reflects the lack of a consensus within the American foreign policy "establishment" about how to deal with the world-wide Soviet challenge. Will U.S.–PRC security cooperation compromise prospects for detente with the Soviet Union and trap the United States in the Sino-Soviet feud? And will an active Sino-American security relationship undermine America's ties to its traditional allies and friends in Asia such as Japan and the states of ASEAN (Indonesia, Malaysia, the Philippines, Singapore, and Thailand)?

There is no more controversial aspect to the further development of U.S.–PRC relations than the matter of cooperation on defense issues. Some observers believe that American efforts to help China strengthen its military capabilities in the face of

Moscow's troop build-up along the Sino-Soviet frontier will increase China's security and caution the Soviet leadership. Others believe that such defense cooperation will incite Moscow and threaten the security interests of our other Asian allies and friends. Some analysts assert that the U.S.–PRC tie cannot be sustained in the absence of some concrete evidence of American willingness to help China deal with its needs to modernize an underdeveloped economy and obsolete and ineffectual defenses. After his visit to Peking in June 1981, Secretary of State Alexander Haig reaffirmed America's interest in a strong and secure China. He emphasized that defense cooperation between the U.S. and China, a country of a billion people, could not be subject to the veto of any Soviet objections.

Assuming that the Taiwan issue remains quiescent, the most difficult and controversial issue in Sino-American relations during the 1980s will be how to view the China factor in America's defense planning. As is suggested by Strobe Talbott in chapter 3, the development of this aspect of the Sino-American relationship is most likely to evolve in reaction to threatening initiatives of the Soviet Union. Yet this volume is designed to provide the background for a considered rather than a reactive approach to the development of this and other aspects of the U.S.–PRC relationship: to replace our fantasies about this remote and fascinating country with a realistic appraisal of what China and the new Sino-American relationship mean for the U.S. and the world.

America's Changeable China Moods

As every American child knows, if you dig a hole through the center of the earth, China will be on the other side. The very distance of the country, in both geographical and cultural terms, has given Americans a set of esoteric images of China and the Chinese for more than two centuries. This has been a land of cultured Confucian Mandarin officials in flowing silk robes, multitiered pagodas, hard-laboring peasants in terraced fields, and an exotic cuisine. There are, as well, dark images of China derived from the country's millennial poverty, periods of political turmoil, and recent decades of revolution and confrontation with the United States: hordes of "blue ant" laborers, rioting student Red Guards, and fanatical soldiers who attack in "human waves" and "brainwash" their enemies.

As Harold Isaacs observes in his classic study *Scratches on Our Minds,* "American images of the Chinese tend largely to come in jostling pairs. The Chinese are seen as a superior people and an inferior people; devilishly exasperating heathens and wonderfully attractive humanists; wise sages and sadistic executioners; thrifty and honorable men and sly and devious villains; comic opera soldiers and dangerous fighters." These contrasting images are associated with sharp changes in political mood and perception that have characterized two hundred years of American dealings with the Chinese.

During the American Revolution China's political institutions were viewed as a model worthy of emulation. The federal government's civil service examination system was patterned on China's imperial examinations for scholar-officials. This "age of respect," as Isaacs terms it, gave way to a time of contempt for China as the country degenerated into chaos during the nineteenth century.

Americans subsequently adopted a benevolent view of China during the days of Sun Yat-sen's Republican revolution in the 1910s and 1920s, an attitude reinforced by active American missionary work in China. An "age of admiration" characterized American attitudes during the period of the war against Japan when Chiang Kai-shek sought to lead his beleaguered and politically fragmented country against both the foreign invader and domestic revolutionaries. This perspective was replaced by disenchantment as Chiang lost the civil war against the Chinese Communists in the late 1940s. Sino-American relations then degenerated into more than two decades of hostility during the 1950s and 1960s as "Red China" allied itself with the Soviet Union in February 1950 and entered the Korean War in the fall of that year.

What perhaps will be seen as an "Age of Friendship" began in 1971 when President Nixon and Chairman Mao Zedong initiated the process of normalizing U.S.–PRC relations with Henry Kissinger's secret mission to Peking. Suddenly, images of "ping-pong diplomacy," the artistic wonders of China's imperial past, and opportunities for trade and tourism with a talented and hard-working people replaced the hostile visions

of marching hordes and rioting Red Guards which had dominated the cold war years and China's turbulent Cultural
Revolution. A truly remarkable transformation in attitudes
occurred during the 1970s which now provides an entirely new
basis for popular support of American China policy.

FROM INTERNATIONAL OUTLAW TO QUASI-ALLY

There have been three major and sequential changes in
American attitudes toward the PRC since its founding in 1949.
Beginning with the Korean War, and reinforced by the Taiwan
Strait crisis in 1958 and the Sino-Indian border war of 1962,
China was viewed as an international outlaw. Year after year
its efforts to replace the Republic of China on Taiwan as the
representative of China in the United Nations were defeated
by votes of the General Assembly. The American people supported the PRC's exclusion from the U.N., as indicated by the
public opinion data in Figure 1. By the spring of 1971, however, for the first time more Americans thought that Peking
should represent China in the U.N. than opposed (45 percent
to 38 percent), thus establishing the basis for acceptance of the
PRC's long-resisted admission in the fall of that same year. As
Henry Kissinger prepared to depart Peking on October 25, at
the end of his second (and first public) visit to the PRC, the
General Assembly voted to expel Taiwan from the China seat
and replace it with the People's Republic.

A second and subsequent change in American perceptions of
China has been the transformation from a tendency to view
the PRC in much the same unfavorable light as the Soviet
Union to a much more favorable view of China in and of itself,
and especially in comparison with the USSR. As is suggested
by the data in Figure 2, it took most of the 1970s for China to
free itself of the legacy of the cold war era alliance with the
Soviet Union and the fanaticism of the Cultural Revolution of
the 1960s in the eyes of the American people. In contrast, the
Soviet Union continues to be seen in a highly unfavorable
light.

This contemporary difference in perceptions of China relative to the Soviet Union is the basis for a third major change
in American attitudes toward China's security. As late as 1977

Fig. 1. American attitudes toward "Communist China's" admission to the United Nations, 1950–1971.

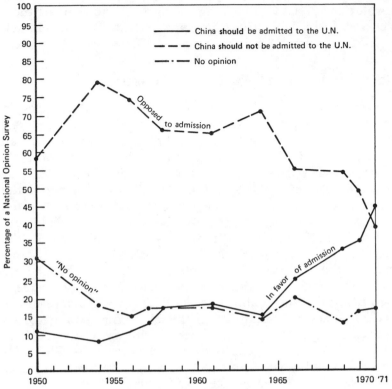

Data Source: *Public Opinion Quarterly,* Summer 1980.

only 11 percent of a national sample of Americans thought that the U.S. should help China build up its military strength so as to resist Soviet power and influence; 70 percent thought the U.S. should *not* help China; and 19 percent had no opinion. In 1980, not long after the Soviet invasion of Afghanistan, however, 47 percent thought the U.S. *should* help China in its security needs, while 40 percent objected (and 13 percent had no opinion).

Thus at the beginning of the 1980s the American public had come to see China as a friendly country in the world community and in its relations with the United States. Moreover, there was growing support, but divided opinion, on the issue of security

Fig. 2. *American attitudes toward China and the Soviet Union.*

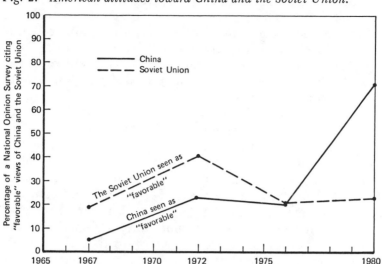

Data Sources: *The Gallup Opinion Index* and *Potomac Associates.*

cooperation with the PRC relative to the Soviet Union. This mix of attitudes provided a firm foundation for sustaining normal relations between China and the United States, and perhaps for making the China factor one element in America's foreign and security policies.

At the same time, we must not ignore the volatile quality of this highly changeable public mood. There is a high level of uninformed or mistaken opinion about China—as well as many other foreign policy issues—in the United States. A Potomac Associates poll in 1977 found that nearly 30 percent of a national opinion survey did not know whether "Mainland China" had a Communist government; and in 1980 nearly 60 percent believed erroneously that China was among America's fifteen largest trading partners (it ranked thirty-third in 1979; Taiwan was twentieth).

The American public's attitudes toward China, as with other countries, are strongly influenced by current events and—as Michel Oksenberg details in chapter 2—by presidential leadership. During the 1970s the public responded with enthusiasm to the Nixon administration's initiation of the normalization process; and China's leaders skillfully reinforced this inclination of the American people to view China as a friendly and cultured country. Thus, barring some presently unforeseen development, such as a change in American or Chinese policy on an issue like Taiwan or strongly negative views of the PRC disseminated from the White House or Department of State, we can anticipate a continuation of trends of the past decade in popular support for U.S.–PRC relations.

If there is any cause for concern, it is that the enthusiasm of the American public for contact with China will lead to unrealistic expectations and possible disappointments. The history of American views of China and the Chinese has been characterized by sharp swings of mood, and today's high hopes for U.S.–PRC relations in the areas of trade, cultural contacts, or even cooperation in foreign policy and national security activities may not be met. At the same time, students of China point out a tendency of the Chinese people to look to their friends for generous levels of support and assistance, to view a more developed and powerful country as a model for their own modernization—as they did of the West in the early decades of the twentieth century, or of the Soviet Union in the 1950s. There is thus the potential for renewed Chinese disenchantment with the relationship if expectations are not fulfilled.

Thus it is vital for the stability of the U.S.–PRC relationship that the expectations each country holds of the other be realistic, that sharp swings of mood characteristic of the past be minimized through policies of prudence and balance that reflect the limits, as well as the opportunities, of normal Sino-American relations.

What Kind of a Relationship with China Do We Want?

When the process of normalizing America's relations with the People's Republic of China began in 1971, there was in essence a clean slate on which to draw the dimensions of a new relationship. The two countries had severed virtually all forms of contact more than two decades earlier. There was no trade or social contact, only the military confrontation across the Taiwan Strait and political vituperation expressed in various international contexts. The sporadic and unproductive

U.S.–PRC diplomatic exchanges at Warsaw provided the only forum for direct and official contact—until the breakthrough meetings of January and February 1970.

ARE THE INTERNATIONAL OR BILATERAL ASPECTS
MOST IMPORTANT?

The small group of Chinese and American leaders who built the normalization dialogue clearly saw the reestablishment of Sino-American relations as a strategic maneuver which would contribute to the security of their respective countries. For PRC leaders, some prospect of resolving the issue of Taiwan, which had been the major obstacle to even minimal contacts between the United States and PRC for more than two decades, was critical for establishing the domestic political basis of a new relationship. Yet the national security implications of normalization were at the heart of the opening initiated by PRC leaders and the Nixon administration. As Mao Zedong told Richard Nixon and Henry Kissinger in various meetings during 1972 and 1973, "We can do without [Taiwan] for the time being, let it come after one hundred years." "Why such great haste? This issue [Taiwan] is not an important one. The issue of the international situation is the important one." "The small issue is Taiwan, the big issue is the world." Such bilateral dealings as cultural exchanges and trade were seen as merely the secondary and supporting elements of a major realignment of international relationships. They were vehicles for publicizing and gaining domestic political support for a dramatic reversal of U.S.–PRC relations "from confrontation to negotiation," and to supporting some degree of collaboration on international issues.

The American public's response to the normalization dialogue, however, tended to focus on the bilateral dimensions of the breakthrough: the backing away from two decades of political and military confrontation; the esoterica of the President and other senior officials visiting the Forbidden City and meeting with long-forbidding revolutionary leaders, acupuncture anesthesia for reporter James Reston, stricken with appendicitis during one of the first visits by an American journalist to Peking, and opportunities for tourism and trade. Only gradually as the 1970s progressed did the emergence of the "strategic triangle" and possibilities for "playing the China card" as an element in American foreign policy enter into the public's consciousness as significant aspects of this new relationship. (We can only speculate at the reactions of the Chinese people—still reeling from the political turmoil of the Cultural Revolution, and less intensively exposed to the symbolic trappings of normalization via television than the American public—to this dramatic about face in their country's political alignment.)

By the late 1970s, however, something of a reordering of priorities occurred in the emphasis of leaders in Washington and Peking on the international security aspects of the relationship relative to its bilateral significance. With the passing away of Mao in 1976 and the purge of the radical "Gang of Four" a few weeks later, China's leaders under Vice Premier Deng Xiaoping attempted to reduce some of the more provocative elements in China's confrontation with the Soviet Union (although the security threat from Moscow clearly endured). They shifted emphasis to highest priority on China's economic development, the establishment of social order through the re-creation of legal and educational systems, and experimentation with a broad range of "pragmatic" approaches to putting China back on the road to social and economic modernization.

This shift in China's political orientation intersected with a Carter administration in Washington that was divided of opinion about the strategic significance of the U.S.–PRC relationship. One perspective, expressed by Secretary of State Cyrus Vance, held that development of the U.S.–PRC bilateral relationship was a valuable end in itself, and that it was inappropriate to make America's relationship with China a function of the Soviet challenge. The other perspective, articulated by the President's national security adviser, Zbigniew Brzezinski, held that the U.S.–PRC relationship constituted one point of American pressure on the Soviet Union. After Moscow's invasion of Afghanistan, Brzezinski's stress on the security significance of the relationship prevailed, as was dramatized by Secretary of Defense Harold Brown's visit to Peking in early 1980.

Uncertainty about whether and how to emphasize the strategic aspects of the U.S.–PRC relationship returned as the Reagan administration assumed management of American foreign policy in early 1981. While the new President and his secretary of state, as noted earlier, expressed recognition of the strategic significance of the China connection, they gave little indication, beyond permitting arms sales, of how this aspect of the U.S.–PRC relationship was to be developed. And President Reagan's campaign comments about Taiwan, combined with various Chinese statements about the need to give priority to achieving the reunification of Taiwan with the mainland in the 1980s (as in a speech by Vice Premier Deng Xiaoping to a leadership conference in Peking on January 16, 1980), imply that the bilateral relationship could be strained in the coming decade if the Taiwan issue is not handled with great skill by both sides.

ACTIVE AND DIRECT OR PASSIVE AND INDIRECT BENEFITS
FROM THE RELATIONSHIP?

As one reviews the development of U.S.–PRC relations during the 1970s it is clear that both countries gained a great deal, in an indirect or passive sense, simply from the elimination of two decades of confrontation. The withdrawal of American military forces from Taiwan, essentially completed in the summer of 1975, freed up one strategic frontier for both China and the United States, imparting greater flexibility to defense planning and allowing resources to be focused on more threatened borders. U.S.–PRC normalization also removed a major source of strain from America's dealings with Japan and other allies who wished to establish political and trading relations with Peking. For the Chinese, as well, normalization with the U.S. ended a decade of hostility toward *both* the Soviet Union and United States, with all the political and military burdens of confronting both "superpowers" simultaneously, while also opening up prospects for the development of Sino-Japanese relations.

Little systematic thought has been given, however, to the active and direct opportunities for U.S.–PRC cooperation which are inherent in normalization. While Peking and Washington view each other as a strategic counterweight to the Soviet Union, in fact the impact of the U.S.–PRC relationship on the strategic balance remains more psychological than real. While normalization enabled China and the U.S. to focus attention, resources, and individual efforts on their real security problems, the two sides have only just begun to consider possibilities for developing an active and functioning security relationship. While there is a limited measure of foreign policy coordination between China and the United States, PRC leaders still occasionally describe the U.S. as a potentially threatening "superpower"; and many American officials are skeptical about Peking's proposal to form a united front against Soviet hegemony. And while trade and intellectual contacts between the two countries continue to grow, neither Americans nor Chinese have thought through the implications for the future of a situation in which a generation of Chinese scientists has been trained in the U.S., in which institutional forms such as legal norms or industrial management practices have been borrowed, or in which trade would account for a significant portion of urban China's grain or America's textile imports.

In a rather abstract sense, Americans and Chinese still have a choice about whether they wish to be adversaries, friends, or allies. In terms of public mood, it is clear that the transformation of the 1970s from hostility to friendship was welcomed in both countries. Yet the 1980s present the U.S. and China with very concrete policy choices that will affect whether the positive opportunities of normalization are developed, whether loose relations of "friendship" are maintained, whether under the press of world events the U.S.–PRC relationship is impelled from a political entente to a more explicit security alliance— or whether the relationship will be poisoned by an issue like Taiwan and either stagnate or even gradually drift back into a hostile confrontation.

As a basis for assessing the possible evolution of this relationship, we can identify four areas of policy choice that are most likely to shape its growth in the coming decade: foreign policy coordination; security cooperation; bilateral exchanges in a range of areas, including educational activities and trade; and the "joker" in the deck of China cards, the future of Taiwan.

FOREIGN POLICY COORDINATION

Since the Communist takeover of China in 1949, the PRC has gone through three major phases in its foreign policy: close alliance with the Soviet Union in the 1950s; a period in the 1960s when China confronted both the United States and the Soviet Union and tried to build a third pole in the international community around the "newly emerging forces" of the Third World; and the turn in the early 1970s toward reconciliation with the U.S., Japan, the states of Western Europe, and others who might help China oppose Soviet hegemony.

By any standard, the depth of this most recent transformation in PRC foreign policy is quite remarkable. After two decades of unremitting hostility toward the United States and its allies, China suddenly became a vocal supporter of the NATO alliance. After twenty years of attacking the U.S.–Japan Mutual Security Treaty, Chinese leaders began to tell the Japanese Communists, Socialists, and Liberal Democrats to strengthen their country's alliance with the U.S. PRC leaders became willing to make common cause with the U.S. in supporting the independence of Pakistan; and most ironic of all, after 1975 they began to urge the United States to resist Hanoi's ambition to dominate the Indochina Peninsula. And the Chinese have attempted, in less overt ways, to reinforce American diplomatic initiatives in the Middle East and in Southwest Asia. They also have come to see at least temporary common interest in stabilizing the Korean Peninsula, insuring the security of Thailand, and strengthening the ASEAN coalition.

This is not to slight the fact that significant and potentially serious areas of difference remain between the U.S. and China. Taiwan—as is detailed below—remains an issue on which we may only have temporarily set aside serious differences in order to pursue more pressing common objectives. China's offshore territorial claims on the continental shelf and in the South China Sea affect the interests of America's allies the Republic of Korea, Japan, and the Philippines, as well as friendly states such as Malaysia and Indonesia. And China's longer-term objectives toward Korea or Indochina may not serve American interests or those of our allies.

Yet the fact remains that in less than a decade Washington and Peking have moved along a spectrum in their foreign policies from antipathy to detente and rapprochement, through a phase of "even-handedness" in relations among the major powers, to a rather close alignment of foreign policies which implicitly forms an entente including Japan and the states of Western Europe which could resist political and military pressures from the Soviet Union. A further step in the development of this relationship would be toward the formation of an explicit alliance, but this would be a commitment to China's call for a world-wide "united front" against the Soviet Union that U.S. officials, thus far, have been unwilling to make. Such a development is likely to occur—as William Hyland suggests in chapter 5—only in the context of still greater Soviet pressures against American and Chinese security interests.

PRC leaders, most foreign observers agree, would far prefer "self-reliance" to alignment in their international relations, if not to be the leader of the Third World of developing states of Asia, Africa, and Latin America. Yet realities have imposed on China the need for coalition, if not alliance, with more powerful and economically developed states in order to attain a balance against its adversaries. Peking's foreign policy remains highly sensitive to the play of the strategic balance (as William Hyland and Michel Oksenberg detail), and while the United States remains a somewhat distrusted "superpower," Peking's tilt toward the U.S. in the early 1970s greatly enhanced the flexibility in China's—as well as America's—foreign relations.

Even without a closer association than exists at present, the U.S. benefits from China's current foreign policy. Third World states seeking an alternative to alignment with the Soviet Union or the United States have a third option in a China which is friendly yet unallied to the U.S. (Harry Harding notes in chapter 9, however, that the closer China moves toward the U.S., the less credible it becomes as a nonaligned model for those who would avoid entrapment in the rivalries of the "superpowers.") And William Griffith documents China's appeals to those ruling and nonruling Communist Parties of Europe who wish to assert their autonomy from a Moscow-dominated international communist movement.

For the immediate future, U.S.–PRC foreign policy coordination is likely to be based on official consultations focused on opposition to the expansion of Soviet influence or resistance to political and military pressures from the USSR. Yet this constitutes a negative or reactive approach to building a relationship. A continuing question for Chinese and American policy makers is whether the relationship can be put on a more positive and enduring foundation so that matters of regional stability in East Asia, amelioration of North-South tensions, measures for coping with the global energy crisis, environmental and food problems, or the management of strains in international trading patterns can be dealt with, in part, through coordinated efforts of the United States and PRC.

A common thread to the interpretations in this volume of the PRC's role in the affairs of Europe, Asia, and the Third World is that at present China's power, and therefore her influence, is quite modest. As William Griffith details in chapter 6, the PRC is not a major factor in European politics despite Peking's diplomacy of the past two decades. And as we discovered at the time of Soviet interventions in Africa and Southwest Asia—from Angola in 1975 to Ethiopia, Somalia, and Afghanistan at the end of the decade—China's world outreach is limited. Even countries in which Peking had invested considerable foreign assistance, such as Tanzania and Mozambique, chose to follow Moscow's lead in policy toward Angola, presumably because of greater Soviet economic and military resources. Even in an area on its own borders of considerable strategic importance—Indochina—Peking has been unable to thwart the designs of a minor power like Vietnam when backed by the Soviet Union.

Thus while China can contribute to a broadly balanced American foreign policy, we cannot look to the China factor as a substitute for U.S. actions. Both Lucian Pye and Robert Scalapino emphasize the need for the United States to cast its policies toward Korea, Japan, and ASEAN on the assumption that the U.S. has an enduring role to play in preserving regional stability and the security of our allies. An active American presence in these regions is crucial to constraining the impact of the Sino-Soviet rivalry; and China is too limited in her outreach at present to pursue its interests alone, quite apart from helping us to realize our own.

At the same time, we share sufficient common interests with the PRC to make coordination of aspects of our foreign policies an important and positive supplement to our own actions, even if a supplement of limited effect. Moreover, it should not be minimized that a positive U.S.–PRC relationship avoids the strains in our foreign relations that characterized, for example, two decades of American efforts to develop coordinated policies for Asia with a Japan, Philippines, or Thailand reluctant to be drawn into Sino-American feuding. China's influence in Asia and the world will grow, however slowly, and American interests will be far better served if that growth leads to more active foreign policy collaboration with the U.S. rather than opposition to it.

SECURITY COOPERATION

Sino-American cooperation in matters of national security and defense was implicit in the development of the normalization dialogue in 1971, for this process began in the context of the world-wide growth of Soviet military power and China's fears of the militarization of the Sino-Soviet frontier. The Soviet invasion of Czechoslovakia in 1968 and the Sino-Soviet border clashes of the following year were the prime movers in the Sino-American reconciliation; and Moscow's direct and proxy interventions after 1975 in Africa, the Middle East, and at a series of points surrounding China—from Afghanistan and Indochina to Japan's northern territories—have heightened the motivation of policy planners in Washington and Peking to explore the defense implications of their now normal relationship.

As with foreign policy coordination, the U.S. and China have now moved along a spectrum of actions from military confrontation through political rapprochement to low-level forms of security cooperation. As Strobe Talbott analyzes in chapter 3, Washington and Peking now tend to view each other as strategic counterweights to Soviet military pressures. Moscow's invasion of Afghanistan in late 1979 finally drove the U.S.–PRC relationship into limited forms of military cooperation, as was emphasized via a series of visits by high-level defense officials beginning in January of 1980 with Harold Brown's trip to Peking. At that time, the Carter administration decided to permit sales to PRC military end-users of "dual-use" technologies such as computers with both civilian and military application, as well as nonlethal defense materiel such as communications and transport equipment, defensive radars, and military-industrial processes. And in June 1981 the Reagan administration decided to consider sales of lethal weaponry to China. Yet this security relationship remains inchoate rather than active. Significant sales of military hardware to China from the U.S. or its allies have yet to take place.

As stressed earlier, the matter of defense cooperation remains controversial and lacking in strong political support in the United States. There are many reasons for this tentativeness: lingering distrust of China's long-term strategic intentions because of its communist political orientation and its capacity eventually to be a major Asian power center in its own right; concern with signs of instability in the Peking leadership; a desire not to complicate the security needs of allies and friends such as Japan or Taiwan; an interest in not precipitating an adverse Soviet reaction or foreclosing future options for improving Soviet-American relations; apprehension that—as was the case with Soviet security assistance to the PRC in the 1950s —Peking may turn against a friend that is not fully forthcoming in its assistance; and a belief that the political and economic costs of significantly aiding China in her defense modernization are beyond America's capacity to assume.

At the same time, serious arguments endure for some form of U.S.–PRC defense cooperation: to secure China as one element in a regional and global balance of power that will be less vulnerable to Soviet pressures; to stabilize the Sino-American relationship by being responsive, in some measure, to the security concerns which impelled China's leaders to normalize relations with the U.S. in the first place; to caution Moscow by communicating in a significant manner America's intention to respond to Soviet threats to our interests; and to create a global coalition, of which China would be one participant, which will counter Moscow's evident efforts to build alliances and military bases capable of projecting Soviet power in Europe, the Middle East, Africa, Latin America, and Asia.

Given the divisions of opinion evident in these arguments for and against U.S.–PRC security cooperation, there are in essence three policy guidelines that the United States can pursue regarding this aspect of the relationship: do nothing; do anything that the Chinese want; or develop some modulated or conditional approach to security cooperation. The "do nothing" alternative has fallen prey to the growing and demonstrated global Soviet military threat, while a policy of all-out defense assistance has failed to gain active support in the face of the inhibitions and doubts about U.S.–PRC security collaboration noted above. By default, American policy makers have evolved an incremental, reactive set of policies in the security field that has seen the relationship grow in step-by-step fashion as Soviet expansionism has eroded political and policy inhibitions and generated support for defense cooperation.

How is the security aspect of the relationship likely to evolve in the future? The basic infrastructure for its development is now in place. Senior officials will continue to exchange views on the defense needs of the two countries and on areas where they might collaborate to mutual advantage. Out of this capacity for dialogue might evolve a shared conception of an appropriate way to enhance security cooperation. Military attaches in Peking and Washington can sustain information exchanges; and PRC state trading corporations can explore American and allied technologies which might enhance China's defense modernization program.

Further movement along the spectrum of increasing security cooperation, however, will require positive decisions at the highest levels in Washington and Peking. The most immediate choices will be for American actions which would help China strengthen its defense industrial base with more liberal transfers of production processes and dual-use technologies, and improve ground and air defenses, command, control, and communication facilities, and transport capabilities. Such defense-oriented activities of long-term effect would not directly or immediately heighten China's capacity to threaten any other regional or global power; yet they would enhance the PRC's long-term military potential and would signify to all observers the strategic significance of the U.S.–PRC relationship.

American or allied sales to China of lethal but defensive military equipment such as antitank rockets, air-to-air missiles, or short-range fighter aircraft may now be initiated on a limited scale, especially in response to some highly threatening Soviet initiative such as an invasion of Poland or Iran. Such sales, of course, would have a major symbolic impact on world-wide perceptions of the strategic balance, even if their practical effect were less meaningful than long-term measures which would strengthen China's industrial and scientific capabilities.

The evolution of this relationship into a full-fledged military alliance, complete with joint strategic and regional defense coordination, sales of unambiguously offensive weaponry, and the signing of a defense treaty, seems unlikely to occur in present circumstances. Neither China nor the U.S. is inclined to tie its security so closely to the other; neither wishes to confront the Soviet Union with such an alliance; and it is not clear how either Washington or Peking would respond to the really dire circumstance of a Soviet invasion of Europe, China, or the Middle East/Persian Gulf. Moreover, both Peking and Washington now agree that the U.S.–Japan security relationship has primacy in Asia.

Above all, the analyses in this volume reach the same conclusion in the defense field that they do in the realm of foreign policy: while the U.S.–PRC relationship can contribute in significant ways to the security interests of the two sides, the China factor cannot be a substitute for an effective unilateral American defense program. The Chinese would not want to collaborate with a vulnerable and uncertain United States in any event; and the U.S. cannot mortgage its defenses to the actions of others. It cannot rely for its security on the instabilities of the strategic triangle and the uncertain future of the Moscow-Peking feud. Under circumstances of either a Sino-Soviet war or rapprochement, the United States would lose out if it lacked the capacity to defend its own interests and those of its traditional allies.

Yet the China factor can be a positive element in our efforts to attain a stabilizing power balance in Asia and to countervail the global Soviet challenge. The task of American policy makers is to cast the security dimensions of the U.S.–PRC relationship, as William Hyland concludes in chapter 5, in that considerable area for maneuver between actions which are so provocative to Moscow that they stimulate a preemptive Soviet attack on China, or measures which are so slight that China feels compelled to accommodate to Soviet pressures. The objectives of such cooperation will be to heighten China's long-term security, strengthen the U.S.–PRC relationship, and convince the Soviet Union that its actions will affect, to a significant degree, the pace and direction of Sino-American security collaboration.

PARTICIPATION IN CHINA'S SOCIAL AND ECONOMIC DEVELOPMENT

The striving for national security has been the primary motive in China's opening to the U.S. Yet as the leadership in Peking has heightened its own priority on domestic economic and social development, such aspects of the U.S.–PRC tie as trade, technology acquisition, and the training of a new generation of scientific and managerial talent have acquired enhanced significance. Chinese leaders began to realize as early as the mid-1950s that if they followed the Soviet pattern of economic development, with its stress on the creation of heavy industries and a large defense sector, they would very likely *decrease* their security and national independence by failing to increase agricultural production relative to population growth and by constricting the development of light industries. Thus Mao Zedong developed the concept of "people's war" as an alternative to Soviet-style defense construction, a perspective that persists today in Deng Xiaoping's relatively low priority on defense modernization and the greater stress on the development of agriculture and light industry.

In addition, both Chinese and American leaders have gained some sense that the U.S.–PRC tie is less stable if it is based solely on security and foreign policy issues. Slight changes in either country's external relations would then have a much more unsettling effect on the other in the absence of economic and cultural contacts that broaden the base of domestic political support for the relationship. As Michel Oksenberg stresses in chapter 2, American participation in China's economic and social development can impart greater stability to the relationship by developing more diverse bureaucratic constituencies than if it were based on the support of only a few senior leaders and solely on the policy of opposition to "hegemony."

China's openness to diverse social and economic contacts

with the United States and other noncommunist countries was significantly enhanced after the purging in 1976 of the radical "Gang of Four." Under Deng Xiaoping's slogan "seek truth from facts," ideology has been downplayed in favor of a self-critical and pragmatic search for alternative approaches to social and economic modernization. Some measure of the degree of commitment of the current Chinese leadership to more open dealings with the U.S. is contained in the fact that such senior figures as Deng himself and Foreign Minister Huang Hua have sent their children to the United States for advanced education.

Nonetheless, there remains a tentativeness or uncertainty about the commitment of the two elites to the relationship that is based, in part, on their expectations of the other. From a Chinese perspective, there have been repeated signs of sluggishness or uncertainty in the commitment of successive American administrations to normal U.S.–PRC relations, as in the Carter administration's delay into mid-1978 in initiating negotiations on the normalization of relations, or candidate Reagan's stress on the Taiwan issue. From an American perspective, continuing signs of political factionalism in Peking, the ongoing debate in China about modernization priorities, and the degree to which the country should open up to the West, the leadership's communist orientation, and China's presumed great power ambitions reinforce doubts about the stability of the PRC leadership's commitment to a long-term relationship with the United States.

Thus, a kind of "catch 22" attitude underlies further development of the U.S.–PRC relationship: a concern that if we *do* help the Chinese develop, eventually they may turn against us; yet an awareness that if we hold back, the Chinese will surely conclude that the U.S. connection holds little of value for them.

Unless one believes that China is too weak and unreliable to be a useful factor in America's foreign relations, perhaps the most useful perspective on developing the relationship is provided by Dwight Perkins in chapter 4. Perkins concludes that the question for the U.S. is not whether China will modernize, but at what pace and with what orientation toward the United States. An active U.S.–PRC relationship in economic and educational areas will not determine whether China succeeds or fails in its development efforts, but we can have some impact on how rapidly modernization occurs, and whether the Chinese see the U.S. as having helped or remained aloof from that process. (The alternative perspective, that China's modernization is bound to lead to developments highly threatening to world peace—and therefore should be actively opposed, or at least not facilitated—is supported by few states other than the Soviet Union.)

There are two broad areas where public policy can have some effect on American involvement in China's domestic development: trade, technology transfers, and financial policies that support them; and cultural exchanges, technical assistance, and educational policies as they are affected by government-funded programs supported by such agencies as the National Science Foundation (NSF), the National Endowment for the Humanities (NEH), and the International Communications Agency (ICA), and by private foundations such as Ford and Rockefeller. The United States is hardly in a position to underwrite the staggering costs of China's economic and social development; yet we can have some impact on the orientation of the leadership through educational and cultural exchanges, and on the degree to which China's economy develops linkages to our own and to regional Asian trading patterns.

In the year and a half after normalization, nine major agreements were concluded between the U.S. government and the PRC which established the basic infrastructure of economic relations. The "claims-assets" issue was resolved. Aviation, maritime, and grain import agreements were reached. Textile import ceilings were negotiated. The Congress passed trade legislation that granted the PRC most-favored-nation (MFN) tariff status. And a joint Sino-American Economic Commission was established. These agreements helped to facilitate a doubling of U.S.–PRC trade during the two years 1979 and 1980.

Further growth of two-way trade will depend primarily on China's own economic development plans, its capacity to absorb foreign technology, and its ability to develop export markets which will earn foreign exchange. Dwight Perkins notes that the Chinese are unlikely to be major exporters of oil during the remainder of the century given difficulties in exploiting their offshore resources and requirements for domestic use; and China will likely be a major importer of foreign grain. Thus there will be severe limits to the country's ability to generate foreign exchange through energy sales and the need to use a significant portion of its hard currency earnings to purchase consumables. In view of these constraints, actions which the U.S. government might take to strengthen China's export earning capacity, or to finance imports from the U.S., will be important to developing two-way trade.

Vice President Mondale indicated in 1979 that the U.S. would make available $2 billion over a five-year period to finance imports via the Export-Import Bank. The Chinese have yet to avail themselves of such credits, or Commodity Credit Corporation loans to finance imports, as they find the interest rates too high. Concessionary rates cannot be developed for China alone; although the government may find that it has to lower its overall loan rate if the United States is to compete with countries such as France and Japan which provide still lower rates to finance their own exports.

Similarly, the U.S. can facilitate the availability of World Bank loans for the Chinese via the International Development Association if it participates in the IDA-VI and VII replenishments. Executive branch or congressional action could also facilitate China's access to U.S. technical assistance and to Public Law 480 grain grants or sales, which currently are prohibited by law, through either a presidential determination that the PRC is not a country dominated by international communism and is friendly to the U.S., or a change in existing legislation which would make China eligible for grain sales at better than commercial rates.

The most significant actions that the U.S. government can take to strengthen U.S.–PRC trade are in the areas of import quotas and tariffs for Chinese exports to the U.S. While China, as noted earlier, is now eligible for MFN tariff rates, still more preferential tariffs would be gained through PRC membership in the GATT (General Agreement on Tariffs and Trade) which would make China eligible for GSP (Generalized System of Preferences) concessionary tariff rates for developing countries. Action in this direction will require both PRC efforts to gain a seat on the GATT, and a presidential determination that GSP rates for China are in America's interest.

Other actions that the U.S. government can take to facilitate trade with China are the negotiation of import quotas or tariffs on politically sensitive items (such as individual textile categories, rubber footwear, menthol, and mushrooms) and the easing of export controls on "dual-use" and other defense-related items manufactured in the United States which the Chinese deem essential to their modernization efforts. In sum, there is a need for the government to monitor the development of U.S.–PRC trade, and to keep in mind China's recent entry into American markets when negotiating import quotas or establishing tariffs.

Several conclusions can be drawn from this rather detailed discussion of the technical mechanisms involved in developing Sino-American economic relations. First, multiple specialized bureaucracies will now play important roles in managing the relationship. Gone are the early days of the normalization process when one or two senior political figures could quickly resolve issues with a simple order. Cumbersome interagency processes are now required to effect changes. Second, politically sensitive domestic economic issues that are often the preserve of narrowly focused interest groups (such as the textile lobby) will involve themselves through special pleading to executive branch agencies and by lobbying in the Congress. The relationship will thus be affected by groups who do not bring a broad national perspective to the pursuit of their special interests. And third, multilateral economic problems such as market access and credit availability will require China-related issues to be weighed against the interests of other U.S. trading partners as well as the economic and foreign policy interests of the country as a whole.

For example, America's traditional trading partners in Asia —especially South Korea, Taiwan, Hong Kong, and the ASEAN countries—will be affected in varying degrees by the growth of Chinese export capabilities. The U.S. will have to reconcile the need to give the PRC greater access to American markets, in part to enable Peking to pay for its growing purchases of U.S.–produced goods, with equitable arrangements for established trading partners. Similarly, a country like India may be significantly affected by large PRC borrowings from the World Bank. The U.S. will thus have to monitor a range of economic effects of China's anticipated entrance into the world trading and financial scene and take certain measures to insure that existing economic patterns are not severely disrupted to the detriment of the interests of other countries.

Management of these issues will involve complex interagency coordination within the U.S. government (as the often conflicting interests and perspectives of the Departments of State, Treasury, Commerce, Labor, and Defense will be involved) and congressional support. This means that a broad and integrated national policy on China will require presidential decision making and leadership. The alternative will be piecemeal and contradictory policies that destroy any coherent sense of direction to the relationship, or paralysis induced by bureaucratic delay and domestic political infighting.

These qualities of highly technical, bureaucratic, and yet politically loaded processes involving the Congress and special interest groups also increasingly dominate the Chinese side of the relationship, thus compounding tendencies for the U.S.–PRC tie to become captive of mechanisms that induce delay and the assertion of narrow interests. For the Chinese this requires, among other things, greater stability in economic policy, an awareness of how commercial practices of recent years have eroded the interest of American businessmen in the China trade, and a willingness to develop export products and markets in order to maintain balanced trading relationships. In short, if the U.S.–PRC economic relationship is to further develop, dedicated and clear-sighted senior political leadership on both sides will have to jointly facilitate decision making.

Cultural and educational exchanges take place in an atmosphere less affected by government policy than do trade relations. Such exchanges have been facilitated on the American side for a decade by two private organizations, the National Committee on U.S.–China Relations and the Committee on Scholarly Communication with the PRC, which parallel the role in the economic area of the National Council for U.S.–China Trade. The National Committee and the Committee on Scholarly Communication have been funded by a combina-

tion of foundation grants and government agency support
(through the State Department, ICA, NSF, and NEH). As the
number of visiting delegations and students involved in cultural and educational exchange programs—as well as tourism—
has swelled, the management and funding of these contacts, on
the American side, have increasingly devolved to the private
sector and to individual universities, friendship societies, tour-
ist agencies, and artistic management concerns. This is as it
should be, given the workings of American society, but it does
mean that—as with trade—decisions affecting the future growth
of the relationship will be made on a highly decentralized basis
with individual interests rather than a larger sense of national
purpose shaping the pattern of exchanges.

Financial stringency on both sides of the relationship will
constrain if not lead to a retrenchment in the further development of cultural exchanges and trade. For example, while a
joint Sino-American Scientific Commission was established in
1979, its work remains seriously underfunded. And while many
of the advanced Chinese graduate students now in the U.S.
have been supported by research fellowships (some funded by
government research contracts), if student exchanges are to
expand, especially at the undergraduate level, the Chinese
government will have to provide increased levels of tuition and
living support. Yet such educational programs provide probably the most cost-effective way for the United States to contribute to the modernization of Chinese society, and to build
strong personal links to new generations of PRC leaders.

Thus U.S. interests will be well served by supporting educational and cultural exchange programs with either foundation
or governmental funding. The willingness of these funding
agencies to do so, however, will be affected by perceptions of
the degree to which the objectives of the particular foundation,
government office, or private institution are served by a given
exchange, as well as by financial limitations. Considerations of
reciprocity are usually high on the list of concerns of individual
funders. Yet as Michel Oksenberg notes in the January 1981
issue of *Foreign Affairs,* strict reciprocity in U.S.–PRC relations
is very hard to achieve—or even to define—in view of the disparities in social and economic organization of the two countries and their different levels of development. It is difficult to

expect individual institutions in the U.S. to take a broad view of their contributions to the exchange process when they may gain relatively little from it directly; yet the striving for reciprocity must not be mindless. Thus, here again, senior governmental leadership will continue to be important in articulating for the country the importance of the U.S.–PRC relationship and in providing financial support for various cultural and educational exchanges that serve the national interest even if they are not strictly reciprocated by the Chinese side.

The Taiwan Time Bomb

Where cooperation in national security and foreign policy matters and the development of trade and cultural exchanges hold the promise of building a constructive U.S.–PRC relationship, the residual issue of the status of Taiwan holds the potential to disrupt if not destroy the still fragile Sino-American tie. The normalization process of the 1970s only set aside this issue, which is so freighted with the emotions of nationalism and sovereignty for the Chinese and weighted for Americans with a sense of loyalty and fair treatment if not the right of self-determination for a small and hard-working population in the face of the inexorable power of a great state.

America's protective relationship with the Nationalist government of Chiang Kai-shek was the principal issue that stalemated any amelioration in the U.S.–PRC confrontation throughout the 1950s and 1960s. The U.S. Mutual Defense Treaty of 1954 with the Republic of China effectively prevented a final resolution of the Communist-Nationalist civil war, which had concluded on the mainland in 1949 with the withdrawal of Chiang's military remnants to Taiwan. And the U.S. military presence on the island, in conjunction with American forces in South Korea and South Vietnam, constituted a three-pronged threat to the security of the PRC. Soviet military initiatives of the late 1960s, however, reordered security policies for both Peking and Washington, leading at last to a break in the stalemate.

The normalization negotiations of the 1970s brought about five changes in America's relations with Taiwan relative to the PRC.

The U.S.–PRC Military Confrontation Was Eliminated—The most immediate and tangible benefit to China and the U.S. of the normalization process was gradual elimination of two decades of military confrontation. In the Shanghai Communiqué of 1972, the U.S. committed itself to the "ultimate objective" of withdrawing all U.S. forces and military installations from Taiwan and to the progressive reduction of the existing force presence "as the tension in the area diminishes." This ultimate objective, however, was unilaterally linked by the U.S. to the prospect of "a peaceful settlement of the Taiwan question by the Chinese themselves."

Following publication of the Joint Communiqué, the U.S. proceeded to dismantle its military presence on Taiwan. In May of 1975 the last offensive weapons, a squadron of F-4 fighter-bombers, were withdrawn from the island; and within a few months of the completion of the normalization process in early 1979 the last element of the American military presence, a PX contingent, departed. America's concern for the security of Taiwan was thus no longer "covered" by either a direct U.S. defense presence or a bilateral treaty with the government of the island.

The normalization agreement which took effect on January 1, 1979, moreover, decoupled the U.S. military withdrawal from the issue of a peaceful resolution of the Taiwan question by the Chinese themselves. The Carter administration merely expressed the unilateral position that the U.S. "will continue to have an interest in the peaceful resolution of the Taiwan issue." The Communist-Nationalist military confrontation across the Taiwan Strait continues, albeit with a substantial reduction in the level of tension that characterized earlier decades. Peking, for example, has ceased alternative day shelling of the offshore islands of Quemoy and Matsu and has substantially reduced its military forces in Fujian Province on the mainland side of the Taiwan Strait.

The U.S. Recognized the Unity of China—In the Shanghai Communiqué (see Appendix 1), American officials artfully responded to China's demand that the U.S. renounce any interest in policies of "two Chinas," "one China, two governments," "one China, one Taiwan," an "independent Taiwan," or the position that Taiwan's status is undetermined by acknowledging that "all Chinese on either side of the Taiwan Strait maintain there is but one China and that Taiwan is a part of China." The Nixon administration said that it did not challenge that position and agreed to Chinese insistence that the formulation state—in an exaggerated fashion—that "*all* Chinese on either side of the Strait" support this view. The U.S., in effect, bound independence-minded Taiwanese on the island to the Nationalist and Communist Chinese position that Taiwan is a part of China.

In the normalization agreement of 1979, the Carter administration recognized the government of the People's Republic of China as the "sole legal government" of China and directly "acknowledged" the Chinese position that there is but one China and Taiwan is part of China. The U.S. thus precluded itself from fostering or backing an independent Taiwan—a position that was consistent with the recommendations of various government studies conducted during the 1950s and 1960s, even at the height of U.S.–PRC military tensions in 1950–51 (before the establishment of the U.S.–Republic of China Mutual Defense Treaty).

The PRC Agreed to American Maintenance of "Unofficial" Relations with Taiwan—The joint U.S.–PRC normalization agreement (contained in Appendix 2) stated that "the people of the United States will maintain cultural, commercial, and other unofficial relations with the people of Taiwan" within the broader context of the U.S. recognition of the PRC as the sole legal government of China. Subsequent to the establishment of U.S.–PRC diplomatic relations and the concurrent severing of American diplomatic ties to the government of the Republic of China on Taiwan, Congress passed the Taiwan Relations Act, authorizing U.S. government funding and laws to sustain social and economic dealings between the island and the United States. These relations are now facilitated by the "American Institute in Taiwan" (also created by the Taiwan Relations Act) and a parallel organization from Taiwan in the U.S. (the Coordination Council for North American Affairs). The American Institute is staffed by professional U.S. diplomats temporarily "separated" from official government service who operate with secure communications, privileges, and immunities as do diplomats the world over—a pattern that also characterizes Japan's post-recognition dealings with Taiwan.

This arrangement, of course, is a fiction of sorts. It provides a way of bridging Peking's demand for sovereignty and the unity of China with American political imperatives and interests regarding Taiwan. It reflects the common desire of both Peking and Washington to establish a cooperative bilateral relationship despite continuing differences on the Taiwan issue, as well as Peking's short-term interest in not destabilizing the current situation on the island. It is this fiction—that America's residual relations with Taiwan are not official—that Ronald Reagan challenged in his campaign statement of August 25, 1980, thus at least temporarily calling into question his willingness to accept the Carter administration's terms (as negotiated with Peking) for U.S.–PRC normalization.

Peking Unilaterally Adopted a "Soft" Posture Toward Taiwan—After nearly three decades of military confrontation and political vituperation between the Nationalist and Communist Chinese across the Taiwan Strait, the normalization negotiations brought about an evident diminution in tensions between the two Chinese regimes. In the normalization agreement of January 1979, the U.S. unilaterally expressed confidence that "the people of Taiwan face a peaceful and prosperous future" and that "the United States continues to have an interest in the peaceful resolution of the Taiwan issue and expects that the Taiwan issue will be settled peacefully by the Chinese themselves." (See the full statement in Appendix 3.)

Parallel with this statement, senior PRC officials expressed for the public record a much more accommodating position on the reunification of China. Dropping use of the term "liberation" (with its implication of the use of military force), Premier and Party Chairman Hua Guofeng stated the "hope" that compatriots on Taiwan would make further contributions to the cause of reunifying China. Hua observed that all Chinese who help in this cause are patriots, "whether they come forward early or late." And in a conversation with American senators in early January 1979, just prior to his trip to the United

States, Vice Premier Deng Xiaoping asserted that Taiwan could maintain its economic and social systems, its political autonomy, and its own armed forces after reunification with the PRC. What is required of the Nationalist government, said Deng, is that it lower its flag and otherwise eliminate symbols of authority which designate it as a rival to the People's Republic of China as the government of all China.

The U.S. Unilaterally Stated It Would Sell Defensive Arms to Taiwan—Peking's moderate approach toward Taiwan and reunification was expressed unilaterally, in a manner that did not compromise the Chinese sense of sovereignty on the Taiwan issue or create an obligation to the U.S. not to use force against the island. It is a posture that could change at Peking's initiative at any time. And while PRC leaders continue to refer upon occasion to their "right" to use force in resolving the future status of the island, to date they have minimized the sense of political or military threat across the Taiwan Strait.

In recognition of this situation, and to give substance to its "expectation" that reunification will not be imposed on the people of Taiwan by force, senior U.S. officials stated publicly in a press backgrounder on December 15, 1978, at the time the normalization agreement was announced, that the continuing but unofficial commercial dealings between the U.S. and Taiwan would include sales by American companies of "arms of a defensive character" to the island on a restrained basis.

In his parallel news conference, Premier Hua Guofeng noted that the U.S. and PRC had "differing views" on the arms sales issue, that "we [Chinese] absolutely could not agree to this," that "it would not conform to the principles of normalization [and] would be detrimental to the peaceful liberation of Taiwan." "Nevertheless," Hua said, "we reached an agreement on the joint communiqué" announcing full normalization.

Subsequent to the establishment of U.S.–PRC diplomatic relations, the U.S. Congress, on April 10, 1979, passed the "Taiwan Relations Act" which wrote into American law the unilateral view that normalization with the PRC "rests on the expectation that the future of Taiwan will be determined by peaceful means" and that the U.S. would "provide Taiwan with arms of a defensive character" in order to help the island "maintain a sufficient self-defense capability." (See Appendix 4.)

The Taiwan issue was thus set aside by the normalization process with a carefully crafted set of statements that bridged irreconcilable political principles in the hope of attaining larger objectives of national security and global political flexibility. Yet the various unilateral statements and political fictions that constitute the Taiwan element of the normalization agreement are a delicate house of cards that could collapse as the surrounding political forces change.

Seen in isolation from the political context of 1979, and on the basis of the public record alone, China would seem to have gotten the better of the normalization deal in an end to the formal American military protection of Taiwan, an explicit American recognition of the PRC as the sole legal government of China, the termination of official U.S. relations with the government of the Republic of China on Taiwan—and all at the cost of no more than a unilateral PRC expression of "hope" for a peaceful resolution of the Taiwan issue and the tenuous unilateral American position on sustaining Taiwan's defenses through arms sales. Even in the context of the times, the PRC may have gained significant short-term advantages in completing normalization just before it "taught Vietnam a lesson" for its invasion of Kampuchea. As William Hyland and Lucian Pye note in chapters 5 and 8, Peking gained security reinsurance from normalization with the U.S. at the end of 1978 in the face of Moscow's backing of Vietnam in its ambition to dominate Indochina.

At the same time, China remains highly constrained in moving away from the normalization understandings on Taiwan. Soviet military and political pressures continue to hold highest priority in PRC security planning; and normal relations with the U.S. and Japan—which Peking would only put at risk through a pressure campaign against the island—remain central to China's national security and economic development planning. And even if the PRC did decide to take the island by force, it would require at least five years of preparation and a very different international environment for Peking to prepare a military campaign. In the interim, the U.S. and other countries would likely react in a manner detrimental to PRC objectives.

The fact remains that China's interests are still served by a peaceful resolution of the Taiwan issue. Events since normalization have sustained the judgment of those American officials who constructed the agreement that Taiwan's security and well-being—in the short term—would not be undercut by normalization: American trade with the island grew from $8.9 billion in 1978 to $11.4 billion in 1980. Political stability has been maintained. Foreign travel to and from Taiwan and foreign investments continue uninterrupted. And there are no signs at present that Peking is building the specialized military capabilities necessary to threaten the island's security. Indeed, implicit in current circumstances is the fact that Peking counts on the U.S. to keep Taiwan from becoming a separate political entity.

At the same time, the generally pragmatic development policies now promoted by PRC leaders are creating an atmosphere much more conducive to some form of reconciliation with Taiwan than in past periods of ideological fervor and political turmoil. Indeed, with thousands of Chinese students from Taiwan and the PRC now meeting on American and Japanese campuses, with professionals from both societies attending international conferences around the world, and with a vigorous indirect trade of more than $200 million per year developing between the island and mainland via Hong Kong and Japan, prospects for a peaceful accommodation of some sort worked out by the Chinese parties themselves would seem to be increasing.

THE AMERICAN PUBLIC'S REACTION TO NORMALIZATION

The reaction of the American people to normalization as it affected Taiwan also bears out the timeliness of the move and its positive effect on public support for U.S. foreign policy. A Potomac Associates poll of 1977 found only 26 percent of a national sample holding favorable views of the PRC, while 56 percent had positive opinions of Taiwan. By 1980 the same polling organization found 70 percent of the public with favorable views of the PRC, although 68 percent were positively inclined toward Taiwan. Another Potomac Associates poll in

September 1979 found that 57 percent of the public considered it "very important" for the U.S. to get along well with the PRC, while only 44 percent gave the same response for "the Republic of China on Taiwan."

In 1977 only 26 percent of a national opinion survey by Potomac Associates supported a policy of establishing diplomatic relations with Peking if it was at the price of a break in relations with Taipei. A Roper poll in January 1979, at the time of normalization, found the public evenly divided on approval versus disapproval of the switch in diplomatic relations from Taiwan to the PRC (32 percent each, with the remainder undecided). A January 1981 Roper poll found 55 percent of a national survey supportive of maintaining official relations with Peking, with only 23 percent favoring the reestablishment of diplomatic ties with Taipei.

Regarding Taiwan's security, the 1977 Potomac Associates poll found 61 percent of a national survey who thought that the island's security was important to them in the context of efforts to normalize relations with the PRC, while 32 percent agreed that the U.S. should help defend Taiwan if it were attacked by the PRC (48 percent disagreed, and 20 percent had no opinion). In 1980 the same polling organization found an increase in those who thought the U.S. should defend Taiwan against China (43 percent, versus 42 percent opposed, with 15 percent "no opinion"), but also significant support for helping the PRC if it were attacked by the Soviet Union (45 percent, versus 42 percent opposed, and 13 percent "no opinion").

Thus to the extent that public opinion both reflects popular judgments about foreign policy initiatives and also responds to presidential leadership, normalization and its impact on Taiwan have thus far gained public support.

FACTORS SHAPING TAIWAN'S FUTURE

It would clearly be in America's interest, as is expressed in the unilateral U.S. statement made at the time of normalization, if PRC and Taiwan authorities could negotiate between themselves some mutually agreeable resolution of their differences which had the support of their people. This would avoid a situation in which the U.S., at some future time, had to choose between support for one or the other Chinese party, or in which the residual and unilateral American expression of concern for Taiwan's security would be tested. It would enable the U.S. to maintain productive relations with both island and mainland. And under circumstances of mutual agreement, such an evolution would very likely best serve the interests of the people of Taiwan and the PRC as well.

History is seldom so accommodating, however, as to present cost-free solutions to humankind's most challenging predicaments. In the case of Taiwan's future, there are four parties whose actions will shape, in some still unforeseeable combination, the evolution of the island's present circumstances. Two of them, the governments of the PRC and the United States, will presumably pursue policies toward Taiwan that are shaped by broader strategic and foreign policy objectives. The other two, the government and the people of Taiwan, will develop policies much more closely tied to their immediate circumstances; and their actions may precipitate developments that will confound even the most far-sighted and well-intentioned leaders in Peking and Washington.

The United States—There are three areas of policy choice that the U.S. can bring to the Taiwan issue. The first is whether to sustain the formal agreements that comprised the public statements and private understandings of the normalization negotiations. Ronald Reagan, during his candidacy for President, called into question his commitment to the "unofficial" character of America's postnormalization ties with Taiwan. Within two months of assuming office, however, he affirmed his commitment to the normalization agreement of January 1, 1979. Should his or a subsequent administration bring about a significant unilateral modification of the normalization understandings and agreements with the PRC, it would almost certainly evoke a response from Peking which would seriously strain if not destroy the U.S.–PRC relationship. (The same should be said, of course, for the likely American reaction to a similar initiative from the PRC—as, for example, the application of military pressure on the island.)

Peking has already demonstrated great sensitivity to actions by other governments which suggest the intention to reestablish official dealings with the authorities on Taiwan or to encourage a separate legal status for the island. Such initiatives will tend to mobilize the potent force of Chinese nationalism and interact with PRC internal politics in ways that are probably uncontainable even by leaders who would invoke the authority of Mao Zedong, Zhou Enlai, or Deng Xiaoping—men who publicly committed themselves to developing ties to the noncommunist West as a way of enhancing China's security and economic modernization.

U.S. implementation of its unilaterally expressed intention to sell defensive arms to Taiwan—a second area of choice—will similarly generate strains in dealings with Peking. This is an issue on which PRC and American leaders in essence "agreed to disagree" at the time of normalization. The extent to which the underlying disagreement will affect the relationship will be shaped by the context within which such sales are made: the state of politics in Peking, the overall condition of U.S.–PRC relations, etc.

The degree of strain will also be affected by the types of weapons sold, and the larger context of U.S.–PRC security cooperation. The Reagan administration will soon face the decision of whether, and when, to sell Taiwan a new generation of fighter aircraft to replace its aging fleet of F-100s, F-104s, and F-5Es. Some argue that if the U.S. were helping Peking deal with its defense requirements—air defense, for example—a decision to maintain a balance across the Taiwan Strait would probably be much less disrupting to U.S.–PRC relations than an American decision to assist Taiwan alone.

PRC leaders will object to such sales to Taiwan on the grounds that they violate the "one China" principle which the U.S. agreed to at the time of normalization, and that they remove any incentive for leaders in Taipei to reach some form of peaceful accommodation—thus enhancing prospects for an eventual "nonpeaceful" resolution of the island's status. To underscore their opposition to arms sales to Taiwan, PRC leaders reduced their level of diplomatic representation with the government of the Netherlands in early 1981 in response to a Dutch sale of two submarines to the island.

A third area of choice for the U.S. is whether to actively create conditions which would "encourage" Taiwan's leaders to work out a negotiated agreement with Peking. It seems highly unlikely that any American administration would pressure the authorities on Taiwan to negotiate with the PRC. The unhappy memory of General George Marshall's mediation mission of the late 1940s, which sought to negotiate an end to the Communist-Nationalist civil war, is only one of many factors which will likely dissuade another administration from undertaking such a thankless task. Yet under certain circumstances, the U.S. could be called upon by one or both Chinese parties to facilitate a negotiation already underway. As such circumstances are impossible to foretell, a decision regarding involvement will be shaped by the expectation of successfully reaching an agreement, the particular role the U.S. was asked to assume, and by a judgment about the degree of support an arrangement would elicit from the people of Taiwan (as opposed to the island's authorities).

The PRC—Peking faces the dilemmas of how to prevent Taiwan from "drifting away" from some form of association with the PRC, and how to entice the island's authorities into a negotiation of their future status as part of a reunified China. The normalization agreement with the U.S., as it affected the status of the island, probably precluded any outside power from reestablishing a protectorate over Taiwan. (Even the Soviet Union has shown little interest in developing relations with the island, given the effect such a step would have on prospects for a future accommodation with the PRC.) Yet Peking must formulate an approach which takes into account the present limits of its military capabilities relative to the island's defenses, the Soviet military threat on other borders, and the need for positive relations with the U.S. and Japan. PRC economic and political enticements are also modest relative to the island's current circumstances.

Consequently, Peking at a minimum seeks to sustain Taiwan's present status pending favorable developments in the balance of military and economic power between the island and mainland. PRC leaders also may anticipate the gradual erosion of American interest in the island relative to growing relations with the PRC. Such an evolutionary strategy, required of the PRC because of the limits of its current military and political outreach, is perhaps most vulnerable to initiatives from the island itself. For this reason, PRC leaders have placed a relatively high priority on the goal of achieving Taiwan's reunification with the mainland in the 1980s—presumably through political action if at all possible.

The Government of the Republic of China on Taiwan—The Nationalist government of Premier Chiang Ching-kuo has shown remarkable adaptability to the increasing political isolation that U.S.–PRC normalization has imposed on it. A dynamic economy and basic domestic political stability have sustained the reality of life on the island even as the symbols of the government's international status as a temporarily exiled national authority fade. Like Peking, the Taipei government seeks to sustain its current circumstances in the hope of some unforeseen but favorable development—and in the absence of any other acceptable alternative.

Candidate Reagan's criticism of the terms of U.S.–PRC normalization, his expressed intention to impart a more official character to America's relations with the island, and his interest in sustaining Taiwan's defenses undoubtedly raised hopes for the Nationalist authorities that they could gain greater support from the new administration than from its predecessors. It can thus be expected that Taipei will seek favorable treatment from the Reagan administration in terms of the level and scope of its representation in the U.S., and in the acquisition of an enhanced defense capability. The longer-term objective of the Taiwan authorities is probably to move the U.S. to a "one China, two governments" policy (a development which Peking will certainly resist), if not to induce strains in the U.S.–PRC relationship.

Given the shifts in U.S. public opinion noted earlier, it is doubtful the American people will support a return to official relations with Taipei if it is at the price of a serious degradation in the U.S.–PRC tie. Probably the only circumstance in which public opinion would back a major shift in support from Peking to Taipei would be if the PRC prepared to use military force against the island. At the same time, there is great residual sympathy in the U.S. for Taiwan, and the American public is likely to support minor adjustments in dealings with the island's authorities that accord with the practice of other nations, as well as efforts to sustain the island's defenses.

The People of Taiwan—Public discussion of the Taiwan issue in the U.S. tends to ignore the fact that more than 85 percent of the island's population sees themselves as "Taiwanese"— as opposed to the "mainlanders" who control the governing structure. Tensions between the Taiwanese community—the descendants of seventeenth century immigrants from Fujian Province across the Taiwan Strait—and the mainlanders who fled to the island in 1947–49 at the end of the civil war were most intense when the Nationalist government of Chiang Kai-shek first imposed itself on the island. Riots in 1947 led to the death of many of the island's indigenous political and intellectual elite. In the subsequent thirty and more years, Nationalist leaders have made significant efforts to ameliorate the division between the two communities and incorporate Taiwanese into the structure of government. However, periodic political riots— as at Chungli in 1977 and Kaohsiung in 1979—attest to continuing tensions and pressure from the Taiwanese for enhanced political power to accord with the wealth they have created with the island's remarkable economic development.

Peking is aware of these internal tensions on the island, and must view with concern the trends toward "Taiwanization" of the island's economic system and political structure, for they strengthen the forces seeking autonomy or independence. PRC leaders probably view the authority of the Chiang Ching-kuo government—with its enduring commitment to "one China," even if a China ruled by the Nationalist or Kuomintang Party— as contributing to the stability of present circumstances. Yet they anticipate that Chiang will pass from the scene during the 1980s, with highly unpredictable effects on the island's political future. For this reason, Peking will hope to engage the Chiang government in negotiations in order to preempt the Taiwanese community from pressing for developments which would reinforce the autonomy of the island, seeking to gain their political independence, or creating conditions of political chaos that could be dealt with only through a PRC military intervention.

The interplay of these various forces, as they will affect the Taiwan situation in the coming decade, is quite unpredictable;

yet it is evident that the Taiwan issue embodies the most
explosive of sentiments for all parties concerned: sovereignty
and the revolutionary impulse for Peking; support for an old
friend and ally, and ultimately the issue of self-determination
for the U.S.; the Nationalist government's very existence; and
basic issues of survival and political autonomy for the Taiwanese. As the potentially destructive element in the complex
equation of U.S.–PRC relations, the Taiwan issue in the 1980s
will require the most delicate and restrained handling by leaders in Peking and Washington. What is needed is a sense on
both sides of the relative importance of the island in the larger
strategic context created by normal U.S.–PRC relations if the
Taiwan issue is not to destroy the foundations of a constructive
U.S.–PRC tie built with the diplomacy of the 1970s.

Conclusion: *The China Factor as a Supplement,*
Not a Substitute

Each reader of this volume will have to evaluate the varied
ways in which China's reemergence on the world scene in the
1970s and the normalization of U.S.–PRC relations have affected international affairs in various parts of the globe. Un-
deniably, however, the changes in world politics initiated by
President Nixon's historic trip to Peking in 1972 were as much
in people's minds as they were in actual alterations in global
political, economic, and military forces. Yet U.S.–PRC normalization initiated processes of change that, if they endure for
several decades, can contribute significantly to the modernization of China and to the building of a new coalition of powers
supportive of the basic goals of American foreign policy.

In retrospect, it is evident that the normalization process
begun in 1971 eliminated the negative burdens on U.S. defenses
and foreign relations of two decades of political and military
confrontation with China. Normalization facilitated our disengagement from Vietnam. And it created a new strategic context for the management of America's long-term competitive
relationship with the Soviet Union. The destruction of normal
U.S.–PRC relations, as a result of whatever development, would
reimpose on both China and the United States great costs
which could not serve the interests of either country.

The positive benefits of normalization will only be realized as the U.S.–PRC relationship develops in the years ahead. Yet the China factor, for all its promise, will be only one element in America's foreign relations. It cannot substitute for an active U.S. role in the political and security affairs of Asia, or for America's own efforts to sustain a stable strategic balance. With foresight and judgment, however, the further development of America's dealings with the People's Republic of China can be a long-term investment in a relationship that will contribute to a stabilizing balance in Asia and in global affairs.

Michel Oksenberg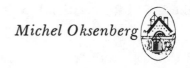

2

The Dynamics
of the Sino-American Relationship

The Instability of American China Policy

Few of America's foreign relations in this century have
exhibited the fragile, volatile quality, the vulnerability to
breakdown, and the susceptibility to rapid improvement that
have characterized our relations with China. For three generations, a web of common interests has linked the United States
to Canada, Great Britain, France, Australia, New Zealand, the
Scandinavian countries, and the Benelux countries. For two
generations, Americans have seen the rise of the Soviet Union
in world affairs as fundamentally inimical to their interests. Only
the common threat to our separate survivals during World
War II brought Washington and Moscow together temporarily.
For a generation, American security has been rooted in alliances
with West Germany and Japan. These alliances were forged

MICHEL OKSENBERG *is professor of political science at the University of
Michigan and a research associate at its Center for Chinese Studies. He
was a member of the staff of the National Security Council, with responsibility for matters relating to China, from January 1977 to February 1980.
He is the coauthor of* Dragon and Eagle *as well as other works.*

following two generations of German-American and Japanese-American conflicts that were concluded on American terms.

In the post–World War II era, continuities have outweighed major shifts in America's relations with most of the developing world. Consider, for example, the stability in American dealings with the ASEAN countries, Pakistan, Saudi Arabia, Zaire, Brazil, Venezuela, and even Iran. Where there have been fluctuations, as with India, Nigeria, Mexico, and Argentina, the oscillations have been of limited amplitude.

To be sure, this presents an oversimplified picture of continuity and stability in American foreign policy. None of these relations has been genuinely constant; each has had moments of great tension. And in some instances, such as with Cuba, Chile, Ethiopia, and Egypt, our relations have gone through sweeping changes. Yet the generality still holds: to a far greater extent than conventional wisdom would have it, American foreign policy has been marked by considerable constancy, and the changes reflect rational responses to profound trends in world affairs.

American policy toward China stands as an exception. From the early 1900s to 1949, Washington's declared policy toward China exhibited continuity. The expressed desire was for a unified, developing, democratic China open to commerce from all quarters. But as the historians of Sino-American relations have constantly emphasized, the reality of American policy departed considerably from the rhetoric, and the way Washington pursued its objectives shifted rapidly from administration to administration. The indifference of Theodore Roosevelt yielded to the active promotion of economic interests under William Howard Taft, which in turn shifted to the moralism of the early Woodrow Wilson, and then to Wilson's sacrifice of Chinese sovereignty at Versailles in order to placate Japan. During the 1920s, Washington adopted diametrically opposed positions on whether the U.S. should or should not renegotiate America's "unequal" treaties with China. In the late 1920s the United States first opposed and then welcomed the rise of Chiang Kai-shek. In the 1930s Roosevelt abandoned the Hoover-Stimson policy toward the Japanese invasion of Manchuria and acquiesced in 1933–34 to the Japanese domination of

China's northeast (Manchuria). But as war swept over Asia, Roosevelt moved to a different vision of the American interest in a unified, independent China. The Truman administration embraced and then distanced itself from Chiang Kai-shek.

AMERICA'S RELATIONS WITH THE CHINESE COMMUNISTS

Moments of comedy, tragedy, and drama symbolize the kaleidoscopic quality of American dealings with the Chinese Communists. No single event can capture the sweep of this complex relationship, but it is useful to recall a few of the moments which encapsulate this rich history.

November 1944: President Roosevelt's special emissary, Patrick Hurley, unexpectedly arrived at the communist wartime capital of Yenan to mediate the dispute between the Nationalists and the Chinese Communist Party (CCP). The comic high point came when the Oklahoman let out an Indian war whoop upon reviewing the hastily assembled honor guard, to the bewilderment of Mao Zedong and Zhou Enlai, who had raced to the airport to greet Hurley. After raising Communist hopes for American assistance, Hurley dashed them upon returning to the Nationalist embrace in Chungking.

January 1947: General George Marshall, as President Truman's special envoy to China, had valiantly sought to reach a compromise between the Communists and the Nationalists and thereby avert civil war. The Marshall mission may have been ill-fated from its outset. Upon his departure from China in January 1947 to become secretary of state, Marshall recognized that a civil war could not be averted. He foresaw the volatility in Sino-American relations that loomed ahead. The United States had neither the will nor the capability to alter China's course.

August 2, 1949: Ambassador John Leighton Stuart departed China. Stuart had been born in China in 1876. He had initiated his career as a missionary to China in 1905, and in 1919 he assumed the presidency of Yenching University. His departure marked not just the termination of an American diplomatic presence on the Communist-dominated mainland, but the traumatic end of American missionary and educational activity in China.

January 12, 1950: Even as Mao journeyed to Moscow to seal the Sino-Soviet alliance, Secretary of State Dean Acheson expressed his desire to "let the dust settle" before the United States resumed relations with China. Excluding Taiwan from the American defense perimeter, Acheson's hope was that the Chinese civil war would soon be settled and the United States could initiate contact with the People's Republic. In June 1950, however, the Korean War began. Fearing that Pyongyang's attack was a prelude to a wider communist initiative, the United States interposed the Seventh Fleet in the Taiwan Strait, thereby reengaging itself in the Chinese civil war. The PRC's subsequent entry into the war—as American forces swept toward the Manchurian border—engendered protracted Sino-American enmity. Instead of months, decades passed before the "dust settled."

April 1954: The major powers assembled at Geneva to seek a settlement of the Indochina War. As Zhou Enlai frequently, bitterly, yet gleefully recalled years later to American audiences, the Chinese Premier encountered Secretary of State John Foster Dulles at a social occasion. He strode across the room, arm extended, to shake the hand of his American adversary. Dulles, determined to survive the conference without recognizing Zhou's presence, turned his back on this brilliant bearer of China's cultural legacy and communist revolutionary traditions. Dulles's behavior foreshadowed the Eisenhower administration's rebuff of China's search in 1954–55 for a Sino-American accommodation over the Taiwan issue. There ensued a fourteen-year stalemate in the ambassadorial talks between China and the United States, first convened in Geneva and later held in Warsaw.

July 9, 1971: National Security Adviser Henry Kissinger boarded a special Pakistani International Airlines 707 to begin his secret journey to Peking. Two and a half years of brilliant diplomatic maneuvering, building on a common apprehension of the Soviet Union, had preceded the mission. Both sides had signaled a readiness to move forward during two crucial exchanges at the ambassadorial talks in Warsaw in early 1970. Both sides had abandoned the sterile formulas which had been repeated in the diplomatic exchanges for fifteen years. In their separate memoirs, President Nixon and Secretary Kissinger describe the subsequent delicate political "signaling" during 1970 and 1971. Upon Kissinger's arrival in Peking, in his first extensive conversation with Premier Zhou, the two men explored their views of the Taiwan issue. Only after ascertaining that both sides were prepared to search for a way to accommodate the sensitivities of the other did Zhou and Kissinger agree that a visit by President Nixon to the PRC would be possible.

February 22, 1972: Mao Zedong and Richard Nixon agreed that their common interests outweighed their differences. The Shanghai Communiqué of February 28th committed the two sides to seek the establishment of diplomatic relations on the basis of the principle of "one China." Implicit in the communiqué was an American commitment not to pursue a "two Chinas," "one China, one Taiwan," or "one China, two governments" policy; the "one China" policy was conditioned on the expectation that the Taiwan issue would be settled peacefully by the Chinese themselves.

December 1975: President Ford and Vice Premier Deng Xiaoping rapidly concluded their survey of global and bilateral issues. The relationship had lost its momentum due to domestic political constraints in both countries. Topics which had been full of promise three years earlier were now covered in cursory, sometimes acerbic, fashion. Yet both sides wished to preserve the facade of harmony, in full expectation that progress could be made after each side had passed through its domestic travails: Watergate and the Vietnam debacle for Washington; the power struggle over Mao's succession in Peking. As a result, having reached the end of their agenda half-way into their last scheduled meeting, Ford and Deng decided to engage in small talk for nearly an hour rather than reveal to the outside world that there was little for them to discuss. The relationship continued to languish for the remainder of the Ford term and into the first year of the Carter administration.

February 3, 1979: At the end of 1978, President Carter and Vice Premier Deng had completed the normalization process within the framework formulated by their predecessors. Weeks later, the decisive and courageous Vice Premier leaned out of a stagecoach and waved his cowboy hat at a rodeo in Houston, Texas. The event was witnessed on television throughout the United States and in urban China. That one calculated act, perhaps more than any other, revealed the extent to which Deng was prepared to go and the personal risks he was prepared to take in order to further Sino-American relations. Working with an equally committed American President, the United States and China in short order established the framework for extensive economic, cultural, and scientific relations.

August 28, 1979: Vice President Walter Mondale became the first American official since 1949 to give a public address in China. He spoke at Peking University, located on the site of the old Yenching University campus where Leighton Stuart, our last ambassador on the China mainland, had presided for so long. The vice president informed his Chinese audience that "any nation which seeks to weaken or isolate China in world affairs assumes a stance counter to American interests." He thereby deliberately echoed the January 12, 1950 speech of Acheson: "We must take the position we have always taken—that anyone who violates the integrity of China is the enemy of China and is acting contrary to our interests." The Carter administration, in short, had returned American China policy to its historical moorings—at least in rhetoric. Once again, the United States proclaimed its interest in a strong, secure, independent China.

January 1980: Secretary of Defense Harold Brown informed the Chinese during his visit to Peking that the United States was prepared to sell the PRC nonlethal military equipment. He had in mind such items as radar, military transport, and communications gear. Mondale's rhetoric was acquiring substance.

August 25, 1980: Following the visit to China of his running mate, George Bush, Republican candidate Ronald Reagan issued a clarifying statement on his China policy. Without knowledge of the negotiating record, Reagan asserted that:

> By accepting China's three conditions for normalization (severance of U.S. diplomatic relations with Taiwan, termination of the defense treaty, and withdrawal of all forces from Taiwan), Jimmy Carter made concessions that Presidents Nixon and Ford steadfastly refused to make. I was and am critical of his decision because I believe he made concessions that were not necessary and not in our national interest.

Reagan also stated that he "would not pretend that the relationship we now have with Taiwan is not official." Finally,

Reagan claimed, "it is absurd . . . that our representatives are not permitted to meet with Taiwanese officials in their offices and ours." These sentences directly contradicted the American government's pledge to the People's Republic at the time of normalization that "the American people and the people of Taiwan will maintain commercial, cultural, and other relations without official government representation and without diplomatic relations." With the ascension if Ronald Reagan to the Presidency, therefore, questions of the credibility and continuity of American policy toward China once again came to the fore.

SHIFTS IN CHINA'S APPROACH TO THE UNITED STATES

While the United States has not pursued a constant policy toward China, neither has China conducted a consistent policy toward the United States. There is little reason to believe, in fact, that American constancy would have elicited a similar commitment from the Chinese government. Of course, both during the warlord period (1911–1927) and under Chiang Kai-shek the weak and faction-ridden central government lacked sufficient control over the country to conduct a coherent, sustained foreign policy.

Vacillation and uncertainty have also characterized the Communist government's America policy. Mao Zedong replaced his 1944–45 interest in an American connection with a tilt toward the Soviet Union by 1946–47. The imprisonment of Angus Ward, the U.S. consul general in Mukden, in 1948–49 and the rough treatment of American diplomats elsewhere undermined the possibility of constructive contacts with the United States. The 1954–55 Chinese probe on the Taiwan issue through the ambassadorial talks never got anywhere in part because of Peking's failure to release all Americans imprisoned in China, as had been agreed. Chinese behavior, which diverged from their more flexible rhetoric, simply confirmed Dulles's suspicion of Communist duplicity. More generally, the moderate Chinese foreign policy of 1954–57—the so-called "Bandung phase"—ended with vituperative behavior toward Japan, the shelling of the offshore islands of Quemoy and Matsu, and Sino-Indian tension in 1958–59. And signs of Chinese interest in expanded contacts with the West in the early 1960s were accompanied by increased assistance to Vietnam and assertive, destabilizing Chinese involvement in Africa and Southeast Asia.

Indeed, China is the only major power which has pursued three different national security strategies over the past three decades: joining the Soviet alliance system in the bipolar world of the 1950s, trying to rely on its own strength while pursuing hostile policies toward both the Soviet Union and the United States in the 1960s, and drawing upon American strength as a counter to Moscow in the 1970s. To be sure, this evolution in Chinese foreign policy and the dramatically altered role assigned to the U.S. occurred for reasons partly beyond China's control, but the changes were also partly the result of choices made in Peking.

SOURCES OF INSTABILITY IN SINO-AMERICAN RELATIONS

We are therefore left with a perplexing question. What explains the volatility or fragility of Sino-American relations? How is it that these two nations have proven unable to sustain a steady course toward each other? Unless the sources of instability are understood and remedied, the current mutually beneficial relationship may prove as ephemeral as previous phases of Sino-American cooperation.

To anticipate the argument, the relationship has proven particularly sensitive to slight shifts in the global balance of power and to internal political changes because neither side successfully forged institutional structures, encompassing substantive interests, which would sustain constructive relations. Further, it has proven difficult to root a constructive Sino-American relationship in our governmental bureaucracies because the constituencies for a positive relationship have tended to be politically weak and because the interests at stake—while considerable—have been hard to translate into concrete, mutually rewarding programs. Finally, because the bilateral relationship has never developed an extensive, deep, and enduring quality, policy makers on both sides have been prone to view the relationship tactically, weighing it against relations of greater importance to each and against their momentary domestic political needs.

Before elaborating on this interpretation, it should be noted that this view, with its emphasis on political structure and interests, parts company from two other frequently offered explanations. The first of these might be called the "human folly" school; the second, the "cultural determinist" school.

The "human folly" argument is that misunderstanding and ignorance, usually on the American side, have resulted in "lost chances" in China. Each interpreter selects his particular moment of misunderstanding: the failure to respond to Mao Zedong's desire to visit Washington in 1944–45; the rebuff of the communist invitation to enter into a dialogue with Leighton Stuart in 1949; the rush toward the Yalu River during the Korean War despite intelligence that Chinese intervention would follow; the Dulles era intransigence of 1954–55; the unwillingness to enter into a serious dialogue with the PRC in the early 1960s. Each "lost opportunity" is attributed to a particular, supposedly rigid person: Hurley, Joseph McCarthy, Dulles, Dean Rusk.

The recitation of these supposed "lost opportunities" exposes the weakness of the argument. With so many missed chances, clearly something more profound than human folly is at stake. Repeated errors in assessment suggest that structural flaws, not individual human error, may be the source of the difficulty.

At the opposite end of the spectrum are the "cultural determinists," who argue that our cultural differences prevent America and China from developing sustained relations. The United States and China seem locked into a cyclical love-hate relationship. There are no lost opportunities in Sino-American affairs, only illusions of them. The relationship suffers from a surfeit of emotion. Each side holds a wide range of superficial, weakly held stereotypes of the other. Moments of friendship quickly turn into euphoria, as all the positive images are called into being. Unrealistic expectations swiftly build, only to be unrealized. A round of recriminations sets in, whereupon all the negative images are called into being. This view, most elegantly and convincingly developed by Harold Isaacs in his classic study of American attitudes toward China, *Scratches on Our Mind,* should not be lightly dismissed. Polls repeatedly have shown very swift changes in public opinions toward China, revealing that attitudes are indeed shallowly held. Because of the missionary legacy, an emotional dimension does exist in Sino-American affairs that seems less pronounced in other relations. Moreover, some truth exists in the observation that both China and the United States suffer from "Middle Kingdom" syndromes and that the closer the two countries come together, the more they repel each other. Chinese passivity and retiring graciousness seem to intensify American assertiveness. American openness and generosity frequently encourage Chinese manipulativeness.

But cultural determinism provides too easy an answer to the instability in Sino-American relations. It precludes the success of such private, binational organizations as Harvard-Yenching, the YMCA, the Peking Union Medical College, and Yale-in-China which had such great impact on China from the early 1900s to 1949. It cannot explain the success of the U.S.–Taiwan relationship. It cannot account for those moments of upturn in the cycle, such as President Nixon's visit to Peking or the 1944 dispatch of the Dixie Mission (a military observer group) to Yenan. As Isaacs and others note, the relationship embodies such a heavy dosage of sentiment precisely because the other dimension of a relationship—a hard-headed awareness of interest—seems so lacking. Hence we must turn elsewhere than culture for our explanation, to matters of interest and structure.

LACK OF INSTITUTIONAL STABILITY

The fact is that a constructive Sino-American relationship has never been institutionalized. The exception was the Taiwan-American relationship, which by the late 1960s was deeply rooted in the workings of the Departments of State, Treasury, Defense, Commerce, and Agriculture, the CIA, Export-Import Bank, and the World Bank, and it had extensive support in the Congress. As Richard Moorsteen and Morton Abramowitz stressed in their seminal analysis, *Remaking China Policy* (1971), the U.S.–PRC relationship was also institutionalized at the time—as an adversarial one. Nearly every agency of the U.S. government had hostile missions toward the People's Republic. Many of these missions were intimately related to the defense treaty with the Republic of China on Taiwan; but others grew out of the trade embargo, immigration restrictions, and outstanding financial claims against Peking.

One vivid example of the obstacles this situation posed comes from the settlement of the "claims-assets" issue in 1979. The United States government had registered roughly $200 million of private claims against the People's Republic for property seized during the revolution and had also blocked approximately $80 million of PRC assets in American banks or foreign banks subject to American law. Naturally, China sought recovery of the blocked assets, while the United States had to obtain a congressionally approved recovery of a portion of the private claims before the United States and China could develop a normal commercial relationship.

The bureaucratic problem was that several officials in Treasury had managed this issue for years, knowing all its details and the myriad problems involved. In 1973, seeking to demonstrate substantive progress in the relationship, Zhou Enlai and Henry Kissinger reached an agreement in principle in which the assets would be swapped. This involved a $17 million Chinese contribution to the American side of the deal as that amount had been successfully drained from third country banks. The Zhou-Kissinger agreement was reached in a morning of negotiation; but that same afternoon, in discussions among the specialists, the agreement began to unravel. The Chinese edged away from the $17 million contribution, while in subsequent weeks Treasury lawyers began to add all sorts of clarifications and limitations to the deal. The Chinese finally concluded they would still have financial liabilities after a settlement.

The Carter administration inherited this complex negotiating record. In January 1979, President Carter and Vice Premier Deng Xiaoping instructed their subordinates to settle the issue, but the subsequent month of feverish activity at Treasury prior to Secretary W. Michael Blumenthal's March trip produced the response from the Treasury career lawyers that no satisfactory solution could be reached. Blumenthal intervened, and with his Chinese interlocutor, successfully developed a different approach during his trip to Peking. But then the bureaucrats on the Chinese side nibbled away at the document the secretary of the treasury and the minister of finance had initialed. When Secretary of Commerce Juanita Kreps visited China one month later, she found the claims-assets issue still unresolved. Raising the issue with Vice Premier Deng Xiaoping, a clearly surprised and exasperated Deng turned to his bureaucrats and said, "I thought this issue had been settled." He then instructed his aides to prepare the agreement for signature. Political will had to triumph over bureaucratic resistance on both sides.

With the pro-Taiwan, anti-PRC orientation of the federal bureaucracies in the late 1960s, only a cabal orchestrated by the White House could break through the barriers created during two decades of confrontation; and this appears to have been the same case in Peking. Indeed, as the 1980s began—a decade after the White House initiative had begun and two years after normalization—the bureaucratic residues of previous anti-China or anti-America missions were substantial in both capitals, while the constructive programs which the leaders on both sides feverishly attempted to implant during 1979–80 were still fresh, tender, and vulnerable to budget slashing.

THE INTERESTS AT STAKE

The absence of a constructive Sino-American relationship rooted in our respective bureaucracies has not stemmed from an absence of common interests. The costs each side has borne when Sino-American relations have been in disrepair or were given insufficient priority are adequate reminders of the interests at stake. After all, the three wars which the United States fought in Asia in the past fifty years at such great cost to both China and the United States were caused, in complicated fashion, by the inability of the United States and China to forge enduring positive bonds. China paid a high price for the officially tolerated outbursts of xenophobia, whether the Boxers in 1900, the antimissionary outbursts of the 1920s, the attacks on Americans in the late 1940s, or the Cultural Revolution of the 1960s. And the United States paid an equally high price for its "anti–Red China" campaign of the early 1950s. While the economic stakes have never been high to either side, therefore, the security interests in this relationship, by any objective standard, have been enormous.

A unified China with positive ties to the United States has enabled the U.S. to develop a constructive involvement in East Asia and has brought stability to the region. A hostile China, on the other hand, has been able to deny the United States a presence on the East Asian mainland unless supported by an American military presence (as in Korea); and even then it has exerted pressure on the American position throughout the region. A divided China has been a source of instability and great power competition.

Historically and today, China also has benefited greatly from a constructive relationship with the U.S. Not only after 1972, but before 1949, it secured access to American technology, skilled manpower, and capital to foster economic growth. It placed large numbers of its students in American universities on favored terms. And it obtained a balance of power, though of uncertain reliability, against the two powers seeking to encroach on Chinese sovereignty: Russia and Japan.

To be acted upon, however, interests must be perceived. And here is the rub. An understanding of the interests at stake has not always been grasped by the leading political figures on both sides. America's China hands both within and outside the government and China's America hands have been advocates attaching primacy to the relationship. Historically, however, they have tended to be mistrusted within their own societies. To the extent that the top political leaders perceived the stakes, domestic political constraints have tended to preclude their acting on their vision. Instead, they have had to subordinate the relationship to other, more immediate and more pressing political needs.

THE VAGARIES OF PRESIDENTIAL LEADERSHIP

We are now in a position to illuminate the issue we posed at the outset—the reasons for the recurring instability in Sino-American relations. The sources of this fragility are somewhat different on each side. For the United States, the factors are the great influence of a handful of individuals in each administration who shape China policy on the basis of untutored sentiment, the shifts in global, strategic views of each administration, the role assigned China under each view, and the fragility of any political coalition in favor of constructive Sino-American ties.

To a striking extent, only a handful of people have managed the relationship on each side. On the American side, the President obviously has had considerable impact. Yet no President has been elected even partly on the basis of his China policy. Eisenhower's pledge to end the Korean War contributed to his victory in 1952, but the electorate was not informed as to how he proposed to terminate the conflict. Kennedy adopted a more moderate stance on the American commitment to the defense of Quemoy-Matsu than Nixon assumed during their 1960 television debates, but again neither candidate spelled out his China policy. In 1968 Nixon assured the public that he had a secret plan to end the Vietnam War, but he did not disclose his plans toward China. The only time China policy per se was an election issue was in 1980, and candidate Reagan's stance clearly hurt rather than helped his campaign.

Further, with the exceptions of Richard Nixon and Jimmy Carter in the post–World War II era, no President assumed office with what might be called a tutored view of the China issue. Nixon had spent considerable time in East Asia, had discussed China with several knowledgeable people, and by 1967 had seen the strategic opportunities inherent in an opening to China. Carter entered office with the view that Sino-American enmity was abnormal (a view reinforced by his own favorable impressions of the Chinese people formed in his youth) and that the opening to China had to be consolidated through normalization lest Washington and Peking again drift apart. One does not have the impression that Eisenhower, Kennedy, Johnson, or Ford had thought carefully about the issue, even though each had been exposed to the problems before assuming office. As Nixon's special emissary to Taiwan from the Republican right, sent to assure Taipei of the earnestness of American intent, Reagan also had experienced the relationship, but solely from Taiwan's vantage. The net result has been that with the exception of Nixon and Carter, China policy has been determined almost capriciously by the often ill-informed views on China the President brought to office.

Beyond the President, in each administration two or three figures emerged who strongly shaped the President's views: under Truman, Dean Acheson; for Eisenhower, Dulles and Assistant Secretary Walter Robertson; in the Kennedy era, Dean Rusk, McGeorge Bundy, and Walt Rostow; for Johnson, Rusk and Rostow; for Nixon and Ford, Kissinger; and for Carter, Zbigniew Brzezinski, Leonard Woodcock, Brown, and—on the desirability of normalization—Cyrus Vance. Yet, none of these advisers was selected for views on China. Again, the element of chance shaped policy.

If personal proclivities toward China introduced discontinuities in the relationship, so too did the global strategic view which each administration gradually came to hold. Each administration since 1949 has had a different perspective on the potential of China in the maintenance of peace. The Eisenhower administration saw China as dependent upon Moscow. Its China policy, therefore, was an extension of a global effort to contain communism. The confrontation was uncompromising, partly in hopes of inducing Sino-Soviet strain, and offered an implicit escape. When Peking escaped Moscow's clutches and was prepared to leave Taiwan in peace, the United States would be prepared to alter its stance.

In a sense, this strategic perspective offered China more hope than the one adopted during the Kennedy administration. To be sure, the Kennedy administration sought to initiate bilateral relations with the PRC. It offered wheat to China during its post–Great Leap Forward grain crisis. It sought an exchange of journalists. It expressed interest in cultural exchanges. The Kennedy administration envisioned these modest proposals as a way to unfreeze the situation, mindful that any first step could evoke an attack from the Republican right.

The Chinese did not respond to these overtures, probably in part because the Kennedy administration had not enunciated a broader strategic view of China which made suggestions for improvements in bilateral relations credible. To the contrary, the Chinese feared with some justice that the real American strategic design of the early 1960s was to reach an accommodation with Moscow at Peking's expense. Particularly after the Cuban missile crisis and the nuclear test-ban treaty signing in 1963, Kennedy and his advisers had concluded that once Moscow and Washington began to contain the dangers of nuclear war and nuclear proliferation, the greatest threat to peace would be limited war, especially wars of insurgency. And the leading exponent in those days of justified limited wars, guerrilla warfare, and nuclear proliferation was Peking. Hence, the Kennedy administration began to develop a counter-insurgency capability and considered Peking to be a greater threat to world peace than was the Soviet Union.

The various memoirs of the Kennedy years obscure this perception, but the conduct of the Warsaw talks and several internal policy memoranda manifest it. Thus the Chinese concluded that the consideration by Maxwell Taylor of a surgical nuclear strike against China, the decisive tilt toward India in the Sino-Indian border war of 1962, the continued American assistance to various resistance groups within China, and the belief that Vietnam was a test case of China's method of indirect aggression which had to be repulsed, all revealed the underlying Kennedy approach to China. With that strategic assessment, the various efforts to improve bilateral relations were rejected by the Chinese as petty, hypocritical moves designed to cover a malevolent policy.

Bogged down in the Vietnam War and then dealing with a China in the throes of the Cultural Revolution, the Johnson administration seemingly never developed a coherent strategic view of China. But the Nixon, Ford, and Carter administrations saw the contribution China might make to the maintenance of a global balance of power. Just as Kennedy helped to create the irresponsible China he perceived, Nixon and his two successors elicited Chinese cooperation because they treated Peking as a responsible, positive force. To an extent, strategic perceptions create their own reality; and shifting views of global strategy and of China's role in it affect the nature of Sino-American relations.

Finally, it has proven difficult to forge a strong enduring domestic political coalition in support of constructive relations with China. Although we have noted the considerable American interest in positive Sino-American ties, they are related to national security concerns which do not easily translate into the coalitions among the private sector interest groups, bureaucrats, and congressional committees which move Washington. Since 1972, China policy has proven susceptible to attack from many quarters:

1. pro-Taiwan elements, so visible during congressional consideration of the Taiwan Relations Act;
2. the vigorous advocates of detente with the Soviet Union who believe China policy should be subordinated to Soviet policy and who, for example, preferred to delay extension of most-favored-nation treatment to China until it could be simultaneously extended to the Soviet Union;
3. the textile lobby, which vigorously and successfully has kept quotas from China low, even though the value of Chinese imports of raw cotton from the U.S. exceeds the value of its textile exports to the United States;
4. assorted Americans with pro-Vietnam, pro-India, and/or human rights concerns who seek U.S. government condemnations of and opposition to those aspects of Chinese behavior that encroach on their priorities;
5. some pro-Israel supporters, who looked askance at normalization out of fear the United States might one day treat Israel as it did Taiwan ("Taiwan is the Israel of the East" is their slogan), and who also react to China's support of the PLO and who seek Taiwan purchases of Israeli military equipment; and finally,
6. some Asian specialists who have urged caution each step of the way since 1972 for the unsettling effects they foresaw—frequently erroneously—upon our relations with Japan, South Korea, and our ASEAN partners.

On the other side have been much of the business community, anti-Soviet conservatives, many foreign policy specialists, the bulk of the academic community, and a good portion of the Chinese-American community. Except on trade issues, this coalition has not provided a strong base of support. As a result, since 1972 the maintenance of a coherent China policy has required strong presidential and on occasion vice presidential involvement. And within the State Department, a vigorous assistant secretary for East Asia and an active China desk have had to defend the policy from encroachment by the Soviet

specialists, the Economics Bureau, the human rights groups (during the Carter years), and so on.   „
An example is the considerable personal involvement of Vice President Mondale, with the active support of Assistant Secretary of State for East Asian and Pacific Affairs Richard Holbrooke, to put the vice president's August 1980 trip together: a visit by Mondale to Vance to secure the secretary's reluctant determination that China was a friendly country, for purposes of the United States undertaking reimburseable aid projects; a visit to Senator Robert Byrd to secure commitment to Senate consideration of the Trade Agreement; conversations with Export-Import Bank officials to obtain a $2 billion commitment for loans to China; pressing the Departments of Energy and Commerce and the Civil Aeronautics Administration to advance negotiations on hydroelectric, maritime, and aviation agreements. Another example is the persistent efforts by Kissinger, Brzezinski, and Brown to loosen export controls to China.
The lesson is clear. Active presidential involvement, or leadership by a strong secretary of state, is necessary to preserve a coherent policy in the face of bureaucratic inertia and diverse interest group activities which tend to erode various parts of the policy. The adverse consequences for China policy of a weakened Nixon during Watergate in 1973–74, of Ford under challenge for the nomination in 1976, and of Carter in his weakness of 1980 simply underscore the point.
But then one must ask what political incentive did these and earlier Presidents have to provide leadership on China policy. Eisenhower, Kennedy, and Johnson all clearly thought overt involvement in an opening to China would be politically risky, although behind the scenes Eisenhower sought to minimize the level of hostility in the confrontation of the 1950s. Nixon, of course, brilliantly assessed the benefits he would obtain from appearing in Peking. It helped assure his reelection. Carter also perceived the benefits, though they were not nearly as great. He seems to have believed that normalization would underscore his competence in managing foreign policy and would reveal his courage and willingness to take on difficult decisions that served the nation well. He hoped to run for

reelection on a record of foreign policy accomplishments. In addition, he believed that normalization would make it easier to sell SALT. He believed that some senators might find SALT more palatable because of the enhanced anti-Soviet posture which normalization would yield. And he probably hoped to enhance his stature through Deng Xiaoping's visit to the United States, although that consideration certainly was not uppermost in his mind in planning for the visit.

With normalization completed, the positive political benefits are likely to be fewer, though a President should be sensitive to the high political costs he would pay if Sino-American relations deteriorated during his tenure, especially if military confrontation returned to East Asia or a Sino-Soviet rapprochement were to occur.

China's Formulation of an American Policy

THE IMPORTANCE OF THE STRATEGIC BALANCE

On the Chinese side, a different set of considerations also produces uncertainties in policy toward the United States. Since 1949, continuity existed in the individuals managing the relationship: Mao Zedong, Zhou Enlai, and Deng Xiaoping (after 1973, excluding 1976), and a number of Western educated foreign policy specialists whose diplomatic involvement with the United States dates to Yenan, the Marshall mission, and the Korean War. The twists and turns stem from China's changing relationship with the Soviet Union, shifts in domestic economic development strategy, bureaucratic politics, and factional strife in Peking.

Since 1949, China has sought its national security within the Sino–Soviet–U.S. triangle. At the outset, Peking sought to draw on the Soviet Union as a counterweight to the United States. An early reason for the Sino-Soviet dispute in the late 1950s was Khrushchev's pursuit of detente with the United States and the related limits Moscow placed on its backing of Peking (as in the Taiwan Strait crisis of 1958). China saw Moscow as willing to sacrifice Chinese interests for an improved Soviet-American relationship. Chiang Kai-shek had witnessed a similar spectacle at Yalta of a Soviet-American condominium determining issues involving Chinese sovereignty (such as foreign involvement in Manchuria). The spectre of Soviet-American collusion against China worried Peking throughout the 1960s, and the Chinese nervously sought their security by competing in hostile fashion with both. The Soviet invasion of Czechoslovakia in 1968 and the enunciation of the Brezhnev doctrine a year later, however, as well as the Sino-Soviet border clashes of 1969, highlighted the dangers of China's exposed position. One measure, in response, was Peking's attempt to reduce Sino-American hostility.

Throughout the 1970s the Soviets persisted in their military build-up along the Chinese border, and their expansionist tendencies became ever more evident. This led China to undertake an increasingly close relationship with the United States. However, this inclination was not automatic. When the United States demonstrated a lack of will, as in Vietnam in 1975, Angola in 1975–76, Ethiopia in 1977, or during the early Carter administration's inclination to reduce military expenditures and withdraw from South Korea, the Chinese stepped back from their American connection out of concern they were not associating themselves with a credible power. During periods of Soviet-American rapprochement, especially following the Brezhnev-Ford summit at Vladivostok, the Chinese also deliberately let their dissatisfaction become public. The appearance of American efforts to attain improvements in Soviet-American relations at China's expense—indeed, improvements facilitated through the Sino-American connection—induced China to disengage slightly from the United States.

Finally, the American handling of the crises in Iran and Afghanistan revealed yet another limit to China's association with the U.S. When Peking perceives that American rhetoric exceeds its strength, or when American activism may benefit the Soviets, the Chinese have not been forthcoming in dealings with the U.S. The Chinese did not support Washington's call for United Nations sanctions against Iran, believing that the Soviets would have benefited from Iran's isolation. And in January 1979, while generally supportive of the American response to Afghanistan, Peking was reserved on some measures. Thus, the Chinese displayed little inclination in 1979–80 to provoke Soviet-American tensions to the point that China might inadvertently be drawn into a conflict.

In short, the Chinese have continually, carefully calibrated the balance of forces in the strategic triangle, and even slight shifts in Soviet-American or Sino-Soviet relations immediately have affected China's posture toward the United States. Thus, an ongoing assessment apparently occurs in Peking concerning the strategic utility of the American connection, but the calculation is not undertaken in "zero based budgeting" terms—that is, a continual, total reappraisal. Rather, there is a constant calculation of appropriate incremental or marginal adjustments in the face of the latest Soviet maneuver and American response. Whether the increments are to increase, decrease, or extend ties to new areas has depended on the context, and has been somewhat unpredictable. This introduces a note of uncertainty at the margins of the relationship.

ECONOMIC DEVELOPMENT STRATEGY AND FOREIGN POLICY

Another source of policy tenuousness, much more severe in impact, has been the continual reappraisal of China's economic development strategy. Since 1949 China has pursued at least six different strategies for economic growth: economic rehabilitation, 1949–52; the centralized, heavy industry-oriented First Five Year Plan, 1953–57; the mobilized Great Leap Forward, 1958–60; the laissez faire Great Leap recovery, 1961–65; the self-reliant Cultural Revolution, 1966–74; and the "Four Modernization" drive, 1975 to the present.

Many factors produced these changes in development strategy—Mao's changing sense of how to keep China on a path of socialist change, power struggles within the leadership, and a changing foreign environment. Another important source of change was an evolution in the objective, internal economic problems faced by China's leaders. Since 1949, reducing the rate of population increase, sustaining growth in agricultural production, removing a changing list of bottlenecks in the industrial sector, training a scientific and technical elite, and increasing management efficiency have been the five major economic problems confronting the leadership, but no single set of policies could possibly have responded adequately to all these problems.

China's performance during the past thirty years reveals that each development strategy perforce has neglected some economic objectives or other worthwhile social goals (such as reducing urban-rural and interregional income disparities) or produced unintended consequences that required modifications of policy.

Moreover, each broad development strategy has had its distinctive foreign policy consequences. Both the Great Leap and the Cultural Revolution helped to engender foreign pressures and produced a hostile environment for foreigners inside China. On the other hand, the First Five Year Plan and the post-Mao era assigned a major role to foreign advisers, trade, technology, and whole plant imports. During the 1950s, the economy was organized in ways congruent with an extensive Soviet relationship, while in the late 1970s Peking sought to shape the economic system for Western involvement through joint venture arrangements, tax laws, and decentralization measures.

These changes in economic policy also had major consequences for defense policy. The emphasis on self-reliance during the Cultural Revolution saw substantial increases in the percentage of the nation's budget allocated to the military, while the post-Mao era witnessed uncertainty in foreign relations as well. In early 1978, Premier Hua Guofeng set forth ambitious targets for the end of the century in agriculture and industry. Chinese ministries embarked on extensive negotiations for myriad projects with Japanese, European, and American firms. During those heady days, Chinese leaders apparently believed that China's growth could be quite rapid and significantly facilitated by swift, extensive involvement of the West. Within twelve months, however, the structural and financial constraints to such grandiose plans were abundantly evident, and Hua's plan was quietly shelved. Throughout 1979 and 1980, the focus was on structural reform: decentralization; expansion of the light industrial and agricultural sectors of the economy; creation of a limited market; management and wage reforms, and price readjustments. A few major foreign commitments for purchases in the metallurgy, transportation, chemical, and energy fields were made. Then, in late 1980, the leadership concluded that these structural reforms were producing inflation, government deficits, and excessive rates of investment. They ordered a retrenchment and cancelled several large orders for foreign imports.

This record of repeated major changes in policy naturally leads to questions about China's ability to sustain a coherent, consistent economic policy toward the West. Nonetheless, several reasons exist for believing that China's turn outward is likely to persist. The two periods of a self-reliant development strategy (the Great Leap, and the Cultural Revolution) were clearly instigated by Mao Zedong, and it is unlikely that any leader for some time to come would wish or be able to emulate his style of leadership.

Aside from these two epochs (1958–60 and 1966–74), it is worth noting that Peking has recognized the importance of expanding contact with the outside world. In addition, the immediate post-Mao plans were highly unrealistic, while the level of foreign involvement envisioned in the retrenchment of late 1980 is sustainable. Finally, the objective major bottlenecks which Peking currently faces are likely to persist for some time in the areas of energy, transportation, electronics, tight urban grain supplies, an educational and research system in disrepair, and a shortage of scientific personnel. These bottlenecks can be significantly alleviated through a Western connection. Some of the previous sources of policy volatility in China's development strategy, in short, have been removed.

At the same time, one must recognize that sources of social instability do exist. Satisfying rising popular expectations for a higher standard of living and securing employment for youth will be pressing problems in the years ahead. Increasing urban-rural income disparities could induce tensions between city and countryside, while administrative decentralization will exacerbate tensions between the developed and the backward regions of the country. The increasing Western presence will also invoke, in some measure, antiforeign sentiments. The management of inevitable social discontent will be a constant challenge for the regime. In short, as with other developing countries, there is a measure of instability to China's modernization process, and the possibility of disorder is always there, particularly if the current development strategy fails to meet expectations.

CHINA'S BUREAUCRATIC BIPLAY

A third limitation to the conduct of Chinese foreign policy has been the fragmentation, inertia, and inefficiency of the bureaucracy. Inevitably, the benefits and burdens of the American opening have fallen unevenly on the myriad organizations whose compliance is essential for the success of the policy. For example, the burden upon the public security apparatus is immeasurably more complex due to the Western presence in China: overseas Chinese meeting relatives, Western journalists talking to dissident youths, American anthropologists nosing about the countryside, and so on. Portions of the military may shoulder increased risks of conflict with the Soviets because of the American connection.

Whether these specific surmises are correct or not, nonetheless, some organizations have been handed added tasks without accompanying increases in budget allocations or manpower or without compensating rewards from the West. It is clear that, given the segmentation of the Peking bureaucracy, such organizations are able to sabotage or delay policies set at higher levels. Moreover, Chinese bureaucrats have demonstrated an awareness of the fragility of Sino-American relations and the policy vacillations of the Politburo over the past three decades. This has induced a reluctance to make a full commitment to current policy, a tendency to hold back, so that a bureaucrat can prove he was less than fully compliant with a policy that may be subsequently condemned.

The converse is also true, with equally damaging consequences. Some bureaucrats and localities have gained a great deal from the American connection. Such units have tended to whet the appetite of their American clients with promises of an ever-expanding relationship. Unauthorized commitments have been made, sometimes in order to enmesh the Americans in lobbying activities at higher levels on behalf of the lower-level unit. Deals which Westerners thought were secure have been cancelled by supervising agencies or have failed to secure the cooperation of a third unit whose involvement had not previously been mentioned. These frustrating aspects of Chinese bureaucratic behavior, which are sometimes accompanied by requests for gratuities, cannot be attributed simply to the influence of a Soviet-style economy. The situation echoes the complaints of Western merchants who traded along the China coast in the early 1800s, reflecting continuities in bureaucratic style. But it does mean that rooting a constructive relationship in China's bureaucratic landscape will be a Herculean task.

One suspects, as with the creation of the Customs Service, Post Office, and Ministry of Foreign Affairs in the late years of the Qing Dynasty, new organizations will have to be developed if any degree of efficiency in dealing with the West is to be obtained. Indeed, the creation of new trading agencies and the call for joint ventures may be a recognition of the problem.

PEKING'S LEADERSHIP FACTIONALISM

The final internal factor causing uncertainty and fragility is the factional basis of Chinese leadership struggles. As with previous Chinese leadership groups, the Communist Party has been plagued by factionalism based as much on personal ties and loyalties as on specific policy preferences. When the Politburo engages in one of its inevitable periodic conflicts over power and position, all issues become game for use in the struggle.

At any point in time, given the division of labor among the senior leaders, certain Politburo members bear special responsibility for America policy. Inescapably, the relationship begins to depend upon their political strength. The managers of the relationship are in an exposed position if the relationship sours. The game can be brutal, and a group that seeks to weaken a Zhou Enlai or Deng Xiaoping can deliberately cause troubles in the American relationship in order to induce a vexing U.S. response. They then can hold Zhou, Deng, or whomever responsible for the trouble.

On at least two occasions, America policy appears to have become entangled in such factional strife. Among the issues dividing Mao's then-anointed successor Lin Biao from Mao and Zhou in the summer of 1971, evidence suggests, was the opening to the United States. Lin lost, but one wonders what would have happened if he had won. And from 1974 through 1976, as Zhou Enlai's political position eroded under attacks from the radical "Gang of Four," the Premier's ability to protect and advance the issues under his control weakened. By 1975, it was impossible for him or for Deng Xiaoping to bring fresh initiatives to the relationship with the United States.

By 1980 Deng Xiaoping was politically exposed because of his deep personal involvement in normalization. His conversations with Leonard Woodcock from December 13 to 15, 1978 had brought the negotiations to a decisive conclusion; and Deng had pushed the relationship forward through 1979 and 1980. Were Deng to become vulnerable on other grounds, such as his management of the economy, it nonetheless would introduce uncertainty into the Sino-American relationship. If he felt his association with the issue had become a political vulnerability, he might even seek to shed his connection with it. Relatedly, were the United States to make a mockery of the normalization agreements which Deng induced his colleagues to accept in the fall of 1978, it would immeasurably weaken his position. Some outside observers believed that Ronald Reagan's assumption of the Presidency and the new administration's lethargic endorsement of the normalization agreement produced political problems for Deng in late 1980.

In such circumstances, it might well be asked whether the leadership in Peking is so endemically faction-ridden that China is simply an unreliable, even impossible, partner with whom the United States can seek to align its policies. Three points should be made. First, the Sino-American relationship has grown and prospered even as Peking was embroiled in the most intense factional strife it can experience. The China opening occurred as Mao eliminated Lin Biao. The relationship survived the intense struggle between the so-called Gang of Four and Deng Xiaoping and his cohorts over Mao's succession in the period 1973–77. This record suggests the United States can proceed on the assumption that China's leaders act on their national interest.

Second, while the struggle for power within the Politburo is ceaseless, Deng Xiaoping has brought to power leaders who appear to share a commitment to pragmatic, growth-oriented policies. Sharp differences may well develop over tactics, and personal power, but the leadership seems more unified over basic policies than at any time in twenty years. Shake-ups in the leadership will continue, but the consequences for foreign policy are likely to be minimal. (The exception, of course, would be a leadership change induced by foreign policy reversals.)

Finally, this leadership has shown some capacity to contain its differences within the Politburo and Central Committee and not to allow its struggles to entail mobilization of popular discontent for power purposes. Circumstances could arise to change this, of course, such as massive failures in the Four Modernizations programs. But at present the leadership even seems willing to court unrest, such as by shutting down unprofitable factories and dismissing unproductive workers, in order to accelerate growth. Mobilization politics, with attendant xenophobic outbursts, seem unlikely for the immediate future.

The military provides another uncertain note. Since Mao's death, the army has seen its budget cut while its burden against the Soviet Union and Vietnam has increased. Military modernization has fourth priority among the Four Modernizations. Some outside observers believe that the military continues to be a reservoir of support for the memory of Chairman Mao, where his contributions are still cherished. Resistance to de-Maoification may come from that quarter. Should the military become more assertive in the formulation of either Chinese domestic or foreign policies, it is not clear what the implications would be for U.S.–PRC relations.

In short, as with China's economic development strategy, an assessment of the current PRC leadership yields a conclusion of caution. Continuity is likely, but the possibility of instability persists.

The Interaction of Chinese and American Policies

THE IMPORTANCE OF THIRD-PARTY ISSUES

Now that we have examined the sources of fragility, one other aspect of the relationship deserves explanation, namely its highly interactive quality. Friendly or hostile actions on one side quickly engender a magnified response from the other.

There has been a repeated tendency to enter into either ascending or descending spirals of improvement or deterioration in the relationship. Why does this happen?

In the absence of a wide range of bilateral ties linking the two countries, either side enjoys wide latitude in developing measures to signal displeasure, to exert leverage, or to enhance the relationship. Each side enjoys only a limited range of responses to initiatives by the other, and the tendency is to respond in kind. Throughout the 1970s the relationship remained sufficiently constrained that at any one moment in time the principal policy makers managing the relationship at the working level in the State Department and the Ministry of Foreign Affairs could effectively handle no more than six to eight issues. That is, there was a sharp limit to the number of issues being actively discussed and negotiated between the two countries at the political level. To be sure, span-of-control problems and time constraints limit any agenda, but the Sino-American agenda was particularly limited because the issues frequently were being addressed for the first time and therefore were particularly complex, thorny, and time-consuming. Each side had a great deal of learning to do, whether the issue was establishing consulates, reaching a civil aviation agreement, or negotiating a tax treaty. Presumably as experience accumulates and agreements are reached governing all areas of the relationship, policy makers will be able to deal with a larger range of issues.

More importantly, with a thin bilateral relationship, the most important interactions between China and the United States tend to take place in third areas where the tangible interests of both sides are engaged: especially Korea, Taiwan, Indochina; and also Japan, Southeast Asia, and South Asia. From this perspective, the real dynamics of the relationship—what has driven the two apart or pulled them together—are to be found less in the bilateral relationship than in the way that China and the United States have interacted in other localities. A few examples will demonstrate the point.

Neither China nor the United States launched the Korean War, but their interests inevitably were engaged in a situation of military conflict. Neither Peking nor Washington fully controlled their respective Korean allies, yet each was compelled to respond ever more firmly to the perceived provocations of the other side in the conflict. The result was a Chinese-American military conflict that neither side sought.

In 1973 the opposite phenomenon occurred. Both sides perceived an interest in reducing tensions between North and South Korea. A positive move by one elicited a response from the other, which in turn induced another constructive response. Particularly as neither side had to cajole reluctant domestic bureaucracies, the sequence of cooperative moves initiated by Peking and Washington to promote stability in Korea unfolded rather rapidly in 1973.

Another important example is Indochina. Where separate backing of North and South Vietnam during the period 1963–65 drove Peking and Washington apart, by 1973 the Indochina situation had altered dramatically. At that point, the U.S. and China shared the common objective of creating a coalition government in Kampuchea. The goal was to bring Prince Norodom Sihanouk back; but to attain that goal the United States and China had to work different aspects of the situation. China backed the Khmer Rouge, while the United States supported Lon Nol. Each side began to deal with its client in ways that would lead to compromises necessary to attain the common objective. But the 1973 Senate imposition of the bombing halt in Kampuchea upon a weakened President precluded the solution toward which both the United States and China had been working. With American leverage on the situation now eliminated, the Chinese had no choice but to abandon Sihanouk and fully back the Khmer Rouge. Instead of an ascending spiral of reinforcing moves, the prospects of Sino-American cooperation on Indochina events rapidly evaporated, and a good deal of the dynamism in the relationship at that time was lost.

Hanoi's turn to Moscow in 1978 provides yet another example. Both China and the United States responded to that development in ways that facilitated the normalization process. After the Vietnamese rejected Peking's effort of late 1977 to negotiate the Kampuchean-Vietnamese dispute, Hanoi turned to Moscow in early 1978 in its search for support to handle the Pol Pot regime. Vietnam began to expel its ethnic Chinese in early 1978, joined Moscow's Council of Mutual Economic

Assistance (CMEA) in May, signed a Peace and Friendship Treaty with the Soviet Union in November, and invaded Kampuchea in December. Faced with a growing security threat on its southern flank, Peking believed a strengthened relationship with the U.S. and diminished tensions in the Taiwan Strait to be in its interest. The Vietnamese actions also affected Washington's calculus. In September 1978 the Carter administration was prepared to normalize relations with Hanoi and had entered detailed discussions to this end. But after Hanoi's December invasion, this was no longer possible. Events on the Indochina Peninsula in 1978 affecting Chinese and American interests—but over which neither the U.S. nor China had control—helped to drive the two countries closer together than either had envisioned ten months previously.

An example of deliberate management of a transitory issue to strengthen Sino-American relations is described in Henry Kissinger's memoirs. The United States consciously responded to the 1971 Indo-Pakistani War in part to increase Peking's then-fledgling confidence in the utility of the American opening. First, Kissinger backed Pakistan, in part out of appreciation for the intermediary role it had played in facilitating the establishment of a channel of communication between the White House and PRC leaders. The Nixon administration wished to make clear that it rewarded its friends. In addition, Kissinger warned the Soviets not to take advantage of the unsettled situation in Peking—where PRC officials remained stunned and mutually distrustful after the September defection and death of Defense Minister Lin Biao—through encroachments on China. The Chinese noted the American posture, which eased Peking's move toward Washington.

Of all the localities where Chinese and American interests are inextricably intertwined and can be acted upon in ways that either buttress or weaken the relationship, none is more important than Taiwan. Judicious handling of the Taiwan issue—as occurred in the Shanghai Communiqué of 1972, in the 1978 normalization agreement, and in the careful selection of American arms sales to Taiwan since 1971—has contributed both to the island's prospects for a peaceful, prosperous future and to improved Sino-American relations. Sale of clearly defensive weapons such as F-5E aircraft and I-Hawk antiaircraft missiles, which Taiwan could not use to threaten Peking but which sustain its capacity to repulse China's available power in the foreseeable future, engenders a measure of confidence but not arrogance in Taipei. This pattern of arms sales has facilitated the initiation of constructive economic and scientific exchanges between the mainland and the island.

In contrast, should the U.S. sell Taiwan weapons with an offensive capability, such as an advanced fighter aircraft or the Harpoon antiship missile, irritants would be introduced into the Sino-American relationship as Taipei could pose some limited security challenge to the People's Republic. Put bluntly, to introduce a military threat on China's eastern flank at a time when Peking is carrying a heavy burden in its military deployments on northern and southern frontiers—deployments which benefit the United States—makes no strategic sense. Offensive arms sales to Taiwan could well induce the deteriorating interactive process we have highlighted in this section.

This cursory review suggests that more weighty American and Chinese interests are engaged in Korea, Taiwan, Southeast Asia, and the South Asian subcontinent than are at stake in the bilateral relationship. Yet neither the United States nor China can fully shape Sino-American interactions in these third locales. The relationship therefore has been highly susceptible to manipulation by others: Pyongyang and Seoul; Taipei; Hanoi and Saigon. Pakistan's Yahya Khan helped bring Mao Zedong and Richard Nixon together because it served his interest; but Taipei or the two Koreas are likely to introduce only irritants into Sino-American relations because their interests are served by heightened tensions between Washington and Peking.

China and the United States face a classic case of great powers whose relationship is subject to manipulation by their adversarial clients. And the relationship of each power to its clients has been too important to subordinate to the Sino-American connection. Thus, to an extent, both Peking and Washington have been willing on occasion to sacrifice Sino-American relations in order to protect their interests in Korea, Taiwan, or Indochina. The sacrifice, however, has usually turned out to be greater than either side envisaged. Conversely, both sides occasionally have subordinated interests in third party relationships for the sake of the Sino-American tie, and with a more beneficial impact on the bilateral relationship than either had anticipated. The momentum that is generated thereby—whether positive or negative—soon affects the state of play of the other issues on the agenda of those officials managing Sino-American relations. This dynamic gives the relationship its highly interactive quality.

Managing the Sino-American Relationship

This analysis of the dynamics of the Sino-American relationship suggests four conclusions for those managing its future evolution.

First, the relationship is inherently fragile, though important to both sides. Constant nourishment and meticulous management have been essential to progress in U.S.–PRC relations.

Second, strong presidential leadership, supported by the secretary of state, has been necessary to give coherence and constancy to the relationship. Moreover, China policy works best when the overall national security strategy adopted by an administration embodies recognition of the constructive contribution which China makes to the maintenance of a global balance of power.

Third, the status of Soviet-American and Japanese relations has had a decisive impact on the Sino-American relationship. Management of all three relationships must be integrated. In addition, American policy toward Korea, Indochina, and Taiwan (especially on the issues of arms sales and the maintenance of a strictly unofficial relationship) has major implications for the future of Sino-American relations.

Fourth, if the relationship is to acquire durability, it must eventually be rooted in more extensive bilateral ties supported by bureaucratic involvement on both sides. Fostering a broad range of economic, cultural, and scientific interactions seems the best way to bring this about.

In drawing these conclusions, we should at least note a paradox which seems to underlie the relationship: the simultaneous need for both presidential leadership and for bureaucratic institutionalization. Without institutionalization, the relationship remains fragile; but with institutionalization, slothful, internally uncoordinated, perhaps culturally incompatible bureaucracies may mismanage the relationship. This paradox is more apparent than real, however. Leadership is still required to give the Sino-American tie political direction and policy content. In that context, problems of bureaucratic implementation and coherence come to the fore. But such problems are far preferable to the political instability and policy discontinuities which have plagued Sino-American relations for the past century.

Strobe Talbott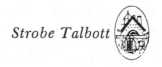

3

The Strategic Dimension
of the Sino-American Relationship

Enemy of Our Enemy, or True Friend?

The Complexity of Triangular Politics

When Henry Kissinger first met Zhou Enlai in Peking in July 1971, the American guest made a point of immediately offering his hand to his Chinese host. Kissinger was making amends for Secretary of State John Foster Dulles's much-publicized refusal to shake hands with Zhou at an international conference in Geneva back in 1954. In atmosphere and sym-

---

STROBE TALBOTT *is diplomatic correspondent of* Time magazine. *Educated at Yale and Oxford, where he specialized in Russian studies, Mr. Talbott translated and edited two volumes of Nikita Khrushchev's memoirs. His interest in strategic and arms control issues developed after 1974 during trips to Moscow, Geneva, and Vienna, where he reported on SALT negotiations conducted by Secretaries of State Kissinger and Vance and President Carter. He published* Endgame: The Inside Story of SALT II. *Mr. Talbott has made a number of trips to China covering the visits of Henry Kissinger in 1975 and James Schlesinger in 1978. In 1980 he interviewed Soviet sinologists in Moscow and Central Asia; and in 1981 he made an extensive tour of the Far East, including a week in Peking, to study regional security problems.*

bolism, Kissinger's first encounter with Zhou could hardly have differed more from Dulles's seventeen years before.

One thing had not changed, however: whether snubbing the Chinese statesman or reaching out to grasp his hand, the men from Washington were both making deliberate and by no means friendly gestures toward Moscow. Dulles regarded Zhou, correctly if not very far-sightedly, as an ally of the Soviet Union and an accomplice of the Russians in the cause of monolithic, predatory, international communism. Kissinger regarded the Chinese Premier as a potential associate of the U.S. and the West in their cause *against* the Soviet Union. Whether the U.S. was seeking to isolate the People's Republic, as Dulles intended in 1954, or to end that isolation, as Kissinger was in 1971, the China factor in American foreign policy has figured primarily in calculations about how to manage the United States' adversary relationship with the USSR.

The America factor has figured similarly in Chinese foreign and security policies. Zhou was receptive to Kissinger's pathbreaking visit not so much because of anything the U.S. had done as because of what the Soviet Army had done first by invading Czechoslovakia in 1968, and then by fighting Chinese border troops in 1969. In short, that first secret, subsequently famous, handshake in the foyer of a government guest house in Peking in 1971 came about because China and the U.S. had recognized a common interest in blocking the expansion of Soviet political influence and military power around the world.

In the decade since the opening between the U.S. and the PRC, that same global, strategic dimension of the relationship has been more important than any strictly bilateral issue. Its unifying influence has overridden a number of extremely divisive problems. Both sides have made extraordinary and often awkward compromises, with each other and with their own principles, for the sake of normalization. In 1979 the United States terminated its defense treaty with the Republic of China on Taiwan and transferred formal diplomatic recognition from a government representing free enterprise to one representing communist totalitarianism. For its part, the PRC accepted a contorted diplomatic fiction that allowed the U.S. to continue dealing, de facto, with Taiwan as a sovereign state despite

Peking's insistence that the island is a province awaiting return to the embrace of the motherland.

Certainly the Soviets have recognized that they are the main reason the Americans and Chinese have come together. The Kremlin has complained loudly and repeatedly about the anti-Soviet basis of U.S.–PRC normalization. The leaders of virtually every other country in the world, too, realize that their regions, and in some cases their internal situations, have been strongly influenced by the evolution of the triangular relationship among the U.S., the USSR, and the PRC.

That evolution has been the single most important development in global politics since World War II; and a drastic realignment among the three powers has been the most important development in each of the past three decades: the Sino-Soviet alliance of the 1950s; the Sino-Soviet split of the 1960s; and the Sino-American rapprochement of the 1970s. As the 1980s begin, the next stage is uncertain to say the least, and some of the possibilities are ominous. The evolution could proceed linearly, to a full-scale Sino-American military alliance against the Soviet Union. It could proceed circularly, with the collapse of Sino-American rapprochement and at least a partial return of the PRC to the Soviet fold. Or, "two could divide into three" (to play on a slogan from the Cultural Revolution), with China seeking to distance itself from both the Soviet Union and the U.S. to establish a more independent position in the strategic triangle. Either extreme, while not likely, would be only slightly more surprising than the seismic shifts that have already shaken the Sino-Soviet-American interrelationship.

Even with the greatest of skill and prescience, the U.S. will not be able fully to control the next stage of that interrelationship. Much depends on what the Soviets and the Chinese do—to, with, or despite each other, as well as what they do to, with, or despite the U.S. itself. Their leaderships are secretive gerontocracies prone to factionalism. The only real certainty is that the decade ahead will see generational successions in Moscow and Peking. This fact alone compounds the extent to which both the Soviet and Chinese factors in the calculus of American foreign policy are at least variables and sometimes unknowns; they are never constants.

But the U.S. can have more control over how the triangular relationship develops if it has a clear idea of how it *ought* to develop. With a guiding concept in mind, the U.S. will be better able to manage the complex interplay of its relations with the USSR and the PRC. Any strategy will necessarily require an understanding of the forces which continue to divide the two Communist giants. And it will require taking full advantage of whatever flexibility and freedom for maneuver the U.S. has in each of the two relationships.

Henry Kissinger was certainly playing the Soviets and Chinese off against each other in 1971. He was planning summit meetings for Richard Nixon in both Peking and Moscow the following year. In his mind and in the unfolding of events, Soviet-American detente, Sino-American rapprochement, and Sino-Soviet enmity were coordinated and mutually reinforcing. For the U.S., that intricate three-way dynamic was immensely advantageous. It meant that the interplay of hopes and anxieties on the part of the Soviets and the Chinese alike induced both sides to move closer to the U.S., and farther from each other, in the diplomatic repositioning of the early 1970s.

A decade later, that dynamic had largely broken down. The U.S. had lost much of its leverage for controlling the interplay. Detente with the Soviets was moribund, perhaps dead. From the onset, the Reagan administration repeatedly committed itself to the concept of "linkage": progress in negotiations and improvements in Soviet-American relations would depend on improved Soviet behavior in the international arena. The Soviets, for their part, expressed a willingness to resume detente—but not on the Reagan administration's terms, at least as initially stipulated. The Soviets dug in deeper than ever in Afghanistan even as they menaced Poland, and they showed no signs of calling off their Vietnamese allies in Indochina or their Cuban proxies in Africa. The superpower relationship, in short, was at best stagnant, at worst doomed to further deterioration and escalating confrontation.

The Sino-American relationship, by contrast, was still favorable, although not exactly thriving. Much of the euphoria had gone out of the atmosphere (and good riddance, perhaps, since unrealistic expectations had characterized the China opening just as they had marked the early days of detente). The election of Reagan, a self-proclaimed friend of Taiwan, had cast a shadow over what in the 1970s had become a well-trodden road from Washington to Peking. Once in office, however, Reagan promised to further the process of normalization. He and his foreign policy advisers made clear that the principal reason for this promise was China's potential strategic value vis-à-vis the Soviet Union. Thus, even though its momentum had diminished, the Sino-American relationship was still on the same track which Kissinger and Zhou Enlai had laid down a decade before, while the Soviet-American relationship was either derailed or moving in the opposite direction. Coordination and synchronization of the two policies were therefore immensely more difficult. Intelligent, forward-looking management of China policy became all the more important.

For the foreseeable future, it would probably be impossible—and it would certainly be unwise—to view China as something other than a strategic counterweight to the Soviet Union. China's own leaders see the U.S. much the same way, and Americans would be foolish to pretend that the driving force in Sino-American relations is anything other than a shared distrust of the USSR. Nevertheless, in the long term it would be in the best interest of the United States (and in China's own interest as well) for U.S.–PRC relations to assume a life of their own, as independent as possible of the Soviet connection. For one thing, any bilateral relationship is by definition precarious and constrained as long as it is primarily a function of the two parties' preoccupation with a third party. Between states, just as between individuals, it is a sign of trouble to be glancing nervously over each other's shoulders while pretending to look each other in the eye.

For some time to come, the U.S. will be bound to fear that its own interests might be jeopardized by any amelioration in the Sino-Soviet dispute. Yet some amelioration is not out of the question. William Hyland details, in chapter 5, China's exploration of the potential for a reduction in Sino-Soviet tensions in 1979—even as PRC leaders abrogated the 1950 treaty of alliance and friendship with the USSR and pursued normalization negotiations with the United States. And in early 1981, some Western sinologists thought they detected signs of renewed debate within the Chinese leadership about the advisability of reducing the confrontation along the disputed northern border, if only to permit the reallocation of some resources from the military to the industrial sector of the economy. Auguries of even the slightest shift in Chinese policy tend to touch off nervous speculation in the U.S. about the durability of the China connection.

By the same token, the PRC will probably continue to worry that its interests will be jeopardized if and when the U.S. and the Soviet Union ever reestablish some sort of modus vivendi, as one can only hope they will. Fortunately, China's contemporary leaders have repudiated Mao Zedong's cavalier talk about the inevitability of a superpower war and the virtues of "turmoil under the heavens." The Chinese are now more realistic about their ability to survive a world war, and they have all but repudiated what Mao called the "excellent" chaos of the Cultural Revolution. But they still seem to be a long way from recognizing that an improvement in U.S.–Soviet relations would be a contribution to international stability.

Regardless of whether Deng Xiaoping deliberately tried to sabotage the SALT II negotiations in the way that he handled his end of the Sino-American normalization negotiations in 1978, there is little doubt that the vice premier regarded it as a bonus that normalization did in fact complicate SALT and other aspects of Soviet-American diplomacy. For some time to come, the Chinese are likely to suspect that any thaw between Washington and Moscow may be a harbinger of some sort of superpower condominium. In a private interview in early 1981, a senior Chinese official, commenting on Leonid Brezhnev's just-launched "peace offensive," offered the following prediction, which was a telling indication of the fragility of U.S.–PRC mutual trust: "You wait and see! The USSR wants to entice the U.S. back into a spheres-of-influence scheme. They want a free hand in Afghanistan and Vietnam, and they will give you a free hand in Cuba."

Chinese and American strategic interests converge on the desirability of deterring and if possible rolling back Soviet expansionism; but for the time being at least, their interests seem to *diverge* on the desirability of eventually restoring Soviet-American detente. The divergence generates tension and nervousness between the U.S. and the PRC.

On the American side, there has been a persistent suspicion that the U.S. has been subject to manipulation at the hands of the Chinese. "Either announce normalization with us before you conclude SALT with the Soviets, or else we'll drag out our negotiations and make fewer concessions to you." That threat was almost certainly never uttered during the hectic diplomacy of late 1978, nor was it necessarily implicit. But there was a widespread impression in the U.S. that the Carter administration had allowed itself to be stampeded in the final phase of the normalization negotiations. The timing certainly was suspicious. The Carter–Hua Guofeng announcement of the agreement to establish diplomatic relations, on December 15, 1978, came less than one week before what was supposed to be the conclusive Soviet-American SALT negotiating session in Geneva.

Only later, after the Vietnamese invasion of Kampuchea (Cambodia) on Christmas Day 1978 and China's punitive border attack on Vietnam two months later, did Western analysts come to clearly appreciate that Peking had been in a hurry for normalization with the U.S. to bolster itself against Vietnam and the Soviet Union. But no matter whether Peking's primary tactical consideration was SALT or Vietnam, many Americans came to feel that their government had been outfoxed by a wily Deng Xiaoping, and in both international and domestic politics, impressions and perceptions often have the force of reality.

"Either sell us arms or we'll make peace with the Soviets." That threat will probably never be uttered in future negotiations between Washington and Peking. But as long as Sino-American relations are based on the proposition that U.S. security depends in substantial measure on the perpetuation of the Sino-Soviet dispute, Americans will be sensitive to any whiff of blackmail in their country's dealings with the PRC.

This is not to deny that U.S. security and the global balance of power are indeed enhanced by the simultaneous continuation of the Sino-Soviet dispute and the maintenance of the Sino-American connection. Rather, it is to point out some of the disadvantages inherent in that reality. And it is to argue for a gradual, eventual decoupling of the Sino-American relationship from the Sino-Soviet dispute, or at least a diminution of the extent to which the former depends on the latter. The U.S. must look to a time when it can treat China as something much more than a "card" in a game of poker with the USSR.

It is significant, perhaps, that even though it was the American press and some U.S. policy makers who first began bandying about the image of a "China card," the phrase has since been expropriated by Soviet propagandists and other opponents of closer ties between the U.S. and the PRC. As the Russians would say, that is no accident. The connotation of the "China card" cheapens the Sino-American relationship while emphasizing its anti-Soviet character. The very notion of a "China card" should also serve as a cautionary reminder that there are other players and other cards at the table, and that in such a game the U.S. is always vulnerable to being bluffed, having its own bluffs called, or possibly losing its considerable stake in normal relations with the PRC.

The strategic implications of the Sino-American relationship apply to other countries beside the USSR. America's allies in Japan and Western Europe, along with the neutral nations of the Third World, have mixed feelings about the motivations and consequences of cooperation between Washington and Peking. Certainly the allies, and many neutrals as well, fear Soviet expansionism and welcome anything that will deter it. But most of them seem skeptical about the unabashed predisposition of the Reagan administration, at least in its first few months, to belabor the anti-Soviet angle of virtually all its foreign-policy initiatives. That tendency seemed gratuitously provocative and polarizing. The last thing these nations desire is to be caught in the middle of a confrontation of the superpowers; and the heightened dangers of Soviet-American conflict encompassing a China allied to the U.S.—and therefore involving Asia—are evident enough to them. Therefore, the prospect of a U.S.–PRC entente against Soviet "hegemony" has questionable benefits for their security, and it raises the prospect of the U.S. placing greater emphasis on its new relationship with China at the expense of America's traditional alliances.

It is noteworthy, however, that Reagan, in contrast to some officials in the Carter administration at first showed more muted enthusiasm for developing the security aspects of the

Sino-American relationship. His antipathy toward Soviet-style communism carried over into a skeptical view of the possible benefits to be gained from a defense relationship with a Communist PRC. And while Secretary of State Alexander Haig has stressed the strategic value of the China connection, it was not clear at first how the new administration would handle the security dimension of normalized U.S.–PRC relations. Presumably Soviet actions would have a significant effect on the evolution of Reagan's China policy, just as it did in the case of his predecessor.

It was clear, however, that Reagan intended to place primary emphasis on the strengthening of U.S. defense capabilities and to avoid undue reliance on ties to countries which do not share America's basic values, political philosophy, and social structure. This caution was evident even as the Reagan administration moved toward an upgrading of its security ties to the PRC.

Spokesmen for many nations of the noncommunist world have made clear that they look forward to the day when the U.S. will discard such simple-minded notions as "playing the China card" and adopt instead a more sophisticated strategy toward the PRC. The goal of such a strategy presumably would be to promote the development of China into a nation that is politically stable, economically strong enough to feed its vast population, commercially vigorous enough to participate in and profit from international markets, militarily powerful enough to defend itself and to play a responsible role in ensuring regional security, and generally supportive of the industrialized democracies. It is certainly in the interest of the U.S. to encourage such a development. With luck and wise leadership, it may even be in America's capacity to reinforce the tendency of China's current leaders to work toward that same goal, and then to help them achieve it.

Bilateral Sino-American Security Cooperation

In the late Carter administration and the early Reagan years, two of the most persistent and controversial questions about Sino-American relations were whether the U.S. should enter into security cooperation with the PRC and, more specifically, whether it should sell arms to China. The public

debate tended to overplay and at the same time oversimplify
both issues.

The first question—whether the U.S. should enter into
security cooperation with the PRC—had already been answered
affirmatively. It had been answered, in fact, repeatedly and
consistently by three administrations. The rapprochement
initiated by the handshake between Henry Kissinger and Zhou
Enlai in 1971 represented security cooperation of practical as
well as symbolic importance. From that point forward, neither
side regarded the other as a likely enemy in the event of international hostilities. Each could concentrate its defense planning on contingencies involving the Soviet Union. Moreover,
the PRC was tying down forty-six Soviet divisions—somewhere
between 750,000 and a million troops—as well as supersonic
Backfire bombers and mobile, multiple-warhead SS-20 inter-
mediate range ballistic missiles. Those Soviet men and machines
were deployed primarily (though not necessarily solely) in case
of war with China. That fact complicated the Kremlin's defense planning and correspondingly simplified that of the U.S.
and NATO. For the first time in two decades, the U.S. no
longer faced a two-front strategic challenge. That was the good
news. The bad news was that the Soviet challenge had grown
by an order of magnitude as the leaders of the USSR prepared to meet their own two-front challenge and built up an
ability to project power world-wide.

In the face of that somber reality, prospects for Sino-American
security cooperation assumed a considerably more active and
risky character in 1971, albeit in secret. One of the more intriguing revelations in Kissinger's memoirs, *White House Years,*
was that during the India-Pakistan War of November 1971,
the Nixon administration warned the USSR—which was backing India—of serious consequences if it attacked Pakistan's ally
China. At the same time, the administration conveyed to China
a willingness to provide assistance if its security were directly
threatened.

Kissinger and Nixon were concerned about more than just
the outcome of the conflict on the Indian subcontinent. They
wanted to give additional, concrete strategic significance to the
still-inchoate Sino-American connection. They wanted to dis-

courage Moscow from trying to nip that connection in the bud, and they wanted to increase Peking's confidence in the utility of normalization in a crisis. Some of Kissinger's critics, many of whom were also skeptics about the wisdom of Sino-American security cooperation, pounced on this episode as a good example of how the China card might well be a bluff—a bluff that, luckily, the Soviet Union had not called in 1971. But the fact remains that the U.S. and the PRC were cooperating against the USSR in the security realm nearly eight years before the formal establishment of diplomatic relations.

As normalization gained momentum during the second year of the Carter administration, talk about cooperation moved from the channels of secret diplomacy into the headlines. Zbigniew Brzezinski, the President's national security adviser, visited Peking in May 1978. He denounced the Soviets as "international marauders" and exuded receptivity to his Chinese hosts' appeals for common cause against "the polar bear." In August 1979, after the consummation of normalization and the establishment of embassies in Peking and Washington, Vice President Walter Mondale, on his own trip to China, declared to his hosts: "Any nation which seeks to weaken or isolate you in world affairs assumes a stance counter to American interests."

One of the next high-ranking American passengers on the Washington-Peking shuttle was Secretary of Defense Harold Brown. He visited China in January 1980, just after the Soviet invasion of Afghanistan. Spurred by that event, the U.S. and the PRC moved to a new stage in their security relationship. They were now, in the words of one observer, "strategic confidants." Brown went well beyond rhetoric. He told Chinese leaders that the U.S. was prepared to sell them nonlethal military equipment, such as radar, transport aircraft, and communications gear. One of Brown's deputies, William Perry, visited Peking later in the year to amplify the Carter administration's policy on military sales. The Chinese were to have access to "dual-use technology" (i.e., technology applicable to military as well as nonmilitary purposes) and additional nonlethal military equipment. The U.S. also approved Chinese military purchases from the West European allies.

When Reagan defeated Carter in November 1980, there was at first uncertainty both in the U.S. and in the PRC about whether the new administration would reverse China policy in any fundamental respect. Not long after assuming office, however, Reagan and Secretary of State Haig sought to assure Peking that they were committed to continuity in U.S.–PRC relations. The new administration decided to sustain a venture begun amidst great secrecy by its predecessor: a jointly operated PRC–U.S. intelligence-gathering effort located at sites along China's northwest frontier designed to monitor Soviet missile tests with sophisticated American-made equipment.

However, the new administration's assurances to the Chinese and its apparent willingness to keep various channels open left unresolved the issues of what form the security relationship might take in the future and what sort of military equipment the U.S. would provide. The Chinese position for several years had been to avoid the word "alliance" but to urge "a united front against hegemony" involving the U.S., Japan, NATO, and possibly other nations as well. For its part, the U.S. not only avoided the word "alliance," it repeatedly disavowed the idea of one. Serious consideration of a formal alliance between the U.S. and a communist, albeit anti-Soviet, country would almost certainly disturb American public opinion. It would also exacerbate lingering concerns about the future of Taiwan and raise questions about the primacy of U.S. security ties to such formal Asian allies as Japan.

The matter of arms sales was somewhat more complicated and was likely to become even more so over time. The Chinese refrain on the subject had been, "Of course we want the U.S. to sell us weapons, and we would welcome such sales, but we do not harbor any hopes in this regard." Yet some of the PRC's hopes suddenly seemed closer to fulfillment in June 1981, when Haig, on a visit to Peking, informed Chinese leaders that the U.S. would lift restrictions on arms sales. Dramatic and controversial as this decision was, it deliberately left unanswered such questions as when these transactions might take place and what sorts of weapons would be involved.

For a variety of reasons, the Reagan administration wanted to postpone confronting the details of the arms sales issue. One reason was that it still had to define, and perhaps redefine, the American relationships with Taiwan and the PRC. That meant dealing with another piece of unfinished business inherited from the Carter administration: whether to support Taiwan's request for a new generation of jet fighter aircraft. It was a thorny political dilemma. On the one hand, Reagan was genuinely indignant at what he felt was the Carter administration's shabby treatment of Taiwan at the time of normalization. Reagan had already backed down, in the earliest days of his administration, from his campaign hints that he might upgrade the unofficial U.S. representation on Taiwan to an "official" liaison office; but he still felt he owed Taiwan something. Moreover, he was under pressure to go through with an arms sale from conservative members of Congress, the aircraft industry, and remnants of the Taiwan lobby in the U.S.

Meanwhile, Chinese officials in Peking reiterated their position that U.S. weapons sales to Taiwan would violate the spirit if not the letter of the normalization agreements, and they warned that the sale of modern warplanes to the island would do significant though unspecified damage to the atmosphere of the overall Sino-American relationship. To give credibility to their warnings, in early 1981 Peking downgraded its diplomatic relations with the Netherlands government to the chargé level in response to the sale of two Dutch submarines to Taiwan. Meanwhile, in order to free resources for industrial development, the PRC had cut its defense budget and partially demilitarized Fujian Province on the mainland side of the Taiwan Strait. Even without new American arms shipments and in the absence of formal diplomatic ties to Washington, Taiwan was arguably safer from Communist attack than at any time since Mao Zedong's victory in 1949.

As they pondered this dilemma, Reagan's advisers agreed that a prudent resolution of the arms sales issue might be some sort of package deal, with something for both Peking and Taipei. But assembling such a package involved the most delicate calculations, some technical and military, some political and diplomatic. It also required time. If Peking was to tolerate a substantial U.S. arms sale to Taiwan, it had to be convinced that other elements of Reagan's China policy were overridingly in the interests of the PRC. Time was needed to build such a case for the Chinese. Hence the best U.S. tactic was to procrastinate on any decisions regarding Taiwan.

On the related issue of arms sales to the PRC itself, a number of considerations also militated against moving ahead rapidly. First, almost everyone agreed that it would be a mistake to sell the PRC offensive arms that would pose a potential threat to America's traditional allies in the region. Second, even though Deng Xiaoping and his fellow pragmatists seemed for the time to be firmly in charge, China's internal political situation was still too much a closed book for the U.S. to be absolutely confident that any offensive weapons it supplied would not someday be turned against the U.S. itself. Third, Chinese leaders repeatedly pledged themselves to the goal of peacefully reuniting Taiwan with the mainland at some point in the presumably rather distant future; but given its own continuing obligations to Taiwan—and its strategic as well as economic interests in Taiwan's survival as a strong, prosperous, pro-Western actor on the Asian stage—the U.S. could not provide the PRC with weapons that might facilitate a Communist "liberation" of the island by force if future leaders in Peking should ever change their peaceful tune.

Perhaps the most difficult question was also the most immediate: how to promote American security cooperation with the PRC in the short and middle term in a way that would deter Soviet aggression rather than provoke it. For the U.S. to provide China with even limited amounts of defensive armaments would be little more than symbolism and very likely counterproductive. That is, instead of staying the Soviet hand, it might force it. Likewise, large transfers of U.S. technology to the PRC, even if technically classified as "dual-use," might so alarm the Soviets that they would decide to risk a preemptive strike against China before the Sino-American security relationship could gather momentum. The Soviets already had good reason to be concerned about China's growing military capability. With the successful testing of a new intercontinental ballistic missile in the spring of 1980, the PRC was on its way toward establishing a credible nuclear deterrent able to cover the entire USSR. (Some Americans noted that the eight thousand-mile range of the new missile was also sufficient to reach the continental U.S. and therefore could represent part of Peking's insurance policy in case Sino-American relations ever deteriorated.)

At the same time, it would be short-sighted, unnecessarily self-constraining, and even self-demeaning for the U.S. to be excessively sensitive to Soviet paranoia and protests. The USSR can be counted on either to mutter or fulminate against any security ties between the U.S. and the PRC. It does not follow that the U.S. must therefore abstain from any defense cooperation whatsoever. For one thing, since such cooperation was already under way when the Reagan administration came into office, American backtracking might very well lead the Chinese leaders to conclude that the U.S. is unreliable and that the PRC has no choice but to make its own accommodation with the USSR. A loss of Chinese confidence in the American connection might induce the PRC back to the negotiating table with the Soviet Union over the disputed border. In and of themselves, such negotiations would not necessarily be a strategic setback for the U.S. and the West; but they would be precisely that if the Chinese, out of disillusionment with the U.S., let the Soviets pressure them into a partial drawdown or pullback of forces along the border, or some other compromise regarding the disputed frontier. Such a development—remote but not inconceivable—would make it easier for the USSR to reinforce its deployments elsewhere.

At a minimum, the U.S. must keep its security cooperation with the PRC moving forward slowly but surely. The pace and form that progress takes should reflect an awareness on the American side of a fundamental, sobering fact: despite its masses under arms—and in some ways because of them—China is extremely backward militarily. Nothing that either China or the U.S. can do will bring about any time soon the technological modernization of the People's Liberation Army. It will be a slow, sometimes politically disruptive, and expensive process. Foreign experts who were given unprecedented opportunities to inspect the most sensitive installations in the PRC have come home shaking their heads at the primitiveness of China's defense industries and weaponry. Less privileged visitors have come away telling tales of the biplanes they saw on the military runway at Harbin, or the obsolete naval vessels that make the mouth of the Huangpoo River in Shanghai look like the back lot of a Hollywood set during the shooting of a World War II movie.

An additional impediment to bilateral defense cooperation is the incompatibility of Chinese and American military cultures. The People's Liberation Army, as the nostalgic overtones of its name suggest, is still imbued with a faith in the invincibility of peasant guerrillas and the strategy of enveloping an invader with sheer numbers. American military experts have found that they must sometimes overcome a second language barrier in communicating with their Chinese counterparts. The doctrine and techniques of modern warfare sometimes seem as alien to the Chinese as the English language itself. China's underwhelming performance in its 1979 attack against Vietnam vividly demonstrated the shortcomings of its military wherewithal and the outmoded attitudes of many senior PLA commanders.

The consensus of Western experts is that China's military-industrial base is ten to twenty years behind that of the USSR Even if China could afford massive amounts of American or West European armaments—which it definitely cannot—the infusion would not do much good in redressing the Sino-Soviet balance in modern weaponry and firepower, which substantially favors the USSR despite China's advantage in manpower. That balance continues to tip toward the USSR because of obsolescence on the Chinese side and concurrent Soviet advances in both the technological sophistication of weaponry and in numbers deployed against the PRC. One American specialist has hypothesized that even if the U.S. were to supply China with ten thousand antitank missiles, the PRC would be only slightly less vulnerable to a Soviet armored attack. Another expert has speculated that two thousand American F-15 fighters would at best be a stopgap measure for modernizing China's inadequate air defenses. And such a sale, even if the Chinese could finance and absorb the weaponry (which they cannot), would carry risks of provoking the Soviets that would negate the short-term, marginal benefits to Chinese air power.

Other quick-fix measures might be less risky and more practical. For example, the U.S. could help the Chinese extend the service life of their own aircraft and tanks by providing certain kinds of industrial technology, some classified as dual-use, which would improve engines and munitions fairly quickly. But the emphasis of U.S. security assistance should be on the long-term process of modernizing China's industrial base and training new generations of specialists rather than on stopgaps and quick fixes.

Even among those who favor such a general policy of security assistance, there is disagreement over whether the U.S. should, from time to time, sell China arms in response to Soviet actions that threaten common Sino-American interests. The proposition underlying the so-called step-by-step approach to arms sales—that the Soviets should pay a cost for aggression in the coin of increased U.S.–PRC military cooperation—makes sense as one of a number of guidelines for policy. As long as the Sino-American relationship is perforce impelled by the Soviet threat, increases in that threat will—and should—provoke higher levels of U.S.–PRC security cooperation.

Certainly it would be foolish for the U.S. to proclaim its intention to insulate Sino-American security cooperation from considerations of Soviet behavior. A major objective of U.S. policy should be to make the Soviets understand that their actions will have some influence on how the security aspects of the U.S.–PRC relationship evolve. It would be undesirable for the Kremlin to believe that the United States was determined to increase China's military capabilities irrespective of Soviet behavior. Conversely, however, it would very likely embolden the Soviets if the U.S. declared a policy of no security assistance to the PRC under *any* circumstances. The leaders of the USSR must come to live with the knowledge that the U.S. and the PRC are likely to accelerate their security cooperation in response to Soviet expansionism.

At the same time, it would be a mistake to go to the other extreme—that is, to threaten specific U.S. arms sales to China as retribution for specific Soviet transgressions. It has been suggested, for example, that the U.S. might provide China with the equivalent of any new weapon that the Soviet Union gives Cuba. Or that the U.S. might respond to a Soviet invasion of Poland by demonstratively upgrading its military relations with China across the board. There are numerous problems with this purely reactive, tit-for-tat approach to arms sales. One is the implication that since Soviet misbehavior can trigger steps forward in Sino-American defense cooperation, Soviet good behavior—or the pretense of it (a partial pull-out of Afghanistan, for instance)—ought to be rewarded with a step backward in Sino-American defense cooperation. That implication is logically compelling, as no doubt the Soviets would point out; but it would be politically absurd, in effect, to punish the Chinese by suddenly withholding military assistance just because the Soviets had made some tactical concession. It was Vladimir Lenin, after all, who made famous the slogan of "two steps forward, one step back."

If U.S.–PRC defense cooperation were governed by a simplistic approach to arms sales, the Soviets would probably try to make the best of it by trying to trick the Chinese and Americans into stepping all over each other's toes. Whether or not the Soviets were to succeed, the continuity and credibility of U.S. policy would almost certainly suffer.

There would also be the quite different danger of a vicious cycle of action and reaction: the USSR misbehaves; the U.S. responds by selling more arms to China; the USSR feels newly threatened and either becomes even more belligerent, at the risk of war, or launches an all-out campaign to seek an accommodation with the PRC. Furthermore, an overly explicit and rigid U.S. policy of linking security cooperation with China to Soviet behavior runs the risk of squandering piecemeal American influence on the Kremlin. Once the U.S. has registered its displeasure with some Soviet action by ratcheting up its military relationship with Peking, it may well have foreclosed future opportunities for dealing with the USSR. Even advocates of the infamous China card have admitted that whatever value it has is greatly diminished once it is face-up on the table.

But the biggest problem with a reflexive, mechanistic policy on military cooperation with China is that it would deepen and prolong the impression that Sino-American relations derive their importance and their momentum solely from the grand obsession with the Soviet threat. While that impression is rooted in reality, it should be an aim of U.S. policy over the long term to diminish both the impression *and* the reality— and to give the relationship with China a standing of its own.

The Limited Partnership

The view of the world from the Middle Kingdom is compatible with the view from the U.S. in some ways, but in others it differs markedly. There are, without question, certain opportunities for the U.S. and the PRC to pursue complementary foreign policies in various regions, but neither side is under any illusion that their shared opposition to Soviet expansionism can easily be translated into a global diplomatic partnership.

Nevertheless, the Chinese have deliberately sought to downplay the differences and exaggerate the overlap between their outlook and that of the United States. They have sometimes resorted to rather artificial attempts to tailor their world view to the American market. For example, it has been a point of dogma with Chinese officials that the principal targets of the Soviet challenge are Western Europe and the oil-producing region of the Persian Gulf. China and East Asia, they say, are of lesser importance in the grand scheme of the Kremlin hegemonists.

In 1980 and 1981 American visitors to Peking who inquired about the menacing Soviet naval build-up in the Far East were reminded that Zhou Enlai had predicted eight years before that the USSR would "feint to the East, but attack in the West." When Senator John Glenn, the ranking Democrat on the Senate Foreign Relations Committee's Asian subcommittee, declared that the eighties would be "the decade of Asia," a number of Chinese officials demurred. The U.S. should think globally, not regionally, they said. "Remember," cautioned Zhang Yuanzheng, a foreign affairs specialist on the staff of the *People's Daily,* "East Asia is only the side flank of the Soviets' frontal thrust toward the Persian Gulf from their base in Afghanistan."

Listening to such lectures on geopolitics, an American visitor might suspect that his Chinese instructors were telling him what they thought he—and the U.S.—wanted to hear. They were emphasizing the Soviet threat to Europe and to Persian Gulf oil partly because they figured that, in the final analysis, the U.S. cares more about Europe and oil than it does about the fate of the PRC. The Chinese are shrewd enough to guess that most Americans tend to look eastward, toward their ancestral homes in Europe and, with greater anxiety if less sentimentality, toward the turbulent lands of the Middle East from which the U.S. imports so much of its energy needs.

China's own priorities are similarly a matter of geographical propinquity and often narrowly defined self-interest. For example, in early 1981 Chinese officials were publicly urging the U.S. to provide military assistance to the anti-Vietnamese guerrillas in Kampuchea. At the same time, they either dismissed as unimportant or criticized as unwarranted the Reagan administration's policy of military support for the beleaguered junta in El Salvador against Cuban-backed insurgents. The Chinese seemed unimpressed by Reagan's decision to draw the line against Soviet expansionism and to treat El Salvador as a test case in meeting Moscow's global challenge—even though that was just what China was urging the U.S. to do in Afghanistan and in Indochina, which are on the PRC's own borders.

Pressed on this apparent inconsistency, some Chinese officials explained privately that they regarded the regime in El Salvador as unsavory. More unsavory than Pol Pot's genocidal Khmer Rouge forces who dominate the anti-Vietnamese resistance in Cambodia? "Well," replied one Chinese official, "you must remember that we have to think of our reputation in the Third World, where U.S. policy in Central America is considered imperialistic. And besides, El Salvador is a long way away from us." Whatever the legitimate case that can be made against the Reagan administration's handling of the crisis in El Salvador, the Chinese reaction to the episode illustrates the limits of agreement between Washington and Peking on foreign policy objectives, to say nothing of actual coordination of initiatives.

JAPAN

One crucial point of harmony between Washington and Peking is the overarching importance of U.S.–Japanese relations. Since 1973, the PRC has supported the American defense tie with Japan, thus easing the Japanese's discomfort about proclaiming "equidistance" in their foreign relations yet living under the nuclear umbrella of one of the superpowers. In 1978 Japan defied heavy-handed Soviet pressures and signed a treaty of peace and friendship with the PRC. Since that event—and according to some analysts, partly in reaction to it—the Soviets stepped up their naval activity around Japan and stationed ten to twelve thousand ground troops on the disputed islands north of Hokkaido. The USSR occupied those territories in the last days of World War II, but Japan still claims them. These and other Soviet moves subtly but significantly altered the political climate in Japan: to a far greater extent than only a few years before, it was now possible for politicians and even military leaders to discuss security cooperation with the United States and an increased role for Japan in regional defense. Japanese officials also began talking openly about the possibility of joint exploration with China of offshore oil in the Yellow Sea.

Officials of the Foreign Ministry and Defense Agency in Tokyo were also quietly supportive of security cooperation between the U.S. and the PRC, although always with the caveat that the U.S. neither sell China offensive arms nor rush to upgrade the current level of its security cooperation. Shortly after the inauguration of President Reagan, Hisahiko Okazaki, a principal security strategist of the Japanese government, offered the following assessment, with its veiled advice to the new administration in Washington: "China is serving a useful purpose for the Western countries and Japan as it is now. I don't share the enthusiasm of those who want to strengthen China as a counterweight to the Soviet Union in the short term, nor do I share the fear others feel of a China rearmed by modernization. Modernization is a long-term proposition. The best policy is to take China as it is and to find, and then build on, common interests between China and the industrialized democracies."

At about the same time, an official of the Japanese Foreign Ministry suggested that if the U.S. pushes its security relationship with China too far, Japan might see it as a tacit admission of American weakness: "We go along with the current U.S. policy of defining China as a friend and not as an ally. Frankly, if the time came that the power equation were so fragile as to require the U.S. to define China as an ally, that would raise very serious questions in our minds."

Cautions of this sort coming from Tokyo have occasionally annoyed some Americans who feel that Japan has been excessively deferential to the USSR, excessively passive in regional security affairs, and excessively reliant on unilateral American efforts to preserve the military balance in East Asia and the Pacific. But by early 1981 Japan seemed to be changing for the better in respect to each of these complaints. Japan has an important role to play in the strategic interaction among the U.S., the PRC, and the USSR. If the trends of 1978–1981 continue, by the end of the decade Japan should be shouldering a far greater share of the burden for patrolling its territorial waters and defending its air space. That should give the USSR additional pause and the PRC additional heart, and it might allow the U.S. to concentrate its own limited air and sea power elsewhere.

Furthermore, as an economic superpower, Japan can make a vital contribution to China's industrial development and its gradual emergence as a participant in the commercial life of the Pacific Basin. In short, Japan can help China evolve into a strong, secure, and supportive member of the international community, which is a goal of the greatest strategic importance to the U.S. Therefore it behooves Washington policy makers to be especially sensitive to Japan's perspective on U.S.–PRC relations and to consult closely with their counterparts in Tokyo *en route* to Peking, rather than just to inform them ex post facto on the way home.

THE KOREAN PENINSULA

The U.S. and the PRC find themselves in an awkward, somewhat ambiguous position on the Korean Peninsula, which remains—some thirty years after the Korean War—a potential flash point of military conflict. In one sense, American and Chinese strategic interests regarding Korea converge dramatically. Both the U.S. and the PRC want to see North Korea remain as independent as possible of the Soviet Union. Neither wants North Korea to permit the Soviets to establish military bases on its territory. Both the U.S. and the PRC want to see South Korea prosper, stimulating the economic life of the region in ways from which China itself might eventually benefit. Neither the U.S. nor the PRC wants to see another war on the Peninsula. In private, Chinese officials are candidly unsentimental and utterly nonideological about their putative comrades in Pyongyang. On occasion they even express humorous contempt for Kim Il-song's anointment of his son, Kim Chong-il, as heir apparent ("social-monarchism," as one official Chinese observer has termed it).

For all this coincidence of view between Washington and Peking, however, the U.S. cannot expect the PRC to support the American defense commitment to South Korea or the stationing of U.S. troops there. China can best contribute to the equilibrium of power on and around the Korean Peninsula by maintaining its own political influence in Pyongyang and thereby keeping the Soviets in check. Ever since the Sino-Soviet split in the early 1960s, Kim Il-song has performed a delicate balancing act between his Chinese and Soviet neighbors. North Korea has the dubious distinction of being one of only three nations sharing common borders with both the USSR and the PRC. The fact that the other two—Mongolia and Afghanistan—are both Soviet satellites has not been lost on Kim.

Because of Kim Il-song's presumed ambition to reunite Korea by force before he dies (the "Great Leader" turned 70 in 1981), and because of North Korea's advantages over the South in military manpower and firepower, it is critical that the U.S. maintain its own deterrent in the form of GIs and aircraft stationed in the Republic of Korea. Jimmy Carter's decision in 1977 to keep a campaign promise to withdraw U.S. forces from the ROK was arguably one of the worst and potentially most disastrous mistakes of his Presidency. It emboldened the North, terrified the South, and sent shudders throughout the region—including in Peking. Carter's subsequent suspension of that decision and Ronald Reagan's cancellation of it altogether caused corresponding relief—once again, including in Peking. But the Chinese expressed their relief only very privately and obliquely. Publicly, the Chinese must oppose the stationing of forces in South Korea. Otherwise, they will complicate Kim

Il-song's balancing act—or that of his successors—since the
Soviets can, and probably do, point to American troops in
South Korea as a reason why they should be allowed permanent
bases or at least access to military facilities in the North.

Starting in 1978, the Soviets have been using the North
Korean port of Najin, which is ice-free year-round, as a backup
to Vladivostok when it is frozen during winter months. The
North Koreans have allowed only Soviet merchant ships to put
in at Najin, but there is no question that the supplies sent from
there to Vladivostok by rail have helped the USSR support its
huge military establishment in Eastern Siberia. The Chinese
see it as their role to prevent any further North Korean tilt
toward the USSR, and if they succeed, they will be aiding
American interests as well as their own.

South Korean officials, for their part, have been cautiously,
discreetly supportive of U.S.–PRC normalization, although
they, like the Japanese, warn against moving ahead too quickly
with arms sales or formal defense arrangements. In February
1981, Hahm Pyong-choon, a former South Korean ambassador
to the U.S. and foreign policy adviser to Presidents Park Chung-
hee and Chun Doo-hwan, issued his own warning to Washington: "Trying to use China as a strategic counterweight to the
Soviet Union could create problems of its own, especially if
Deng Xiaoping's modernization program seems to fall short of
its goals and therefore fails. In that event, his other policies—
including his American card—might be called into question.
Therefore arming China one-sidedly could backfire on the
U.S., and against all of us in this region."

SOUTHEAST ASIA

The emergence of ASEAN, the Association of Southeast
Asian Nations, has been a positive and promising development
not just for its five member-states (Thailand, the Philippines,
Singapore, Malaysia, and Indonesia), but for the U.S. as well.
The association has managed to achieve more internal coherence and regional influence than most observers predicted
at the time of its founding in 1967, and it has generally used
its influence in ways favorable to the economic and political
interests of the industrialized democracies. ASEAN has helped

to stimulate brisk trade and growing prosperity among the noncommunist nations of the Pacific Basin. The organization has also served as a contact point between America's allies in the region and the Nonaligned Movement, since its members include three nonaligned states (Singapore, Malaysia, and Indonesia) as well as two with defense ties to the U.S. (Thailand and the Philippines).

In a number of international forums, including the Nonaligned Movement and the United Nations, ASEAN has held together as a firm bloc in opposition to the Vietnamese occupation of Kampuchea. At the same time, its members are unanimous and emphatic about the limits of their collective ability to guard regional security. They have repeatedly ruled out the formation of a multilateral military force, for example. But especially in the wake of Vietnamese aggression in Kampuchea, and the establishment of what amounts to permanent Soviet bases in Vietnam, ASEAN has been receptive to the United States' playing a more visible and vigorous security role in the area. In short, it is a strategic imperative for the U.S. to foster the further development of ASEAN and to cultivate the best possible relations with its members. The U.S. should keep an especially watchful and sympathetic eye on ASEAN as it deals with the PRC.

Sino-American security cooperation in the late 1970s and at the beginning of the 1980s generated mixed feelings in ASEAN. Had it not been for the dramatic Soviet military build-up throughout East Asia during that period, ASEAN might have regarded the growing relationship between the U.S. and China with dismay and perhaps outright opposition. However—thanks to an upsurge in Soviet naval traffic through the Strait of Malacca and in the South China Sea—ASEAN leaders were far more tolerant of talk about U.S.–PRC security cooperation than they otherwise might have been.

Just as the Soviets had unwittingly made it possible for Japanese politicians to talk openly about increasing Japan's defenses, so the Soviets made it possible for Indonesian politicians to climb off of their neutralist fence and criticize the USSR. In part because of widespread resentment against Indonesia's prosperous ethnic Chinese minority, and in part because of bitter memories of the abortive and bloody coup attempted by the pro-Peking Indonesian Communist Party in 1965, the government in Jakarta has traditionally regarded China as the principal menace to Southeast Asia. But in early 1981 the climate of opinion had changed sufficiently for Vice President Adam Malik to say, "The Soviet Union now presents the greatest threat to the area because it is helping Vietnam realize Ho Chi Minh's old dream of a single Southeast Asian Communist grouping."

But mistrust of China lingered. Malik, for all of his prestige as Indonesia's best known statesman and a former president of the United Nations General Assembly, was speaking as a civilian. His military colleagues who dominated the government, particularly President Suharto, continued to worry that the PRC would someday use Indonesia's overseas Chinese community as a fifth column for leftist subversion and that the Chinese might fill any vacuum created by the eviction of the Soviets from the area. As one Indonesian general commented wryly, "Better the hegemonists from far away than those from nearby."

Similar concerns were felt in Malaysia and elsewhere in the region. There was also apprehension that the U.S., in what some ASEAN officials termed its "new love affair" with China, might subordinate its policies toward Southeast Asia to its relationship with the PRC. Even officials in Singapore voiced this concern. Singapore is one of the most outspokenly anti-Soviet and pro-Western nations in Asia. With a Chinese majority, it does not share Indonesia's half-political, half-racial suspicion of the PRC. Yet its leaders still took pains to caution the U.S. not to exaggerate the strategic value of China—and certainly not to take any action that might contribute to a Sino-Soviet conflict. As Prime Minister Lee Kuan Yew's deputy for foreign affairs, Sinnathamby Rajaratnam, put it in early 1981: "Supplying offensive arms to China to take on the Russians would be playing with fire."

On the issue of Kampuchea, Singapore publicly echoed China's urging that the U.S. join in a multilateral effort to aid the anti-Vietnamese resistance. At the same time, however, officials in Singapore and the other four ASEAN capitals seemed to agree that the U.S. must avoid the appearance of allying itself directly with China against Vietnam. Such an appearance, they feared, might stiffen Vietnam's intransigence and leave the Hanoi regime with no choice but to deepen its entanglement with the Soviet Union.

The Chinese have devoted themselves—so far with notable lack of success—to "teaching Vietnam a lesson" and bringing it to its knees. On this point, China's strategy may well part company with that of the U.S. at some point in the future. Washington may decide it is in its long-term interest to resume attempts at normalization of relations with Hanoi in order to woo the Vietnamese away from the Soviet fold and toward ASEAN. Such a goal is at best distant and difficult, given Vietnam's current policy of blatantly colonizing its neighbors in Indochina and given the extent of Soviet penetration there. In the nearer term, the U.S. can reassure the noncommunist states of Southeast Asia (and perhaps even some far-sighted Vietnamese as well) by making clear in word and deed that it does not expect the Chinese eventually to achieve preponderant influence in Southeast Asia, and that it is not America's intention to turn over its responsibilities for regional security to the PRC.

THE THIRD WORLD

China has historical and economic claims to a kind of honorary membership in the Third World. Indeed, it sees itself as a founding patron. Zhou Enlai attended the 1955 Bandung Conference in Indonesia, at which the grand old men of nonalignment—Sukarno, Nehru, Nkrumah, and Tito—declared a plague on the houses of both the U.S. and the USSR. After the outbreak of public feuding between Moscow and Peking in the early 1960s, China sought security and economic development by identifying itself with the so-called newly emerging forces of the Third World. What is more, like most inhabitants of Africa, Asia, and the Middle East, the Chinese people are nonwhite, and they are poor.

Because of China's affinity with the Third World, the U.S. derives some indirect benefits from its improved relations with Peking. At the most rudimentary level, it is a welcome development that China is no longer actively working against American interests in its diplomacy and propaganda among developing countries. Conversely, the U.S. benefits—again, indirectly—from China's constant attacks on the Soviet Union. China's vocal support for NATO and its branding of the Soviets as "social-imperialists" have tended to challenge prevailing myths in the Third World about who is progressive and who is imperialistic.

Until they sponsored Vietnam's invasion of Kampuchea and launched their own invasion of Afghanistan, the Soviets were making headway with their own claim to being "the natural allies of the nonaligned." Singapore officials have commented that their sometimes lonely job of denouncing the Soviet Union and its Trojan horse, Cuba, within the Nonaligned Movement is made somewhat easier by the applause these denunciations elicit from Peking. "If we were just mouthing the American line," remarked a Singapore diplomat at the Nonaligned Summit in Havana in 1979, "it would be much easier for our opponents to dismiss us as running dogs of the Yankees."

In Africa, Chinese advisers and workers assisting Tanzania and Zambia with major development projects distinguished themselves by laboring hard, living modestly, behaving respectfully toward the local populace, and usually abstaining from clandestine mischief-making. This record is in marked contrast to Soviet behavior on all counts. There is, as a result, considerable good will for the Chinese in Africa. Insofar as the U.S. and China are perceived to be on the same side, so much the better.

But all this is part of what might be called the strategic atmosphere. Only rarely is it of concrete or operational utility to the U.S. There may be isolated instances from time to time when U.S. and Chinese interests clearly coincide and when their capabilities complement each other. More often, though, their interests are merely parallel. Because China's economic, military, and covert resources are limited—and because its well-known common cause with the U.S. can be something of a handicap among its Third World brethren—China is likely to steer clear of active collaboration. In the Third World, as elsewhere, it is still little more than shared opposition to Soviet expansionism that makes the U.S. and the PRC partners, and that is the basis of only the most limited partnership for the foreseeable future.

WESTERN EUROPE

America's allies in Western Europe hope that the U.S. will be at least as attentive to preserving the limits as to expanding the partnership with China. The West Europeans are fearful that the U.S., in an excess of anti-Soviet zeal combined with naive enthusiasm for its new friendship with China, might be drawn into an alliance-like bilateral security relationship, which in turn might grow into a multilateral entente embracing Japan, Australia and New Zealand, and the NATO states themselves. Such a development, in the West European view, would confirm the worst Soviet fears of "encirclement." Chinese talk about a "united front against hegemony" tends to make West Europeans wince, especially when the phrase crops up in toasts by senior Chinese at banquets with European defense officials. The West Europeans have warned repeatedly about the dangers of provoking the Soviet Union by selling American arms to the PRC. (However, the Europeans themselves, particularly the British, have not been averse to selling their own weapons to the Chinese.)

The reason for European nervousness about an active program of Sino-American security cooperation—like so many other aspects of the China factor—is evident from the map. Western Europe lives in uneasy proximity to the Soviet Union and its Warsaw Pact allies. It is caught in the middle, both politically and geographically, between the U.S. and the USSR. That position is all the more precarious at times of tense and deteriorating Soviet-American relations. Elsewhere in this volume, William E. Griffith quotes Zhou Enlai as once remarking, "Far-away water cannot put out fires." Zhou was acknowledging that China was still a regional, not a global power. The same is still largely true of Western Europe. China is far away and cannot come to the rescue if fire breaks out in Berlin or in Poland.

This West European perspective on China may be parochial, but it is understandable. In any event, it is not going to change any time soon. American insensitivity to it—or, worse, contemptuousness of it—will only exacerbate transatlantic friction and intraalliance disunity. That does not mean, however, that the United States should be paralyzed by West European anxieties any more than it should be by Soviet paranoia. Rather, the U.S. should take special care to consult closely with its allies as it moves cautiously, purposefully forward with its new-found "strategic confidant." The U.S. must continually reassure the West Europeans (and the Japanese), while reminding the Chinese themselves, that America's goal is a stronger, more secure China that is tied to the West by trade, diplomacy, and a mutual interest in international stability—but not by formal defense commitments. In sum, as the stock disclaimer of the communiqués would have it, the order of the day in Sino-American relations is friendship but not alliance.

Conclusion: Enemy of Our Enemy, or True Friend?

While the "friend-but-not-an-ally" formula serves well the diplomatic and strategic purposes of the United States, it remains the description of a goal rather than of the existing reality. For all the ritualistic toasts to Sino-American "friendship" that have reverberated from banquets at the Great Hall of the People to state dinners at the White House, the U.S. and the PRC are not yet friends. Nor will they be for a long time to come. Constant talk about friendship will, unfortunately but unavoidably, continue to be a smoke screen for the sentiment that really brings them together—a sentiment which is best expressed by the ancient Arab saying, "the enemy of my enemy is my friend." That is a slogan more suitable for tactics than strategy, since the logic of the words themselves implies how easy it is for friends to become enemies. It is a slogan that recognizes the evanescence, not to mention the inherent cynicism and potential for treachery, in friendships formed purely against common enemies.

The U.S. needs a strategy toward China that will hasten the day when the relationship stands on its own and is no longer hostage to the vicissitudes of Sino-Soviet tensions. After all, China has importance—indeed, truly strategic importance—in its own right. Despite its poverty, its susceptibility to turmoil, its hidebound bureaucracy, its secretiveness, its rigid ideology, and its repressive political system, China is the home of one-quarter of humankind. In looking to the year 2000, the U.S.

confronts the prospect of living in a world with a minimum of 1.2 billion Chinese. That staggering figure alone argues for a policy aimed at gradually extricating the China factor from calculations about the Soviet Union and giving it a value of its own.

The emphasis of such a policy should be on building human contacts through technical, scholarly, journalistic, and commercial exchanges as well as strictly official ones; it should be on opening the doors of American colleges, universities, and research institutes to help train new generations of Chinese scientific, managerial, and other intellectual talent. The emphasis should be on encouraging the growth of Chinese industry and trade. That help will involve more than just the United States' playing banker and salesman to China. The harder task will be suppressing America's resurgent protectionist impulses so that if and when China begins to realize its potential as an exporter, it has a market in the U.S.

As Michel Oksenberg argues in chapter 2, the Sino-American relationship needs to be institutionalized so that it will survive the almost inevitable turbulence of leadership feuds and changing political, economic, and strategic circumstances. As a corollary to that guideline, the U.S. must avoid the temptation to invest too much political capital in the success of any one Chinese leader or faction. For one thing, in the inner recesses of China's leadership struggle, it would not necessarily do an individual or a group any good to be too conspicuously identified as "America's choice." That has been a risk in the mutual infatuation between Deng Xiaoping and the U.S.

Without endorsing the Four Modernizations as "Dengism," the U.S. can—and should—support the goals of Deng's economic policy. The first three of the "modernizations" are agriculture, industry, and science-technology. The fourth is defense. The Chinese ordered their priorities in that way not because they regard their national security as the least important of the challenges facing them, but because they realized that improved defenses will depend on a modernized industrial and technological base. It is for the same reason that U.S. strategic interests in the development of Sino-American relations will be best served if strictly military assistance is relegated to second (or fourth) place after programs aimed at helping China strengthen its economy, improve the productivity of its farms, and develop its scientific expertise.

While this general course makes sense at the beginning of the 1980s, no one could pretend to know where it will have led by the end of the century, although there has been tantalizing speculation on the subject from commentators with noteworthy credentials and perspectives. No less an authority on Sino-American normalization than Richard Nixon speculated in his manifesto, *The Real War,* published in 1980 and dedicated "to our grandchildren," that China might eventually become "the world's most powerful nation" and that its political system might evolve into something "more Chinese than Communist." (Covering his bets, however, Nixon also allowed for the opposite: China might turn out "more Communist than Chinese," posing in the long run "an expansionist threat to the West.")

Singapore's Deputy Prime Minister Rajaratnam, after accompanying Lee Kuan Yew to China in 1980, returned home believing that "Deng Xiaoping has come to the conclusion that communism is a total failure and that these have been wasted years. Now he has the practical problem of how to eradicate thirty years of indoctrination." Other Asian observers of China have theorized that de-Maoification is a prelude to de-Marxification. Noting that official Chinese propaganda already emphasizes the goal of a "civilized" rather than a "socialist" society, some of these theorists have predicted that communism might eventually give way as the state ideology to some as yet vaguely conceived mixture of nationalism, Confucianism, and the Four Modernizations.

The Soviets, meanwhile, have been entertaining their own theories about what is going on in China and where the country is headed. Their predictions are in some ways mirror images of those in the West—equally tinged with wishful thinking. Aleksandr Chicherov, a leading sinologist at the Institute of Oriental Studies in Moscow, predicted in 1980 that Deng Xiaoping's policies of encouraging massive infusions of Western technology and seeking to automate Chinese industry will drive more and more Chinese out of work, thus "worsening internal tensions and eventually bringing about a collapse." According to Chicherov, future historians will look back on

Deng's Four Modernizations campaign as the beginning of the end of the anti-Soviet era in China just as the Shah's "White Revolution" and all-out effort in the 1960s to modernize and westernize Iran were the beginning of the end of the Peacock Throne. All the USSR needs to do, Chicherov implied, is sit back, watch the deterioration of China into ever-greater weakness and disruption, and wait for it eventually to fall back into Moscow's arms.

Another Soviet sinologist, Aleksandr Yakovlev at the Institute for the Study of the Far East, said, "China doesn't have the military strength to threaten world peace on its own, and even the military and economic aid of the U.S. and other Western countries won't make a big difference. Besides, the course of the present Chinese leadership will eventually be reversed when the people realize they're on the road to imperialism and colonialism." A Kazakh academician in Alma-Ata, Salyk Zimanov, was equally optimistic: "The Chinese are caught up in a kind of poisonous contamination of chauvinism. The Chinese leaders in general tend toward extreme policies. Right now they're extremely hostile to us. But it should be remembered that China was our best friend not too long ago. With the perspective of history, we know things can change very fast. It's quite possible that China will rather quickly turn again from a friend of the U.S. into a friend of the USSR."

Thus while non-Communist students of the Chinese mystery ponder the notion that China may some day defect from the Red Flag, their counterparts in the Soviet Union look forward to the return of the prodigal comrade. Either way, it is heady stuff—and a bit too visionary to help either American or Soviet policy makers in charting the next ten years of their respective dealings with the PRC. All the U.S. can do—and it will not be easy—is to keep its own policies focused on the long-term goal of making China a true friend of the U.S., rather than just the enemy of our enemy.

Dwight H. Perkins

4

The International Consequences of China's Economic Development

Economics is not the sole basis of national power. Japan in the 1940s and Vietnam in the 1970s are examples of nations that created great military power on the base of a relatively weak economy. Nor does an expanding share of world trade necessarily give the nation whose trade is expanding greater influence over other states. In some respects, expanded trade makes a country more dependent on its trading partners, and hence gives them enhanced influence or reverse leverage. Nonetheless, when all the qualifications are considered, it is the case that changes in the relative economic strength of nations have had the greatest influence on shifts in the international balance of power in the twentieth century. Only the rising spirit of nationalism in former European colonies and semidependen-

DWIGHT H. PERKINS *is director of the Harvard Institute for International Development and professor of modern China studies and of economics at Harvard University. His past positions include chairman of Harvard's Department of Economics and associate director of its East Asian Research Center. He has consulted for the Korea Development Institute, the Government of Malaysia, the World Bank, and the Ford Foundation. Dr. Perkins has authored and edited numerous books and articles on China, Korea, and other parts of Asia.*

cies rivals the forces of industrialization in shaping international relations in the contemporary world.

If industrialization is a key to influence in international relations, where does the People's Republic of China stand today, and where will it be a decade or two hence? The common perception today is that China is poor, backward in technology, and only in the early stages of its industrialization program. Not only is China underdeveloped today, but it will remain so for some time to come because of the enormous obstacles that lie across its future development path. It should give one pause to recall, however, that serious people were making similar statements about the Soviet Union only three decades ago and that American policy makers at the same time were worried whether Japan's economy could be brought to a point where it could meet the minimum consumption needs of the Japanese people. Americans, including policy analysts, are notorious for their lack of historical perspective. Hence, historical analogy will not suffice. The objectives of this analysis are first to discuss what we know about the current state of China's economy and the changes that can be expected over the next decade or two and then to assess the impact of these changes on China's role in the international economy and on Chinese military power.

The Current and Future State of China's Economy

Despite common perceptions to the contrary, the fact is that China's industrial sector is already quite large. Support for this proposition is most readily provided by a comparison of contemporary Chinese industrial output with that of Japan and the USSR in the early 1960s (Table 1). By the early 1960s both Japan and the Soviet Union had fully recovered from the economic effects of World War II, and renewed growth had been underway at high rates for half a decade or more.

As the data in Table 1 make clear, China in 1979, in the aggregate, had an industrial economy comparable in size to that of Japan and the USSR eighteen years earlier. In fact, Chinese industry in 1979—even allowing for the lower quality of its products—was probably a good deal larger than that of Japan in 1961. Electric power generation, as good as any single

TABLE 1.

Product	China (1979)	Japan (1961)	USSR (1961)
Electric power (billion kWh)	281.95	132.04	327.61
Crude steel (million m.t.**)	34.48	28.27	70.76
Cement (million m.t.)	73.90	24.63	50.86
Sulphuric acid (thousand m.t.)	7000.00	4684.00	5718.00
Coal (million m.t.)	635.00	52.00*	373.00*
Petroleum (million m.t.)	106.15	0.71*	204.97*
Cotton yarn (thousand m.t.)	2630.00	545.00	1165.00
Television receivers (thousands)	1329.00	4609.00	1949.00
Motor vehicles (thousands)	186.00	250.00	149.00

* averages for 1961–65.
** metric tons

Source: United Nations, *Statistical Yearbook, 1970;* and State Statistical Bureau of the People's Republic of China, *Report on the Results of the 1979 National Economic Plan* (April 30, 1980).

indicator of industrial progress, was double Japan's level and nearly comparable to that of the Soviet Union.

It is hardly surprising that China's industry has achieved such levels. The industrialization process got underway in the early part of the twentieth century (a few factories were established late in the nineteenth), and between 1912 and the outbreak of war with Japan in 1937 an average annual growth rate of 8 percent a year was achieved. The industrial base was still small in 1952 when recovery from World War II was achieved, but a base did exist. From this starting point, for the next twenty-seven years Chinese industry grew at an average rate of 11 percent a year for an overall 17.6-fold rise in industrial production. The producer goods sector, the one most relevant to military power, grew at an even faster rate of 13.4 percent a year but from a smaller initial base.

It is interesting to speculate why so many visitors to China get such a different impression of the state of China's economy from visual evidence. In part the answer is that Chinese industrial output must be divided among four times as many people as in the USSR and eight times as many as in Japan. Thus Chinese output is large in the aggregate, but the people are still poor in per capita terms. It is also a fact that over 85 percent of China's people live in rural areas and over 70 percent are still members of rural communes. Thus the shift in population from rural to urban areas that normally occurs in the process of economic development has yet to occur in China.

This absence of a rural-to-urban shift is in part a reflection of the stage of industrial development reached by China, but it is also a result of Chinese government policies that prohibited migration and indirectly encouraged urban enterprises to adopt increasingly capital-intensive techniques. If China's industrialization drive had been based on the consumer goods sector as was the case elsewhere in Asia, urbanization would already have been much further along than was in fact the case in the late 1970s.

Finally, American and other foreign businessmen have become disillusioned with commercial dealings with the Chinese and the way that Peking has run the economy in recent years. Contracts worth hundreds of millions of dollars have been cancelled without warning. The decision-making process within the Chinese bureaucracy has been sluggish, erratic, and undecipherable. Moreover, these negative impressions of China's business practices have been reinforced by the existence of only a few first-class hotels and the spartan quality of daily life in China.

As a consequence, the dream of the early 1970s of a billion new customers has given way to a feeling that the Chinese economy is and will remain difficult to deal with and extremely backward for decades. While understandable in the current frustrating climate, these attitudes provide a very distorted basis for estimating both the current state of the Chinese economy and its future prospects.

The reason for going into the above discussion of specific industries and the impressions of foreign businessmen is to provide a clearer picture of the "machinery-and-steel" reality that underlies the gross national product projections that follow. Because gross national product (GNP) estimates must be built up from individual product series using prices that can become badly distorted, there is considerable room for judgment in choosing among different GNP estimates. Such is particularly the case when one is trying to convert GNP in some other currency into U.S. dollars. In addition to the problem of distorted domestic prices, one must add the problem of a distorted exchange rate. In China, where the foreign exchange rate plays only a minor role in China's foreign economic relations, exchange rate conversions of GNP into U.S. dollars are particularly treacherous.

There is little controversy over the magnitude of Chinese national income in Chinese prices measured according to socialist concepts which exclude many services. The total was 301.1 billion yuan in 1978 (in 1978 prices) and 337 billion yuan in 1979 (in 1979 prices, which were 4.6 percent above the prices of 1978). Excluded services that must be added to convert these figures into GNP according to Western concepts would add at least 10 and possibly as much as 20 percent. Thus Chinese GNP in 1979 was nearly 400 billion yuan in current Chinese prices. To simplify and add clarity to the calculations that follow, this is the figure that will be used in the following analysis.

Divided by a population in 1979 of 971 million and converted into dollars at the official exchange rate, one arrives at per capita figures of $224 (national income according to socialist concepts) or $266 (GNP). These are the kinds of figures being published by the Chinese, and they are highly misleading. For reasons not appropriate for detailed discussion in a study of this sort, a more appropriate exchange rate would give China a GNP of $400 to $500 per capita in 1979. The theoretically correct method of conversion—converting each commodity one by one—gives an even higher figure, about 12 percent of U.S. per capita GNP according to one crude attempt. For the purposes of this essay we shall use the $400–500 per capita figure and a total GNP in 1979 of U.S. $400 billion.

Total GNP in the U.S., USSR, and Japan in 1978, by way

of comparison, was $2,100 billion, $1,254 billion, and $969 billion respectively. How long will it take China to reach comparable levels? The answer depends on what growth rate one expects China to achieve. One way to approach this question is to look at past growth rates of national income that averaged about 4.8 percent per year between 1952 and 1979 (in 1978 prices). The growth rate in 1952 prices over the same period is 6 percent per year, but 1952 prices give too heavy a weight to the fast growing industrial sector and hence 1978 prices are preferred. Because these years included the disruption of the Great Leap Forward (1958–1959), the sudden withdrawal of Soviet technicians (1960), and the Cultural Revolution turmoil (particularly 1967, 1968, 1974, and 1976), it is reasonable to presume that if China can avoid comparable disruptions in the future, the growth rate will be at least as high as in the past. A 4.8 percent a year growth rate, it should be noted, is quite respectable in comparative historical terms but low when compared to the spectacular rates of growth attained in the 1960s by China's East Asian neighbors.

How fast is China likely to grow in the 1980s and beyond? There is first the drag of China's agricultural sector. China's other East Asian neighbors have relied increasingly on food imports, but for reasons that will be discussed below, China cannot do the same and hence must invest heavily at low rates of return in the agricultural sector. China also suffers from an energy shortage, although unlike most developing nations China does not have to rely on petroleum and coal imports. Hence the PRC is not subject to the impact of OPEC price increases except in the positive sense that such increases raise the value of Chinese energy exports. Perhaps most serious from the point of view of achieving accelerated growth is the impact of China's problems with its inefficient bureaucracy, inherited Soviet-style system of planning, and limited skilled manpower.

Thus in projecting the growth of Chinese GNP, it comes down to a matter of judgment of how much the advantages of a lower level of political disruption and a greater use of foreign technology will be offset by uncorrected inefficiencies in China's system of planning and management and the drag of the agricultural sector. In my own opinion, if the current emphasis on economic growth is retained by future leaderships, it is reasonable to expect that Chinese GNP growth rates will accelerate to at least 6 and perhaps as high as 8 percent a year over the next decade and even beyond. The 10 percent rates achieved for a time by Japan and South Korea are beyond China's reach. The differences between 6, 8, and 10 percent are not trivial over long periods. A 6 percent rate doubles GNP in twelve years, an 8 percent rate in nine years, and a 10 percent rate in seven years. For illustrative purposes we shall work mainly with a 7 percent rate (which doubles in ten years), but it is a simple matter to use alternative rates if the reader finds them more plausible.

At a 7 percent GNP growth rate, China would have a total GNP of $800 billion in 1990 (in 1979 prices) and $1,600 billion by the year 2000. Per capita GNP would have risen from $400 to over $700 in 1990 and to nearly $1300 by the year 2000 (assuming an average 1 percent population growth rate over the entire period). By way of contrast, if GNP grew only at 4.8 percent (3.8 percent per capita), total national product in 1990 would be $640 billion and in the year 2000, $1,020 billion ($580 and $1020 per capita). These and other alternative projections are presented graphically in Figure 1.

The point of these calculations is to underline the fact that China will have a very large GNP within a relatively short time period barring some major economic catastrophe. The country will be approaching late 1970s Japanese levels of GNP by 1990, and even at lower rates of growth it will reach late 1970s Japanese levels by the year 2000. At a 7 percent growth rate, China by the year 2000 will be well past 1979 Soviet GNP and will be closing in on that of the United States in the same year. In per capita terms, China will still be poor in 1990 and the year 2000, but a doubling and a tripling of per capita income, provided that it does not all end up in investment and armaments, will have a major impact on the standard of living of the Chinese people.

The only events likely to stop this growth in its tracks would be the outbreak of war with the Soviet Union or prolonged political upheaval on the pattern of the Cultural Revolution. China's management, energy, and agricultural problems are serious, but they are the kinds of problems faced and overcome by all developing nations during the growth process.

Fig. 1. GNP Growth Projections.

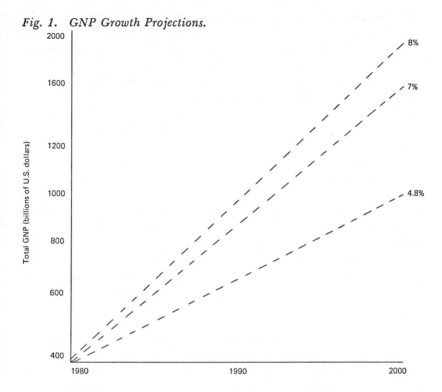

Implications for Foreign Trade

These growth projections also provide the basis for a systematic and quantitative discussion of what is likely to happen to Chinese foreign trade over the next decade and beyond. Much of the discussion of China's future role in the international economy has been dominated either by wishful thinking or fear unsupported by analysis. The wishful thinking has been by Western and Japanese businessmen and bankers dreaming of a bonanza of sales and high interest loans to a billion Chinese. The fear is that of other export-oriented developing nations—a giant China with low wages that will cut them out of their hard won export markets in the United States, Western Europe, and elsewhere.

More recently, Peking's sudden cancellation of several major contracts with the Japanese and others has led to a complete reversal of business attitudes toward the China trade. Instead of a vast market, some businessmen see no market at all, only a billion peasants with little purchasing power and an ineffectual bureaucracy incapable of either sustaining effective policies or doing much of anything to develop foreign trade.

The first issue, therefore, is how large is China's trade in fact, and how rapidly will it grow over the next decade. Data for the late 1970s are presented in Table 2, and China's trade in 1978 is compared with that of other nations and territories in Table 3. The main point to note is that China's trade in 1978 was not much larger than that of India and significantly smaller than the trade of either South Korea or Taiwan. South Korea's trade, and that of Taiwan, has grown rapidly and in the 1970s was large enough to be noticed by protectionists in the United States and elsewhere. Few people talked about this trade as a dominant force in international markets, however, except in the areas of textiles and electronics. Only Japan among Asian nations was spoken of in such terms, and Japanese trade in 1978 was more than eight times the size of Chinese trade.

China in the late 1970s, therefore, was one of many trading nations, not a case apart. China's share of the world's population was 22 percent, but its share of world foreign trade was only .9 percent. It is difficult to see how a nation with less than 1 percent of world trade is going to either swamp world markets with its exports or bring prosperity to large numbers of the world's multinational companies with its imports. China will play a role in world markets; but only if its share rises markedly will that role be fundamentally different from what it has been in the past.

The rate of growth of China's foreign trade over the next decade depends on a number of elements, several of which are not easy to forecast. To begin with, China is a large country, and large countries in terms of population and geographic size tend to have lower foreign trade ratios (exports plus imports divided by GNP) than do small countries. Thus China, like the US or the USSR, is never likely to achieve the dependence on foreign trade of a Netherlands or South Korea let alone a Singapore. Efforts to expand foreign trade in the late 1970s did lead to a rise in China's foreign trade ratio from roughly 8 percent in 1977 to 11 percent in 1979, and the issue for the future is whether that ratio can be raised even further. By way of comparison, the U.S. and Japanese ratios in 1978 were 15 and 18 percent respectively. The issue then becomes one of whether China can achieve ratios over the next decade comparable to that of either the U.S. or Japan.

TABLE 2.   CHINA'S FOREIGN TRADE

Year	Exports		Imports	
	(in millions of U.S. $) *	*(in millions of yuan)*	*(in millions of U.S. $)* *	*(in millions of yuan)*
1974	6,730	n.a.	6,805	n.a.
1975	7,120	n.a.	6,830	n.a.
1976	7,270	n.a.	5,580	n.a.
1977	8,075	13,890	6,605	13,280
1978	9,965	16,760	10,265	18,740
1979	13,505	21,200	14,740	24,300

* The U.S. dollar figures are f.o.b. for imports as well as exports because the figures are calculated from data supplied by China's trading partners rather than from c.i.f., (cost, insurance, and freight) data when the goods arrive in Chinese ports.

Sources: Central Intelligence Agency, *China: International Trade Quarterly Review, Fourth Quarter, 1979* (May, 1980); and the State Statistical Bureau releases on national plan fulfillment of June 27, 1979 and April 30, 1980.

TABLE 3.   INTERNATIONAL COMPARISONS OF FOREIGN TRADE IN 1978

(All figures in millions of U.S. dollars)		
	Exports	*Imports*
United States	141,154	182,787
Japan	97,570	78,776
India	6,113	7,343
Republic of Korea	12,713	15,074
Taiwan	12,687	11,027
China	9,965	10,265

Note: Except for China, all import figures are c.i.f.

Source: These figures are from the United Nations, *Monthly Bulletin of Statistics,* except for data for the Province of Taiwan which are from the *Taiwan Statistical Data Book, 1979.*

To achieve a 15 percent level by 1990, Chinese trade over the next decade would have to grow in real terms at a rate of over 15 percent a year; and to achieve an 18 percent level, real growth would itself have to approach 18 percent. Nations such as Japan and South Korea have achieved growth rates of this magnitude over a decade-long period, but for a number of reasons China is unlikely to do so.

The most important reason is that the Chinese economy is not geared to producing goods for export. The Chinese system, like the Soviet economy after which it was patterned, is best at producing great quantities of machinery, steel, and low-quality consumer goods. Western markets, however, require high-quality goods that are specifically designed for those markets. Until recently Chinese industrial enterprises were not concerned with marketing of any kind; that was the job of separate commercial enterprises. Recent measures designed to promote joint ventures, the establishment of free trade zones, the use of Hong Kong businessmen in Chinese factories, and many other similar activities are all designed to overcome this lack of market, particularly foreign market orientation. Even for the domestic Chinese market the rules have been changed so that enterprises receive bonuses based on what is sold rather than what is produced. It is reasonable to assume that all these efforts will to some degree bear fruit in the form of increased exports of manufactures, but not to the extent of a nation such as South Korea whose whole economic system is geared toward exporting.

A second constraint on the rapid expansion of Chinese exports is the fact that the growth prospects for China's traditional exports are dim. Agricultural products, which made up the bulk of these exports, are in short supply at home, and as indicated above, agriculture is and is likely to remain a slow-growing sector. As incomes rise, however, Chinese consumers will want to spend more on food, and this too will cut into the ability of planners to generate a farm surplus for export. The alternative of holding down domestic consumption through rationing would undermine the incentive impact of wage increases and thus would hurt labor productivity.

There are those who argue that petroleum exports will provide a route out of this impasse, but for reasons that will be explained below, although petroleum exports may increase and the price of those exports may rise faster than the general rate of inflation, such exports are not likely to be a rising share of Chinese trade in the 1980s.

Others have argued that China can borrow its way to a more rapid expansion of foreign trade, at least on the import side. The big jumps in imports in 1978 and 1979 were in part financed by long-term borrowing abroad. Published plans indicate that China intends to continue this practice. But there are limits on the availability of subsidized credits, which are the only ones China has shown much interest in. Even if the World Bank receives the funds necessary to accommodate major International Development Association (IDA) loans to China, and the Japanese and European governments continue to support subsidized export credits, long-term loans of $2–3 billion a year throughout the 1980s would be an optimistic projection. Annual loans of this magnitude would allow China to maintain a balance of payments deficit somewhat larger than that of 1979, and hence imports could expand at a rate slightly, but only slightly, higher than the rate of the growth of exports.

What then is a reasonable forecast of the growth rate for China's exports and total foreign trade? A minimal estimate would be that foreign trade in real terms would grow at the same rate as GNP, that is on the order of 6 to 8 percent a year. Chinese foreign trade in real terms probably grew at a rate at or a bit below GNP during the 1952–1977 period, but that in part was the result of deliberate efforts to limit international economic relations. Indexes of Chinese foreign trade in real terms for this entire period have yet to be calculated. Hence there is some uncertainty surrounding just what the growth rate of foreign trade really was. In current prices the trade ratio rose from 10.6 percent of national income in 1952 to 14.3 percent in 1957, had fallen back to 10.2 percent by 1977, and then rose to 11.8 percent in 1978 and 13.5 percent in 1979. Such figures suggest that foreign trade grew at roughly the same rate as national income over the twenty-five-year period. These figures do not constitute proof, however, because of possible changes in relative prices that would affect these ratios. Presumably now that China's economic planners are working hard to expand those relations, they should be able to do better—

although not as well as the Koreans and the Japanese. Furthermore, world-wide pressures for protectionism are making it harder to expand exports even for the Koreans and Japanese. A plausible forecast, but one that is little more than that, is that China could achieve an annual increase in exports and imports of 10 percent in real terms.

At 6 percent a year, Chinese exports would pass $25 billion (in 1979 prices) by 1990, and total trade would be over $50 billion. At 10 percent, the 1990 figures would be over $35 billion for exports and around $80 billion for total trade. These are substantial sums, particularly from the point of view of individual companies—especially in those countries that manage to capture the lion's share of the China market. If the United States or Japan were to capture or hold 20 percent of the China market (a much higher share is unlikely), that would mean a trade of from $10 to $16 billion per year. Such figures might be as much as 5 percent of Japan's total trade in 1990 or 3 to 4 percent of U.S. trade in that year. This would make China a leading trading partner of each country, possibly even one of the top three or four, at least in the case of Japan.

Exports of $25 to $35 billion a year would also create some problems for exporting nations such as South Korea, particularly if Chinese exports were largely composed of manufactures, as is likely to be the case. But the degree of competition provided by China should be kept in perspective. The manufactured exports of many other nations in Latin America and Asia will also be growing in the 1980s. With respect to exports, China is simply another newly industrialized country beginning to play an increasingly important role on the world economic scene, not a special case several times greater than the others.

China will also be particularly competitive at the low-wage end of the manufactured exports spectrum if it can overcome its marketing weaknesses. The People's Republic is already a major exporter of textiles, and it is quite possible that China over time will cut into the shares of Korea and Taiwan in the U.S. textile market if the U.S. begins to adjust its textile quotas to the benefit of American consumers. But this change, too, is what one expects in the course of economic development. Rapid growth in Korea and Taiwan has pulled wages up to a level where they are no longer very competitive with respect to exports where semi-skilled worker wages make up a high proportion of total costs. If China does not gradually drive them out of these markets, others will, just as Japan did to American textile manufacturers and then later as Korea, Hong Kong, and Taiwan did to Japan.

China by 1985 and 1990, therefore, will be a trading nation with a greater impact on the world economy than it had in the late 1970s; but in no sense will it be a rival for influence with the larger industrialized nations such as Japan or West Germany. Yet even if its overall impact on world markets is limited, is it possible that China will have a disproportionately large impact on such key markets as those for petroleum and grain?

There was a time when Chinese leaders encouraged or at least did not discourage the view that the PRC would soon become a major petroleum exporter. Despite a growth rate in petroleum extraction averaging 20 percent a year throughout the 1960s and 1970s, however, domestic demand for that petroleum managed to nearly keep pace with output. In the late 1970s, out of a total production of two million barrels a day, only 10 percent, or 200,000 barrels a day, could be made available for export, mainly to Japan. Then in 1979 the growth in production of petroleum in China slowed dramatically to only 2 percent that year. The oil fields onshore had reached the limits of their capacity. Exploration offshore and in China's far northwest had only just begun.

It is possible, even likely, that Chinese and foreign companies exploring offshore will find major new pools of oil. The same expectation can be held for exploration in China's northwest. But even if such discoveries are made, they will not have a major impact on Chinese petroleum production levels until the mid-1980s at the earliest. And by the mid-1980s, China's domestic energy requirements will have grown along with GNP, if not a bit faster. Thus, Chinese finds would have to be truly enormous for the PRC to become a major world exporter of oil. Optimists might project Chinese output of four million barrels a day by 1990, with a quarter of that (one million barrels a day) available for exports. A lower figure is more likely unless it turns out that the Gulf of Bohai or the South China Sea really is another Persian Gulf.

China will probably play a larger role on world grain markets, but on the import not the export side. Imports of grain by 1979 had already passed ten million tons a year. This is about 5 percent of the world's grain trade, depending on whose statistics are used. Grain imports of ten million tons represent a substantial rise over the five to six million tons of grain imports each year in the 1960s; and this occurred despite an annual rate of increase in grain output between 1965 and 1979 of over 3 percent. Population growth over most of this same period did average 2 percent (as contrasted to 1.2 percent in 1978 and 1979), but urban wages were stagnant until 1978, and rural incomes rose by only a few percent.

China's future demand for foreign grain will depend on what happens on both the supply and demand sides. On the supply side, there is controversy among Western analysts over whether grain output will continue to struggle upward at 2 percent a year or whether recent reforms designed to improve rural incentives and agricultural management will accelerate growth of grain production to 3 percent a year or even more. Even a 3 percent rate (2 percent per capita) may not be enough to meet consumer needs if urban wages are rising steadily along with a rapid shift in population from rural to urban areas. Higher incomes will lead to greater demand for meat, and it takes three pounds of grain to produce a pound of pork and eight pounds of grain for a pound of beef.

Thus the prospects are that China will feel under steady pressure to raise grain imports, not because of an occasional poor harvest as in 1980, but because of the long-term problem of trying to feed a billion people on only 250 million acres of arable land. The United States, by way of contrast, has nearly 400 million acres in crops for a population of 220 million. While the Chinese will be under pressure to raise grain imports, it does not follow that they will have the foreign exchange necessary for proceeding very far in this direction. There is almost no possibility, for example, that China will go as far as Japan or South Korea in becoming dependent on food imports. In the first half of the 1970s, Korea imported over seventy-five kilograms of grain per person. If China were to do the same, Chinese grain imports would be over 75 million tons a year in the 1980s. Even at current grain price levels, China is not likely to have the foreign exchange available for such large purchases. And needless to say, if China were to make purchases of this magnitude, world grain prices would soar.

There is no basis, therefore, for a concrete estimate of China's demand for imported food in the 1980s. So much depends on the strength of China's overall foreign exchange position, and not just on the performance of domestic grain production or on the rate of increase in urban demand. Barring a miraculous breakthrough on the domestic production front, however, the pressure will be to raise grain imports above the already high levels of the late 1970s.

Technology Transfers: The Importance of Trained Manpower

It is sometimes assumed that foreign trade and technology transfers are virtually identical. Measures that promote foreign trade thus are also measures for the promotion of the transfer of advanced techniques from the industrialized to the less developed world.

While there is some truth to this view, there is more to these kinds of transfers than the import of high-technology products. The key to technology transfer is not so much trade as it is people. When the Communists took over the Chinese government in 1949, for example, there were around one thousand natural scientists with Western doctorates who had remained in China or returned after 1949. Thousands more were trained to roughly comparable levels in the Soviet Union in the 1950s. Two of the returned American-trained scientists headed up Peking's nuclear and missile research and development programs. Others played key roles in research on everything from new rice varieties to aircraft design. Many became teachers who trained the 1950s and early 1960s generations of engineers and scientists.

The greatest damage done by the Cultural Revolution (1966–1976) was not the direct disruption of industry—which was severe only in 1967 and 1968—nor was it the restrictions on high-technology imports. Restrictions on foreign trade did exist as a result of pressure from the Cultural Revolution Group, but imports in the early 1970s included many high-

technology items, including major ones such as complete petro-
chemical plants. The real damage was to the educational and
research systems that trained the people who could absorb
this new technology.

From 1966 until 1978 or 1979, Chinese universities and research institutes were either closed altogether or operated
under such politicized conditions that little in the way of scientific and technical training was possible. By 1980 the youngest
of those trained abroad either in the West or in the Soviet
Union were in their fifties. Many still in active leadership
positions were in their seventies because there was no one to
replace them. The number of first-class scientists trained completely within China is unknown to the outside world, but the
number could not be large given that only in the years 1950
to 1957 and 1961 to 1965 did advanced training operate in a
reasonably unfettered manner. Perhaps a few of the most important military weapons institutes were protected from massive political interference for somewhat longer periods of time,
but even these facilities suffered substantial disruption.

It is only against this background that one can understand
the importance of the thousands of scientists who went to the
United States and elsewhere in the West in the late 1970s for
stays of one or two years and occasionally longer periods. Most
were in their early forties because hardly anyone younger than
that had been able to acquire both a good undergraduate education and some quality postgraduate training. By 1985 at least
as many as ten thousand people with advanced training in the
West will be back in China. Barring another Cultural Revolution tidal wave, these people will be playing leading roles in
hundreds of research institutes spread across the nation. By
1990, if scientists and technicians continue to go abroad as is
intended by current government policy, the number with foreign training may be several tens of thousands. As more well-
trained people return, the quality of training received by those
who remain in China will also improve.

In short, as early as 1985—and certainly by 1990—China will
have a cadre of many thousands of scientists and technicians
familiar with the frontiers of their various fields. Tens of thousands more trained at home as well as abroad will staff the
institutes and enterprises that will implement the programs

required to bring Chinese industrial technology up to the best international standards, at least in strategic areas of activity. Chinese scientists long ago demonstrated that with proper training they could win Nobel Prizes, put satellites in orbit, and develop high-yielding varieties of rice. The problem has been that there are not enough such scientists; many of those who were trained remained in the United States after 1949, while those who did return to China were often misused or persecuted. By 1990 the number of scientists with the equivalent of Ph.D. training should be expanding by several thousand each year, and the annual additions to the roles of technicians with good undergraduate training should number in the hundreds of thousands. They will be working with the sizable cadre of scientists and technicians trained in the 1950s who will not yet have retired.

Scientific exchanges for China, therefore, are not just a matter of promotion of good will through people getting to know each other's cultures better. These exchanges are central to China's efforts to catch up with the industrialized nations of the world. Once trained, these scientists and technicians can to some degree keep up with the frontiers of their fields through publications even if for a time they are once again prevented from traveling abroad. Thus, in no realistic sense is foreign training making China dependent on the West. If anything, these scientists will help to free China from the existing dependency on the West for high-technology products acquired through trade.

The direct benefits of these exchanges to Western scientists are more modest. Specialists in a few fields such as seismology, cancer epidemiology, economic development, and certain of the arts will gain even at the frontiers of their fields from contacts with the Chinese. But there are no comparable benefits in most other disciplines. The case for scientific exchanges with China must rise or fall in the West on the proposition that scientific progress in China is intrinsically a good thing, and the faster the better. The United States and its allies will not determine whether Chinese scientists advance to the frontiers of their field, but they could and probably will have considerable influence on the pace at which that advance occurs.

The Economics of Military Power

Since no reasonable person will argue with the benefits of helping China eradicate cancer in children or developing better plant varieties with which to feed its people, the question of whether more or less scientific progress in China is desirable becomes primarily an issue of how one feels about improvements in Chinese military technology. In a similar vein, few would find it defensible to attempt to hamper Chinese attempts to improve the standard of living of the Chinese people, but many more—the great majority of Russians, for example—do not feel the same way about economic advances that can be translated into greater military power. This analysis is primarily concerned with forecasting what is in fact likely to occur with respect to China's military modernization, and what difference actions by the West might make; but I shall return to the question of what is desirable from an American point of view in the conclusion. First, however, one must come to grips with how the growth of China's economy and advances in Chinese technology will affect PRC military power in the 1980s and beyond.

There are broadly speaking two ways in which the condition of a country's economy affects its military power. On the one hand is the size of a nation's GNP and the industrial share of that GNP which the nation's leaders are able to divert to military uses. On the other hand, even if one has all the money one needs to spend on weapons, a nation may lack the technical proficiency required to develop the kinds of weapons required.

China's military budget in 1979 was 22.27 billion yuan, equivalent to 6.6 percent of national income according to socialist concepts, or around 5.5 percent of GNP. A more realistic figure that would include items excluded from the formal military budget would raise this percentage by an unknown amount. For illustrative purposes, the figures in this analysis are based on a 7 percent rate relative to GNP.

The first point is that China's military budget is currently running at a rate of U.S. $25 to $30 billion, a figure that, to give some comparative perspective, is perhaps double Vietnam's total GNP and nearly as large as South Korea's entire GNP.

(This figure was derived by applying the 7 percent figure to the earlier GNP estimate of U.S. $400 billion. Very different results might be obtained if one attempted to value Chinese military weapons and personnel using U.S. prices.) Even if the percentage share of the military budget is not increased or is slightly reduced, China would be spending over U.S. $50 billion on defense by 1990. And if the situation warranted it, China would clearly be able to spend a higher share than 7 percent on the military. Chinese planners, for example, are currently trying to bring the rate of capital accumulation down from around 36 percent of national income to 25 to 27 percent, a 10 percent drop, in order to increase incentives and growth. In an emergency, the state would be able to divert at least a comparable sum to the military without even having to completely sacrifice economic growth.

In the normal course of economic development—assuming a constant 7 percent of GNP diverted to arms—the Chinese military budget would not reach the U.S. $100 billion level until the late 1990s (if the projections of GNP at the beginning of this paper prove to be correct). But it is also clearly within the Chinese government's capacity to reach the U.S. $100 billion level (in 1979 prices) by 1990 if it so chooses. A defense budget of 12 to 14 percent of GNP would be required. The lower figure (12 percent) is based on the assumption that GNP growth over the decade averaged 8 percent a year. The higher figure is based on a 6 percent growth rate. The United States and the Soviet Union each spent more than U.S. $100 billion in 1980, although not several times more; and no other nation in the world has ever come close to such a large figure.

The other component of the economics-military power equation, China's technological level, goes a long way toward explaining why China has held military expenditures well below what one might have expected given Peking's perception of the danger of war with the Soviet Union. Visitors to the PRC with a knowledge of military technology have returned in recent years commenting on the backwardness of Chinese armaments technology. An air force equipped mainly with MIG-19s, obsolete tanks, and a strategy that still relies on the massive mobilization of a trained militia, all point to a nation that ultimately would have to fall back on guerrilla warfare against the fire power of an army such as that of the Soviet Union. The conclusion of these observers is not simply that current Chinese technology is at least two decades behind the times, but with a leap in logic, that Chinese military technology is likely to remain far behind that of the Soviet Union or the United States far into the future.

Forecasts of technological developments are always treacherous, but the first point to make is that Chinese military technology could be brought up to current levels of the advanced military powers by the simple expedient of the United States or even France giving China the necessary weapons and helping China build plants to manufacture them. Because such a step might so alarm the Soviet Union as to lead it down a path toward World War III, such a development is unlikely to occur. But the point is a useful antidote to those who think that current technology gaps will persist indefinitely.

The second point is that China already has a nuclear and missile force that is substantially less than two decades behind the technologies of the United States and the Soviet Union. Furthermore, this is a force with some deterrent capability, even though it is theoretically conceivable that the Chinese force could be destroyed by a first strike.

Perhaps most important is that history is replete with examples of nations that started far behind in one or many aspects of industrial technology and then caught up in a hurry. In fact, the closing of the technology gap is what normally happens in the process of industrialization. Follower nations do not have to copy all the mistakes or stages of development of the technology leaders. They can skip over most of them, as the Japanese have done with civilian technology. The U.S. did not fire its first ICBM until per capita GNP had passed $5,000 (in 1979 prices). China tested its first ICBM with a per capita GNP of $400.

It would be foolish to attempt a precise forecast of just when China will have the technical capacity to produce aircraft and ancillary equipment that will make its air defenses competitive with an air force at the most advanced levels, or when China will have a secure nuclear retaliatory force. The only point is that, given a continuation of current Chinese policies, that level is likely to be achieved much sooner than most outside observers currently seem to expect.

When Chinese military technology does reach competitive levels, China will have the economic resources to pay for a very formidable military force. Whether China will in fact decide to spend its money in that way will depend on conditions at the time technological parity or something approaching it is achieved. In the meantime, there is little point in increasing purchases of MIG-19s, rifles, cement for underground tunnels, or whatever. Such purchases will not significantly raise Chinese military power relative to where it already is vis-à-vis the Soviet Union.

Implications for the United States

The interests of the United States have been implicit in much of the above discussion, but it is time to make these interests explicit. The trade issues require little further comment. Like the industrialization process of such nations as Japan and South Korea before it, China's industrialization will provide expanding markets for some American manufacturers and farmers, and competitors for others. It will be manufacturers in nations such as Korea, however, who will face most of the Chinese competition since in the 1980s Chinese manufactured exports are likely to be made up mainly of products making substantial use of semiskilled labor working at low wages.

The implications of a rise in Chinese military power are more complex and can only be touched on here. The central point is that China's military capabilities are likely to increase relative to those of both the United States and the Soviet Union, not to mention China's other neighbors, under any likely assumptions about what the US. and the Western Europeans might do to help or hinder the process. Plausible forecasts of what the United States might do to either accelerate or hinder the PRC's military modernization might change the date at which particular weapons systems are acquired by several years, but the United States acting alone or even in concert with its Western allies could not keep the People's Liberation Army technologically backward for decades even if it were deemed desirable to do so.

Would delaying the development of Chinese military technology by a few years be desirable? The Soviet answer would be an unequivocal yes. From an American point of view, however, there would be little to gain. Increased Chinese military capacity to deter a Soviet invasion would lessen the possibility of such an invasion occurring, an invasion that could trigger nuclear strikes by both sides as part of an escalation without a predictable end. China's capacity to support North Korea or settle its differences with Taiwan by force would rise, but so would China's capacity to deter Vietnamese adventurism. But these increases in Chinese power are going to occur in any event, so the question is really one of whether much is to be gained from delaying them until 1995 instead of 1990.

Americans did not determine the outcome of the political struggles that preoccupied the Chinese leadership throughout the 1970s, but American actions will have some influence on the evolution of China's economic and national security policies. More than any Chinese leadership in modern times, the men who came to power after Mao's death in 1976 have committed themselves to the proposition that China has much to gain through increasingly intimate involvement with the industrial nations of the West and Japan. Cooperation by the West in the development of China's scientific manpower, technology base, and economic system will tend to confirm the correctness of that view against those among the leadership who would still prefer to go it alone with minimum contact with the outside world, or repair relations with the Soviet Union. Thus the cost of attempting to restrict technology transfers is that such acts tend to undermine the political standing of those in China who are willing to allow the PRC to become involved constructively with the world community.

It may be that the current leadership will once again turn inward, or that new leaders will come to the fore who will have China's centuries-old fear and disdain of foreigners. But for the present, there is the opportunity to show the Chinese that there is a better way. And the only cost to the United States is that China will become a major world power a few years sooner than would otherwise be the case.

William G. Hyland

5

The Sino-Soviet Conflict:

Dilemmas of the Strategic Triangle

The Emergence of the Strategic Triangle

On April 11, 1980 the formal treaty relationship between
the Soviet Union and the People's Republic of China officially
expired. To be sure, the Treaty of Friendship, Alliance, and
Mutual Assistance negotiated between Stalin and Mao Zedong
in February 1950 had been an empty shell for more than two
decades. Neither Peking nor Moscow had considered itself
bound to come to the defense of the other since at least the
public outbreak of the Sino-Soviet feud in 1960. Nor did the
treaty provide even a rough framework for concerted policies.
The relationship with the prospective aggressor—Japan, or any
state allied with Japan—had long since been transformed from
the unrelieved hostility of the 1950s. But the very act of invok-
ing the formal abrogation clause, which Peking did in April

WILLIAM G. HYLAND *is a senior fellow at the Georgetown Center for Strategic and International Studies. He formerly served as a staff member of
the National Security Council, director of the Bureau of Intelligence and
Research of the Department of State (1973–1974), and deputy assistant to
the President for National Security Affairs (1975–1976).*

1979, symbolized the profound change in the relationship between the two communist allies. Even this last vestige of the alignment of the 1950s had to be exorcised.

Yet in the very act of destroying the legal basis of what once had been described as an unbreakable alliance, Peking initiated an intriguing dialogue with Moscow for the first time since 1964. These new Sino-Soviet talks, which collapsed within nine months of their initiation in the spring of 1979—in reaction to Moscow's invasion of Afghanistan—were followed by a further enhancement of the Sino-American relationship. New momentum was added to the creation of an anti-Soviet entente composed of the United States, China, and Japan. This evolution seemed to return the world to a polarization of strategic relationships, thus calling into question the future of the "triangular" dealings among Washington, Moscow, and Peking which had emerged in the early 1970s.

ENCIRCLEMENT AND COUNTERENCIRCLEMENT

In the aftermath of the Soviet Union's invasion of Czechoslovakia in August 1968, the tense relations between the Chinese and the Soviets had taken a major turn for the worse. In the spring of 1969 there were sharp military clashes on the Ussuri River islands of the Sino-Soviet frontier. It seemed that the Soviets might even go so far as to invade China. The Chinese leaders apparently shared such apprehensions, and they maneuvered adroitly to involve the Soviets in a series of discussions which would defuse the antagonism along the Sino-Soviet border. But this was to a large extent a holding action by the Chinese. The focal point of the diplomacy of both powers was the United States.

The Soviets gradually opened the way to a period of so-called "detente" with the U.S.; and the Chinese, similarly, initiated the process of normalizing Sino-American relations. Thus, in 1971 the strategic triangle was born, with both communist powers intent on exploiting their lines to the United States in order to isolate their adversary. Indeed, in the early 1970s the Soviets made a number of serious overtures to the United States to join in a tacit or even more explicit alliance against China. Hints along these lines were dropped first during the

SALT I negotiations, and then in the meetings between Soviet Communist Party First Secretary Leonid Brezhnev and President Nixon. The Soviet leader made clear both his anxiety about the growth of Chinese power and the desirability of the United States joining the USSR in opposing the expansion of PRC influence.

The refusal of the United States to join in such an adventure was almost certainly a major reason why "detente" began to dissipate after 1974. If the relaxation with the U.S. would lead to no major gains vis-à-vis China for the USSR, then the utility of the American connection was obviously open to question. Among the diverse reasons why the Soviets initiated a more aggressive phase of policy, beginning with the intrusion of Cuban troops into Angola in mid-1975, almost certainly a key motive was Moscow's increasing concern with Washington's China connection.

For the Chinese, however, their "America card" proved to be an effective instrument of foreign policy. It produced a series of Soviet overtures for reconciliation, usually in the form of proposals for a nonaggression treaty. It also served to keep alive, although just barely, the Sino-Soviet border negotiations. And it may have served to keep the domestic Chinese conflict over foreign policy from being dragged into the severe leadership feuds that erupted in Peking in the waning days of Mao's rule. At the same time, while Sino-American relations gradually evolved into a reasonably cordial framework, no major progress or breakthrough could, or would, be worked out—especially as the U.S. election campaign began in late 1975. It may well be that the American failure to thwart the Soviets and their Cuban proxies in Angola, as a result of constraints on a U.S. response imposed by a rebellious Senate, shocked the Chinese leaders, coming as it did so soon after discussions between Vice Premier Deng Xiaoping and President Ford in Peking in December 1975.

In any case, when Mao died in 1976 the triangular relationship was still operative, but its underlying assumptions were weakening. Sino-Soviet hostility had driven both Peking and Moscow toward Washington. It now appeared that Washington could not be won over by one side or the other. But equally important, it no longer appeared that the U.S. could easily exploit the pivotal position of the triangular manager. Washington could not invoke the "China card" against Moscow without having to consider whether a new price would have to be paid to Peking, either in a reduction in the status of relations with Taiwan or in military assistance to China. But the U.S. could not easily return to a Soviet detente without risking the China relationship, particularly in light of the power struggles that followed Mao's demise.

The first break in this seeming stalemate came from Moscow when rather clear signals were sent to Peking shortly after the Chairman's death in September 1976. The Soviet leaders, probably drawing on their own experience after the death of Stalin, may have thought that in a Chinese succession period the opportunities for a change of course would be optimal. Accordingly, friendly gestures were initiated. Brezhnev proclaimed that there were no issues that could not be resolved in the spirit of "good neighborliness." But whatever hopes existed for even a limited reconciliation gradually faded. The Chinese response, after some hesitation, was negative. Peking's conditions for normalization were inflexible: troop disengagement from the border area; resolution of boundary questions; and Soviet force withdrawals from the Far East provinces, from Mongolia, and from Vietnam—thus returning the situation to the condition of the early 1960s.

It is not surprising that this phase ended in failure. The Sino-Soviet dispute had long since ceased to be impelled by the personalities of Mao and Khrushchev, or Brezhnev for that matter. What had been an ideological, and then an internal communist quarrel, had become a struggle for power, in effect a confrontation in which the traditional instruments of national policy—diplomacy, military positions, alignments, and alliances—played their familiar roles. Both Moscow and Peking thus engaged in intensive maneuvering from the spring of 1978 until the end of the year.

In this period the Chinese inaugurated a broad new policy: modernizing the economy; building up the defense sector; and initiating new moves toward Japan, Western Europe, and the United States. In this phase new Premier Hua Guofeng made a trip to Eastern Europe and Southwest Asia. Negotiations for western arms were initiated. The normalization process with the U.S. gained new life during the visit to China of President Carter's national security adviser, Zbigniew Brzezinski, in May 1978. And, most important, a peace and friendship treaty was signed with the Japanese in August 1978. Simultaneously, China's relations with Vietnam steadily worsened as Soviet influence grew. The Chinese were clearly trying to build a coalition against Moscow in which Chinese military modernization would be underwritten by Japan and Europe, if not by the U.S. as well.

The USSR countered with a series of moves of its own. Local Communists seized power in Afghanistan in April 1978. Japan was the target of a series of threats, just before and after the signing of the Chinese treaty in August 1978. And then, for the first time, Soviet troops occupied the Japanese northern islands—thus compounding the territorial dispute which for so long had been the stumbling block to any Japanese-Soviet normalization. But the most aggressive Soviet counterthrust came in Southeast Asia, where Moscow signed a new treaty with Vietnam in November 1978. This was a virtual blank check for Soviet support, which the Vietnamese desperately needed before launching their attack against China's ally Cambodia (Kampuchea). Even though the treaty stopped short of an automatic guarantee of Soviet military assistance, the implication was that if China put pressure on Vietnam, Hanoi could count on Soviet aid, perhaps even military action.

The implication was never fully realized, however. The Vietnamese, of course, did attack and the Chinese "counterattacked," but in the end the Soviets made no overt military move against the PRC. Moscow nevertheless emerged from the crisis with major strategic gains in the form of access to naval and air bases at Cam Ranh Bay and Danang, which were of growing importance in light of the new crisis in the Persian Gulf and Indian Ocean.

The Chinese had taught North Vietnam a "lesson" with impunity. But Peking's flawed effort to sustain a modern military campaign raised serious questions about its defense capabilities. There is some reason to believe that Chinese military mistakes—openly acknowledged by Peking—may have played a role in the decision behind the Chinese diplomatic opening to Moscow. While threatening for several weeks to abrogate the Sino-

Soviet treaty of 1950, the formal notification of an intent to terminate was interestingly coupled with an offer to negotiate (in a note of April 3, 1979). This overture coincided with a period of probable weakness in the political position of Deng Xiaoping and the emergence of serious revisions in China's economic development program—the "Four Modernizations."

THE FAILURE OF DIPLOMACY

Whatever the precise Chinese motives in offering to negotiate in the wake of the Vietnamese-Chinese conflict, it was now up to Moscow to reject or to explore the offer. The Soviets, of course, were mindful that they were entering into the final phase of the SALT II negotiations and that a summit meeting with President Carter would likely be the context for the treaty signing. They were also aware of growing speculation and interest in the U.S. in "playing the China card," including a revived interest in developing the military dimension of the Sino-American relationship. Hence, it was both opportunism and prudence that dictated the Soviet negotiating stand.

The Soviets probed Chinese intentions in their reply of April 17, 1979. On May 5, Peking suggested general negotiations without conditions. The Soviets responded on June 5, proposing that talks at the deputy foreign minister level begin in July or August in Moscow (i.e., after the proposed U.S. summit). The note defined the objectives of the negotiations: improvement of relations based on "the principles of peaceful coexistence" and publication of a proposed agreement on these principles in an "appropriate document."

There was no great expectation in Moscow that the Chinese would respond positively to the proposal. A commentary of June 4 in the Soviet press indicated that talks with the Chinese would not be easy, "as the weight of contradictions is too great, too much distrust has accumulated. . . ." At the June 18th session of China's National People's Congress, Premier Hua Guofeng equivocated. He noted the earlier period of Sino-Soviet friendship, but put the burden for any improvement in relations on Moscow.

The Soviets reacted angrily, but the diplomatic exchanges continued. Moscow's media speculated that the Chinese would advance "certain preliminary conditions." In the wake of the signature of the SALT II treaty and the Carter-Brezhnev summit (where Andrei Gromyko claimed China was discussed), Peking responded on July 16 by proposing the initiation of talks in Moscow in mid-September—at the vice ministerial level as proposed by Gromyko, but without proposing any preconditions. The cat and mouse diplomacy continued for a while longer; and not until late August were the days of September 18–20 finally accepted for the beginning of negotiations.

The agreement of the two communist antagonists to negotiate seemed to engender a certain nervousness in Hanoi. Just before the arrival of the Chinese delegation in Moscow, Politburo member Le Duc Tho arrived to meet with his Soviet counterpart Mikhail Suslov; and then Vietnamese Premier Pham Van Dong came a few days later to meet with other Soviet leaders. Some reinsurance against a Sino-Soviet accommodation at Hanoi's expense must have been a major item in the discussions.

In due course, on September 23, PRC Vice Foreign Minister Wang Youping arrived in Moscow. Three days later, in typical Soviet negotiating style, Gromyko presented the United Nations with a grandiose scheme for an international agreement prohibiting "hegemonism." The irony of Gromyko's pressing China's favorite slogan could not have been lost on Peking, and it did not augur well for the formal negotiations that were about to begin.

The course of these negotiations, which lasted until November 30, has not been revealed by either side. There were five preliminary meetings which ran through October 17, when the formal negotiating sessions began. There were six sessions thereafter that concluded on November 30, 1979. Shortly after the final session Gromyko met with Wang Youping to discuss "some questions connected with the Soviet-Chinese talks."

It appears that in the talks both sides held more or less firmly to their general positions, while expressing some nuances. The Soviets argued for an agreement on principles which could then form the basis for further negotiations. The Chinese argued for more specifics, but did not reject a formal document. (This position had been foreshadowed in June in Hua Guofeng's speech to the National People's Congress.)

Peking did not press for preliminary conditions but apparently held to its general demand that Soviet forces withdraw from the border area. The Soviets countered with a limited proposal in which some thinning out of their troops might be exchanged for a nonaggression treaty.

At the same time it was thought by some outside observers that the Chinese were, in fact, seriously interested in the talks. This was suggested by the tone of Hua Guofeng's speech in June, the lack of Chinese preconditions, and the fact that the talks did indeed take place in Moscow—despite some serious military incidents along the border in the period prior to negotiations.

Both sides also maneuvered in the international arena to exploit the talks. The Chinese negotiated a visit to Peking by American Secretary of Defense Harold Brown in early 1980. This was announced shortly after the preliminary Sino-Soviet discussions began. And a "secret" U.S. report, urging American arms sales to Peking, was leaked to the American press in early October. As noted earlier, Gromyko began an anti-Chinese campaign in New York at the United Nations. And in November the Soviets began informing outside observers that the talks were "not going well."

According to an American reporter traveling through Moscow, the Soviets proposed that each side agree not to attack the other with nuclear or conventional weapons and that each adopt a policy of not seeking hegemonism in Asia or anywhere else. This would be incorporated into a statement of principles, similar to the Soviet-American statement of May 1972. The Chinese replied with their standard demand for a withdrawal of Soviet troops, especially those stationed in Mongolia, and then added the condition that all Soviet aid to Vietnam be halted. This, of course, had to be rejected by Moscow. Even to hint at such a bargain would lead to a collapse of the Soviet position in Asia.

Even before the final meeting of November 30, 1979, *Pravda* had attacked the Chinese in a long article (published on November 24) claiming that the root of tensions in Southeast Asia was Chinese policy and that the situation could only be normalized by removing the root cause—"by stopping Peking's expansionist aspirations." Even so, several Yugoslav journalists emphasized the positive significance of the fact that for the first time in fifteen years there had been "serious" negotiations between Peking and Moscow. It was officially announced on December 5 that talks were to be continued in the Chinese capital "at a time coordinated by the two sides." Somewhat strangely, the official Chinese delegation did not depart Moscow until December 10. This departure came in the wake of a long *Pravda* commentary published two days before under the pseudonym of "Alexandrov" which gave a highly pessimistic appraisal of the future course of the talks.

The *Pravda* commentary seems to have been in fact a reprise of the Soviet negotiating position. For example, the commentary strongly reaffirmed the necessity ("reality") of maintaining Soviet defenses along the Chinese border, including the stationing of troops in Mongolia—thus suggesting that a thinning out of these forces, as a precondition, had once again been rejected. And the Soviets repeated their standard position that the issue of Soviet forces in Mongolia would only be resolved when the Chinese abandoned their policy of territorial annexation.

The territorial issue also seems to have remained stalemated. *Pravda* revived the dormant charge that Peking still claimed a "historic right" to millions of square kilometers of land and sea belonging to "practically every one of its neighbors," including the maritime provinces of the USSR, Sakhalin Island, and parts of Kazakstan and Central Asia. The Soviet commentary characterized Peking's denunciation of the Sino-Soviet treaty as an action that "could not be regarded as anything other than hostile." This act, of course, was contrasted with Moscow's supposedly positive desire for normalization of relations as reflected in the Soviet proposal for an agreement on principles of peaceful coexistence. Any "sane person," *Pravda* argued, would recognize that the normalization of state-to-state relations required a "definite legal foundation of principles agreed and recorded in an appropriate document." This objective, *Pravda* insisted, had to become "central to the effort at normalization." Precise principles were spelled out: equality, respect for national independence and sovereignty, territorial integrity, noninterference in internal affairs, nonuse of force or the threat of force, and mutual advantage. The antihegemony slogan was incorporated as one of the Sino-Soviet principles, along with a commitment to do everything necessary to prevent the emergence of a situation that could cause a dangerous aggravation of relations (a commitment very similar to that included in the Soviet-American statement of principles of May 1972).

In short, the Soviets at the end of the first round of negotiations gave a pessimistic estimate of the future course of the talks, but stopped short of predicting their collapse. Indeed, the Soviets included in their commentaries the announcement that the discussions would be continued in Peking on an agreed date—suggesting that the date had already been fixed. Interestingly, a somewhat later version only announced that the talks would be continued "in the future." So the exact degree of commitment to the next phase of negotiations was unclear, or not settled.

In any case, in the days following the adjournment of discussions in Moscow—presumably in the period when the Soviets were preparing to invade Afghanistan—Soviet comments became sharper. On December 11 the ubiquitous *Izvestia* commentator Alexander Bovin wrote an article entitled "Warning," in which he accused China of attempting to create a hostile encirclement of the USSR. With the passing of only a few days, however, the Soviet invasion of Afghanistan made Moscow's reservations and the prospects for the talks academic.

AFGHANISTAN AFTERMATH: A SINO-AMERICAN-JAPANESE "TRIANGLE" AND STRATEGIC POLARIZATION

In a strategic sense, Moscow's invasion of Afghanistan was aimed in part at thwarting the "encirclement" of the USSR that the Soviets were warning against. While the immediate problem of domestic political instability in Afghanistan required drastic Soviet action, the advance of Moscow's troops to the Khyber Pass created a new strategic situation. One of China's principal friends, Pakistan, was now directly confronted with Soviet power. Iran, already in increasing turmoil, was now pressed by the Soviet Union on two flanks. And the entire Persian Gulf—an obvious strategic energy source for Europe, the U.S., and Japan—was threatened by the USSR. Whether the Soviets chose to move further was almost academic when compared to the psychological impact of Moscow's military advance beyond the USSR's own borders and post–World War II sphere of control in Eastern Europe.

The Chinese certainly recognized that the Soviet move was a severe challenge, comparable to the invasion of Czechoslovakia in 1968. The Soviets were, in effect, announcing that they were arrogating to themselves the right to decide through military means the fate of "socialism" in all countries on their periphery. The Chinese met the problem head-on by calling off any further negotiations. This meant, in practice, that the treaty with Moscow would then lapse automatically on April 11. Their general posture, however, was rather cautious. The formal statement merely noted that continuation of the talks would not be "appropriate" under the circumstances. But no other aspect of the tattered Sino-Soviet relationship was suspended.

The principal effect on policy, however, was a distinct drawing together of Washington and Peking. In January, U.S. Secretary of Defense Harold Brown visited China. One result of his trip was a decision by the Carter administration to permit sales of "dual-use" technology and nonlethal military hardware to the PRC. China's Vice Premier Geng Biao reciprocated the Brown visit in May 1980; and the secretary of defense, in welcoming Geng to Washington, announced that the U.S. looked forward to the "continued step-by-step strengthening of ties between our two defense establishments as an integral part of efforts to normalize all facets of our relationship." Geng Biao publicly speculated that the Chinese might buy American arms "in the future," and the Pentagon released a list of equipment that would be freed from export restraints. American officials conceded in the press that a new defense relationship had begun. At almost the same time, the Chinese announced during Hua Guofeng's visit to Japan a determination to "break the nuclear strangle hold of the superpowers."

These two trips—Geng Biao to Washington and Hua Guofeng to Japan—were intended to demonstrate a new "triangular relationship" comprised of China, Japan, and the United States. Hua reportedly informed the Japanese that the Sino-

Soviet talks were dead and would not be resumed as long as Soviet troops remained in Afghanistan. One practical consequence of the new anti-Soviet triangle was Hua's announcement that North Korea would not attack South Korea. In other words, the Chinese, in return for political and military support against the Soviets, were reassuring both Japan and Washington that they would guarantee the status quo in Korea.

American officials then moved further in a major policy statement that was designed to end the old Sino–Soviet–U.S. triangular interplay. Assistant Secretary of State for East Asia and the Pacific Richard Holbrooke, in a speech on June 4, stated that the "famous triangular diplomacy of the early 1970s is no longer an adequate conceptual framework in which to view relations with China. . . . In short, relations with China are not a simple function of our relations with the Soviet Union. . . ." Yet a clear policy of tilting toward China was evident in Holbrooke's assertion that "we can and will assist China's drive to improve its security. . . ." One further, fortuitous step which reinforced this new security entente was President Carter's meeting with Hua Guofeng in Tokyo after attending the funeral of Prime Minister Ohira. While of no great substance, the impromptu Sino-American summit meeting in Japan was fraught with great symbolism.

The Soviet response to these trends, quite predictably, was hostile. In February, Prime Minister Aleksei Kosygin warned that the USSR would pay "unremitting attention to the question of the defense capability of the USSR." "No one," he said on February 21, 1980, "must be left in any doubt that the Soviet Union will not allow any disturbance of the balance of forces which has come about in the world to the detriment of its security." In June, the Soviets defended their actions in Afghanistan on the principle that certain situations "demanded extraordinary solutions and the courage to adopt them." Moscow took note of the new triangle being forged by Carter, Hua, and the Japanese by, in effect, countering with a new $1.6 billion arms supply agreement with India. Pakistan became the object of a new peace campaign over Afghanistan, supported by warnings from Moscow about being dragged into the conflict. And even Washington was cautioned that Chinese ambitions, independent of the status of U.S.–PRC relations, would be a source of potential conflict from which the United States would not be able to stand aside. In short, the Soviets saw the leverage in the relationship shifting from Washington to Peking. There was, as *Pravda* put it, an "emerging American-Chinese military alliance."

In what for the Soviet Union was a gloomy prospect, there was at least one element that raised questions about the durability of the enhanced Sino-American rapprochement: the instability of the Chinese leadership. Not only were serious problems of economic policy at issue among the leaders, but the whole anti-Maoist trend reflected in the various rehabilitations of Cultural Revolution purgees pointed to an increasing struggle between Deng Xiaoping and Hua Guofeng. Gradually the domestic political struggle in China deepened. The campaign against Mao Zedong's legacy intensified and became more overt, and there was a debate over whether to put the Gang of Four—including the Chairman's wife, Jiang Qing—on open, public trial. All of this must at least have given the Soviet leaders pause, if not generated hopeful speculation that out of the internal turmoil might come still another reversal of verdicts on Sino-Soviet relations.

In late August 1980, Brezhnev took public note of China's internal problems. He stressed that the Cultural Revolution had been openly appraised as the greatest of catastrophes for China, but that "unfortunately all this does not *as yet* tell in China's foreign policy. As before, it remains hostile to the Soviet Union. . . ." Almost this exact formulation was repeated seven months later by Brezhnev at the Twenty-Sixth Soviet Party Congress; but he softened his remarks somewhat, noting Soviet negotiating proposals remained on the table. In addition, the Soviets must have been intrigued by the modification of the "Four Modernizations" program for economic modernization: a lessening of attention to defense industries and cutbacks of imports of technology. Moscow may have concluded there was less urgency in the Chinese military build-up. According to some Soviet commentaries, there was opposition in Peking to foreign economic dependence (meaning close ties with the United States). The outbreak during the American election

campaign of 1980 of a dispute over Taiwan policy no doubt
further fueled Soviet hopes of a disruption in U.S.–PRC relations. Deng Xiaoping's veiled threat to improve relations with
Moscow if the Taiwan dispute continued was certainly noted
in Moscow, even if the obvious tactical circumstances of Deng's
warning required some discounting of its seriousness.

In sum, following the death of Mao two efforts were made
to achieve some degree of reconciliation between Moscow and
Peking: in the spring of 1977 and the fall of 1979. Both ended
in failure. At the same time one major crisis, the Sino-
Vietnamese military conflict, passed without a Sino-Soviet military clash. But the overall trend has been in the direction of a
Sino-American entente at Moscow's expense. This may be the
most profound change brought about by the events of the late
1970s. The original justification for the American opening to
China was to stimulate an improvement of relations with *both*
communist powers; hence "triangular diplomacy." By the end
of 1980 it seemed that the China connection had less and less
value for the U.S. as a lever against the USSR. The strategic
environment had been polarized in reaction to Moscow's interventions of the second half of the 1970s, from Angola to
Afghanistan.

Moscow's China Dilemma

What options are left for Moscow, and Peking, in the
evolution of the Sino-Soviet feud? The late 1970s demonstrated
that some effort to achieve even limited rapprochement was
not inconceivable, even if exceedingly complicated. But it also
confirmed what must have been Moscow's worst fears, that a
genuine U.S.–Chinese–Japanese alliance, with links to Europe,
was indeed emerging. Much of the aggressiveness in Soviet
diplomacy during the 1977–79 period was aimed at countering
or thwarting the emergence of this new entente. As long as
China was weak or relatively isolated, some Soviet accommodation might be arranged; but once China embarked on a
path of serious military modernization and external alliance-
building, its threat to the USSR would inevitably grow. Relations could continue, of course, on a middle ground for years,
but the basic choice remained: conciliation or confrontation.

CONCILIATION OR CONFRONTATION?

In assessing their basic options toward the PRC, the Soviets must answer two questions: will the strategic threat from China worsen and, if so, at what point will it become intolerable?

It is difficult to assess the real military threat to the USSR from China, for Soviet leaders undoubtedly view the PRC with a large measure of subjective fear and apprehension. Yet a major theme in their appraisals is that China's foreign policy is inherently expansionistic and that sooner or later, with or without U.S. support, the Chinese will challenge the Soviet Union. "Despite the change in leadership from Mao to Hua, the summons for war against the Soviet Union is still to be heard from Peking," wrote one prominent Soviet propagandist.

Official and semiofficial American appraisals rate China's military capabilities as quite limited. A study for a congressional committee, for example, emphasized the technological and economic backwardness of the Chinese as a major constraint on the early emergence of greatly improved military capabilities. Even if the Soviets have also come to recognize the constraints on China's military modernization, time remains an essential variable. Given outside technological assistance, the Chinese will almost certainly reach a position to neutralize Soviet military options in a decade or two. It may already be too late, in the sense that the few Chinese ICBMs constitute a crude deterrent against the Soviets.

Soviet leaders may very well feel that the 1980s will be the crucial period in dealing with the long-term challenge from China. For example, Brezhnev discussed the Chinese threat with President Nixon in 1973. He speculated that Peking would be a major power in about ten years (i.e., 1983). A subsequent evaluation, from Soviet political commentator Victor Louis in his book *The Coming Decline of the Chinese Empire* suggested that sooner rather than later the Soviet Union would have to deal with the Chinese threat:

> So if for China what is a disadvantageous gap in military technology and armaments is closing, the other, and extremely favorable, gap in manpower is just as inexorably widening. Therefore, it would be far more difficult to achieve a military victory over China today than it

was a decade ago. And it will be immeasurably more difficult in another decade than it is today. One highly placed Soviet official has been reported as saying that it would even be unjust and cowardly to leave the solution of the Chinese question for the next generation to cope with.

Soviet preparation for a showdown sometime in the 1980s is also suggested by the carefully constructed phases of the Soviet military build-up against China. The initial period, following the overthrow of Khrushchev in 1964, stressed the build-up of a basic structure of army divisions and air support. This phase had at least some semblance of a precautionary measure, although this clearly was not the main motive. Initially, the Soviets put into place along the Sino-Soviet border the structure of several field armies, increasing their deployments from about twelve to fifteen divisions in the mid-1960s to over forty-six in 1980. Between 1968 and 1970 the number of divisions doubled, and then increased by a further 50 percent in 1971 when the build-up began to level off.

This build-up was followed by a second phase of adding modern equipment and raising the level of preparedness of the deployed divisions. In the early 1970s the Soviets turned their field army into a garrison force, completing the construction of permanent installations and support facilities. The authoritative International Institute for Strategic Studies, in its annual *Strategic Survey* of 1973, described the Soviet military presence along the Sino-Soviet frontier as a "balanced, hard-hitting, and effective force which is trained and equipped for nuclear and nonnuclear operations." It was said to be capable of providing the "nucleus of an offensive force able to repeat the successful Soviet campaign against the Japanese Kwantung Army in Manchuria."

Nevertheless, it appears that a successful Soviet offensive against China would require about eighty divisions, nearly double the present deployment. Thus, a major prior reinforcement would be necessary. Soviet nuclear forces, however, are the compensating advantage, offsetting conventional weaknesses. The build-up of nuclear forces in the Soviet Far East has gone beyond tactical weapons in recent years with the appearance of the "Backfire" medium bomber and mobile SS-20 IRBMs. The Soviets have begun to put in place a modern nuclear force that could operate against *all* of China, without resorting to the central weapons targeted against the United States (i.e., ICBMs). This represents a major increase in Soviet military capabilities in the Far East.

In 1980 a further strengthening occurred in all phases of these Soviet deployments. According to American reporting, about half of all the Soviet army divisions along the Chinese border reached full strength, with their equipment including the new T-72 tank, the most advanced helicopters, and new surface-to-air missiles. SS-20 IRBMs are reported to have been deployed in two different Soviet military districts bordering on China—the Siberian and the Transbaikal. Soviet ground forces are now supported by 500 bombers and 1,400 fighters. The naval forces in the Far East have increased by five attack submarines and several more major surface combatants. There are eight missile cruisers and sixteen missile destroyers and frigates in the Pacific Fleet. And Soviet forces on the Kurile Islands, landed after the signature of the Sino-Japanese treaty, have reached a level of about ten thousand troops.

An evaluation of the Soviet military potential published in the New York *Times* on May 21, 1980 concluded:

> The consensus at headquarters here [NATO] is that, if the Russians were sufficiently worried by the prospect of a Chinese-American alliance, they could attack and take Manchuria, which produces half of China's oil and a third of its steel.

> The Soviet Union, it is said, is so superior in nuclear weapons that it may carry out the Manchurian operations without nuclear strikes. The other side of the coin is that the Chinese may feel impelled by their weakness in conventional forces to loose nuclear weapons on cities in western Siberia and the Urals.

It is impossible to predict whether the Soviets, reaching a peak in their military build-up in the mid-1980s, will feel compelled to stage a confrontation, or even an attack, before Chinese ICBMs reach a point of strategic invulnerability. On the one hand, the Chinese themselves have moved away from a proclaimed program of rapid military modernization. As Hua Guofeng announced in September 1980, "It will not be possible to increase the expenditure on national defense by a big margin; the aim should be to make our army an impregnable

Great Wall." This, of course, is a more moderate posture than the goal of achieving superpower status, and it comes against a background of disenchantment with the performance of the People's Liberation Army during the Vietnamese conflict. On the other hand, a more rational economic plan may actually improve China's longer term prospects for military modernization. Thus, the latent threat remains.

In this light, a possible effort by Moscow to exploit its presently favorable military position relative to the Chinese cannot be ruled out. But it is also possible, as in 1969, that the Soviets will use military pressure to extract a political advantage by once again holding out the prospect of a rapprochement with Peking. There are a number of long-term factors which make another round of negotiations plausible.

First, there is the continued waning of the ideological component in Chinese and Soviet politics. While long since transformed from an ideological struggle, the Sino-Soviet dispute continues to be influenced by the need to express disagreements in acceptable Marxist-Leninist guise. In China the ideological problem is complicated by the need to revise the history of the past fifteen years of Cultural Revolution. A number of senior leaders who in the past were supposedly sympathetic toward Moscow—men like Liu Shaoqi or Peng Dehuai—have been rehabilitated, albeit posthumously. At the same time, China's main antagonist of the Soviet Union, Mao Zedong, is being denigrated, and the policies of his successors are increasingly pragmatic if not "revisionist." Thus, as time passes, the need to defend old positions lessens on both sides of the Sino-Soviet feud. The irony, therefore, is that the end of ideology makes possible an accommodation between two formidable ideological protagonists.

Second, there is the waning of the territorial issues. China's claims to Soviet territory have not been abandoned, but they have been scaled down and muted. Of course, from Moscow's vantage point any claim to Soviet territory is a challenge and therefore is totally unacceptable, but this figures less and less in the debates and/or the negotiations. Moreover, the build-up in Soviet defenses has to reduce some of Moscow's apprehensions about China. Compared with the early 1960s, the Soviet

Far East is vastly more secure. And the prospect of a Chinese ICBM threat makes the struggle over minor river islands and tracts of desolate borderland seem rather peripheral.

Third, there is the uncertainty generated by changing leaderships in both Peking and Moscow. The successors to Soviet leader Leonid Brezhnev will have had less indoctrination in the early, polemical phases of Sino-Soviet bitterness. They are likely to view China in the terms of a great power challenge—admittedly a potentially alarming prospect—yet one that might be dealt with through such traditional measures as diplomacy, military capability, economic enticements, alliances, and so on—but not an intractable ideological problem, as leaders of the older generation might have believed. (It can easily be argued, however, that Russian fears of China are too deeply ingrained to be subject to generational amelioration.)

On the Chinese side, the discrediting of many of the policies of the revolutionary generation may make the dispute with the Soviets seem less central, or at least more subject to management through diplomacy and maneuvering. At a minimum, a new set of leaders may want to gain time for economic construction. This would require keeping the Soviet front under some political control.

The real variable, however, would seem to be the international balance of power. Sino-Soviet hostility is open to influence by major outside powers in that both Moscow and Peking will alter their policies in accordance with international trends. Deng Xiaoping, in the midst of the Taiwan dispute with the Republican candidates in the 1980 election, made it clear that he was not adverse to playing a "Russian card." Deng warned Japanese officials that it was an illusion to believe that Peking was automatically tied to anti-Soviet positions advocated by the United States, or that China would be incapable of reviewing its frozen relations with Moscow. While such hints obviously had a manipulative motivation, it is nevertheless interesting that Deng would invoke the "Russian card" at a time of considerable domestic political struggle in China.

In short, the prospect for a Sino-Soviet rapprochement may depend as much as anything on American actions. If China retains confidence in Washington's policies, then its clear national interest is to hold to an alignment with the U.S. against the growing military threat from the north and potential encirclement from the south.

Even if the two Communist powers see an interest in easing tensions, are the likely terms of detente within the realm of a negotiated settlement? After all, both sides have consistently put forward harsh demands which are not easily abandoned. From the Chinese side there has been a determined effort to force a Soviet military withdrawal from the border areas and from Mongolia. Thus far the Soviets have only agreed to thin out their military deployments in return for a major political concession. What would that be? Probably a firm, unequivocal renunciation of any territorial demands. Even so, this leaves the more critical question of China's program for military modernization and Peking's security alignment with the United States and Japan. Can these issues be resolved? And then there is the Chinese demand for a Vietnamese withdrawal from Kampuchea, which would amount to a renunciation of interest in dominating Indochina—a most unlikely turn of events. In short, China must want Southeast Asia as its primary sphere of influence; but what would Russia receive in turn? What the Soviet Union might exchange for giving Peking a free hand in Southeast Asia would be a significant reduction in Chinese ties to the U.S. and Japan—a major shift in international alignments.

In sum, the heart of the Sino-Soviet conflict remains: Russia wants a weak, relatively isolated China, while China, in turn, is determined to attain security in the short run through ties to the West and Japan, and in the long run by achieving the status of a major—if not the dominant—power in Asia. Moscow cannot concede this without putting large areas of critical territory in Siberia at some risk, not to mention the impact on Soviet global political ambitions. But the alternative for Moscow is grim: a possible military conflict with a huge country that has been the graveyard of all previous invaders. This will be a bitter choice for the next generation of Soviet leaders, who will inherit an intractable problem that neither Stalin, Khrushchev, nor Brezhnev was able to resolve.

The America Factor and the Stability of the Strategic Triangle

As noted, the Chinese will carefully weigh the status of their relations with the United States before making any turn toward Moscow. And almost certainly the Soviets, in constructing a policy toward the Reagan administration, will want to test the solidarity of the Peking-Washington relationship. Thus, tactical maneuvering within the strategic triangle will continue in the 1980s.

The more basic question for the future of U.S.–PRC relations is whether the U.S. can avoid being pulled increasingly into an alignment with China as part of a new containment of the USSR, thus polarizing strategic relationships in an anti-Soviet entente. The announcement of the Carter administration in the summer of 1980 that U.S.–PRC relations were now decoupled from the triangular play of the Sino-Soviet dispute was an effort to regain some strategic flexibility for the United States and to make the China relationship less dependent on fluctuations in Soviet-American relations. Yet it was enunciated at a time of severe deterioration in Soviet-American relations and growing speculation about Sino-American security cooperation. Inevitably, the U.S. will be called upon to decide whether the military dimension of its relationship with the PRC will grow, and if so, what its impact will be on Moscow.

There is little doubt that significant American military assistance to China would be regarded by the USSR as a most severe challenge, seriously threatening any prospects for U.S.–Soviet accommodation. It could be the catalyst in moving Moscow to take preemptive action against the Chinese. But it is also an implicit American bargaining chip of considerable value. The American policy dilemma is that to renounce any military assistance to China out of deference to Soviet sensitivities—even in return for significant gains—would raise agonizing questions for China about the future of its relations with Washington.

On the other hand, it is naive to believe that there is no strategic triangle. It continues to exist and to be a major influence on decisions made in Moscow and Peking. It will continue to play its role in Washington as well. While an open or blatant American manipulation of the strategic triangle is neither desirable nor feasible, the United States still retains the pivotal role. China can be driven into the arms of the USSR if Washington insists on a "two Chinas policy," if it slights Peking's striving for economic modernization and security, or if it suffers severe losses in its international position. And Moscow can be driven to severe measures if Washington embarks on an extensive build-up of Chinese military power. But within these limits, the U.S. retains a large area for maneuver in the context of the on-going Sino-Soviet conflict.

William E. Griffith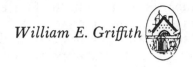

6

China and Europe

"Weak and Far Away"

China and Europe: The Flow of Influence

China is a regional, not a global power. It is far from Europe; and as Zhou Enlai once remarked to a Yugoslav journalist, "Far-away water cannot put out fires." Inevitably, therefore, the relations of China with Europe are politically as well as geographically peripheral.

Even so, this is the first time in five centuries that China has played any role at all in the affairs of Europe. It is also the first time in a century and a half that Europe, exclusive of the Soviet Union, has played *no* significant role in China. Those who know Cracow will remember that every noon a trumpeter plays a tune from the tower of St. Mary's, the great church on the marketplace which is the home of Wit Stwosz's great

WILLIAM E. GRIFFITH *is Ford Professor of Political Science at the Massachusetts Institute of Technology, and an adjunct professor of diplomatic history at the Fletcher School of Law and Diplomacy of Tufts University. He serves as a consultant to the National Security Council, and is a roving editor for the* Reader's Digest. *His recent publications include:* The European Left: Italy, France, and Spain; The Ostpolitik of the Federal Republic of Germany; *and* The Soviet Empire: Expansion and Detente.

altarpiece. But the tune is cut off suddenly, in mid-phrase, in memory of the time in the fourteenth century when the trumpeter's throat was pierced by a Mongol arrow. Cracow did not fall to the Mongols, however, and from then until 1956 China played no role in European politics.

China did exercise some cultural influence, however, in the French enthusiasm for *Chinoiserie* in the eighteenth century. Ever since Marco Polo's voyage to Cathay in the thirteenth century the West had known that there was a great but mysterious civilization in China; and trade contact was maintained, first over the land routes and later by sea. But the most significant effort to bring European influence to China in early modern times, the Jesuit mission beginning in 1582, failed when the Vatican refused to allow Father Ricci to adapt Christianity to Chinese culture. It was thus not until the early nineteenth century that Europe began to have an impact on China, primarily the British from the sea and the Russians from the north. Thereafter China, underdeveloped and ruled by the decaying Qing Dynasty, rapidly became an object of European (including Russian) imperial ambitions. By the end of World War II, however, only the Soviet Union still had significant influence in China. Under American pressure, the British and French had surrendered their concessions there; and the Japanese presence was totally eliminated by the results of World War II, just as the German presence had been removed after World War I.

Yet Western Europe, like the United States, had great influence on modern China's intellectuals—an influence which was to revive after the death of Communist Party Chairman Mao Zedong. But this influence was technological rather than cultural. The overwhelming Chinese sense of cultural superiority was only limited, but not destroyed, by the realization of the modernizing Chinese intelligentsia that it was European technology which had enabled Britain to defeat China. Therefore China needed, as the late nineteenth century western-educated defense thinker Yen Fu said, "wealth and strength" to withstand the foreign barbarians. (Paraphrasing this view, Deng Xiaoping asserted in 1979 that "socialism brings wealth and strength.") The Kuomintang learned this lesson in theory, but it was too traditionalist, corrupt, and weakened by the Japanese invasion to put it into practice.

Great Britain and France won World War II in theory, but lost it in practice. They withdrew from China and Southeast Asia because they were too weak to remain. France fought a fruitless rear guard action in Indochina, and Britain gradually withdrew from Malaya. Hence, when the Chinese Communists entered Peking in 1949, Western Europe was no longer a significant factor in the politics of East Asia. European influence had been replaced by that of the United States, whose long, checkered record of relations with China falls outside the purview of this chapter. So does that of the Soviet Union, toward which Mao Zedong "tilted" in 1949 for lack of a better alternative, despite his resentment of the way that Moscow had treated the Chinese Communists during their long march to power.

The PRC in the Socialist Camp

Thus the People's Republic of China became a part of the "camp of socialism headed by the Soviet Union." Soviet credits, aid, and technical experts flooded into the PRC. Similar influence, in smaller amounts, also came from the developed East European communist states, notably East Germany and Czechoslovakia. Politically, China had entered into what was for it a new kind of relationship, a member of the "socialist community." It had become a full ruling-party member of the "international communist and workers movement," and an observer in the Warsaw Pact and the Moscow-dominated Council of Mutual Economic Assistance (CMEA). Nevertheless, until the death of Stalin in 1953, China's dealings with the East European party-states, with the very limited exception of economic ties, were minimal.

Although there is some indirect evidence that the Soviet Union did not approve of certain Chinese ideological formulations in the 1949 to 1953 period (notably that of the "people's democratic dictatorship"), it would be far-fetched indeed to think that this had any significant impact on Chinese–East European relations. Meanwhile, Chinese contacts with Western

Europe were practically nonexistent. This was the height of the cold war, and the weak Western European states were under the influence of a strongly anti-Chinese Communist America. Chinese involvement in the Korean War, which at the time was believed by many Western Europeans as well as Americans to be just the prelude to a Soviet attack on the NATO states, intensified anti-Soviet and anti-Chinese feelings in Western Europe. The view was widely held that China was indeed, as Dean Rusk put it at the time, a "Slavic Manchukuo," a political dependency of the Soviet Union. France had a special reason for accepting this view, for China was supporting Ho Chi Minh in his struggle against French rule in Indochina.

In retrospect, Stalin's death was the great watershed not only in Sino-Soviet relations but also in Chinese and Russian policies toward the rest of the world. In addition, China's recovery from the disruptions of the civil war, Khrushchev's determination to initiate detente with the United States, and the destabilization of Eastern Europe which resulted from his toleration of liberalization there led to the return, after so many centuries, of China as a factor (even if far from a decisive one) in the politics of Eastern Europe. While Peking's initial opportunities were primarily the result of domestic East European developments, Chinese motives arose from growing tensions in Sino-Soviet relations—and after 1959, the overt split.

The first instance of Peking's post-Stalin involvement in the affairs of Eastern Europe which is publicly known involved Yugoslavia in 1954. Given what occurred thereafter, it may be assumed that the Chinese were both opposed to Yugoslav policies and used the country as a "surrogate" for criticism of the Soviet Union in their growing differences with Khrushchev. In a letter to the Soviet Communist Party in June 1954, which was a response to a Soviet circular letter announcing Khrushchev's intention to work toward a rapprochement with Tito, the Chinese expressed serious reservations about "Yugoslav revisionism." It seems likely that this attack was not only against Tito and his policies but also against Khrushchev's intention to promote detente with the United States.

A more important Chinese move occurred in the summer of 1956, when the Chinese indicated to Polish Communist Party First Secretary Edward Ochab, during a visit to Peking, that they looked favorably upon the wave of liberalization then sweeping Poland. This led to the return to power of Wladyslaw Gomulka in the following October, despite Soviet pressures to the contrary. This Chinese attitude of support for the Polish moderates could only have been regarded by the Soviets as an attempt to interfere within their sphere of influence in Eastern Europe.

The second Chinese move, also in 1956, was the then secret visit of Mao Zedong's deputy, Liu Shaoqi, to Moscow at the height of the Hungarian Revolution. The initiative in this event apparently was Khrushchev's, in view of the subsequent Soviet concessions to the Chinese immediately before the Moscow meeting of ruling Communist Parties in 1957 (including a promise of assistance to China's nuclear development program). Liu, judging by subsequent Chinese articles, probably advised that Moscow allow Polish developments to proceed on the (correct) assumption that Gomulka would gradually bring them under control, but that the Hungarian Revolution should be crushed—as indeed it was. In both instances, a new level of Chinese influence in Moscow regarding developments in Eastern Europe was marked.

The most important sign of rising Chinese involvement in Eastern Europe in 1956, however, was Peking's role in the Soviet-Albanian break. It has only recently become clear, as a result of the publication of Albanian leader Enver Hoxha's memoirs, that the Soviet-Albanian dispute had as its background the hostility of Hoxha and his associates to Yugoslavia. The Soviets lost Albania, and the Chinese—also hostile to Yugoslavia—gained it for a time as an ally in Eastern Europe because of a typically fierce Balkan rivalry. Hoxha also makes clear that one of the principal reasons for his rivalry with Tito was Albanian territorial irredentism—Tirana's violent resentment of the fact that since before World War I one-third of all Albanians lived in the Yugoslav-ruled provinces of Kossovo and Metohija, also known as the "Kosmet." Moreover, Hoxha was then, as now, in a "super-Stalinist" phase, and he therefore had much more sympathy for radical, guerrilla-based Chinese communism than for Khrushchev's policies of de-Stalinization and detente.

Beginning in 1971, the year that Henry Kissinger first visited Peking, however, the Sino-Albanian alliance became a victim of China's decision to carry out rapprochements with the United States and with Yugoslavia. (So much for the ideological factor in Sino-Albanian relations!) While that alliance lasted it was an example not only of China's influence in a small, underdeveloped part of Europe, but also—and more importantly—of China's global, rather than regional, ambitions in international politics, communist and otherwise. Since it was highly unlikely that the Soviet Union would agree to a Chinese outpost in Eastern Europe (any more than either the United States or Yugoslavia did at that time), the Sino-Albanian alliance of the 1960s was a major obstacle to any Sino-Soviet rapprochement—much as the current Soviet-Vietnamese alliance continues to preclude an improvement in Moscow's relations with Peking.

The first indication of an Albanian effort to escape from Soviet control was in early 1956, when the Albanian press, like the Chinese, did not mention Khrushchev's de-Stalinization program and was far less vigorous than the Soviet leader in criticizing Stalin. The Albanian-Soviet dispute, like the growing Sino-Soviet differences and resultant Sino-Albanian entente, became much clearer in early 1958 on the issue of relations with Yugoslavia. Both Tirana and Peking took a far harder line than did Moscow toward the "revisionist" Yugoslav party program. As the Chinese themselves stated some years later, Peking and Tirana were using the Yugoslavs primarily as a whipping boy to attack Khrushchev's "revisionist" policies, especially regarding detente with the United States. By that time the competition between Moscow and Peking to gain influence in the Albanian leadership was fierce. It broke out into the open in 1960 when Hoxha purged two pro-Soviet figures in the Albanian leadership and violently denounced the Soviet position, and supported the Chinese, at the meetings of Communist Party leaders in Bucharest and Moscow that same year. In the late 1950s Chinese aid to Albania rose rapidly, and after 1960 Soviet aid sank even faster—thus demonstrating that China was prepared, within the modest limits of what was needed to keep the Albanian economy afloat, to put its money where its mouth was.

China's next—and perhaps in the long run most important—

move in Eastern Europe occurred in 1964, when the Romanians published their "declaration of autonomy" from Soviet hegemony, thus establishing themselves as "Communist neutralists" vis-à-vis both the Soviet Union and China. Romania's motives were essentially nationalist: a determination not to remain an unindustrialized raw-material producer within CMEA; resentment at Soviet political domination; frustrated fury over the 1945 Soviet annexation of Romanian Bessarabia (which the Tsars had annexed in the late nineteenth century and Romania had taken over in 1918); and the historic anti-Slav, and particularly anti-Russian, sentiments of the Romanians.

The traditional Romanian good timing in betraying its allies had stood Bucharest in good stead in the two world wars. But this time Romania's game was both more complex and more global: it succeeded in becoming a neutral between Moscow and Peking—a substantial feat considering that the Red Army was an overwhelming power on its borders and that Romania had no major military allies. It rapidly improved its relations with the United States, West Germany, France, and most of the Third World. And it remained neutral between Israel and the Arabs during and after the 1967 Middle East War.

China's role in the Romanian deviation is more difficult to determine than in the Albanian case. What is clear is that by 1964 Chinese hostility to the Soviet Union was so total that Peking had every incentive to cultivate Bucharest. The Romanians, like most other Communist Parties, were reluctant to see a Sino-Soviet split. They preferred to be "communist neutralists" on the pattern of North Korea and North Vietnam, to balance between Moscow and Peking. Surely China would have preferred that Romania break completely with Moscow, as had Albania. But the latter had no land boundary with the Soviet Union, and Romania had. Thus Peking had to satisfy itself with Bucharest's "communist neutralism," as it did with Pyongyang's and Hanoi's, and to rejoice in the fact that Soviet influence in Bucharest had been greatly reduced.

On balance, then, China's forthcoming policies in Albania and Romania successfully reduced Moscow's influence in Eastern Europe during the 1960s, even if its own influence remained limited.

China and Western Europe: The Tentative Flirtation

The Sino-Soviet split also brought about, slowly but in-
exorably, the revival of relations between China and the governments and Communist Parties of Western Europe. The
process was delayed by the Cultural Revolution and, to some
extent, by the Vietnam War. It was continually limited by the
desire of the West Europeans to minimize the offense to the
Soviet Union of being cordial to its bitter enemy. However,
exactly because Western Europe, including the West European
Communist Parties, was not anywhere near as subject to Soviet
pressure as was Eastern Europe, the chances for improved relations with China seemed much better than in reality they have
turned out to be.

On the Chinese side, the initial motivation behind Peking's
desire to improve relations with Western Europe was its need
for trade and technology to compensate for Moscow's cutoff
of economic contacts with the PRC in 1960. (The agricultural
crisis which followed the collapse of the Great Leap Forward
in the early 1960s also forced Peking to turn to Canada and
Australia for grain.) With the United States and Japan excluded as alternatives at least for the time being, Western
Europe was Peking's only alternative. Moreover, with West
Germany still self-bound by the Hallstein Doctrine (which held
that Bonn would not take up or maintain diplomatic relations
with any country which had them with East Germany, with
the one exception of the Soviet Union) and with Great Britain
in economic decline, France was China's logical first candidate.

A China initiative also held attractions for General de Gaulle,
who had become President in 1958 as a result of the Algerian
War, and who in 1962 had withdrawn France from the NATO
integrated command (although not from the alliance). His
policy was one of restoring France's grandeur based on the
country's historic claim to a world-wide mission; his objective
was to free France, and Europe, from *le double hégémonie*
of Soviet-American domination.

De Gaulle had no illusion that he could totally dispense with
American protection, as was demonstrated by his immediate

and total support of President Kennedy in the Cuban missile crisis. But as a result of the American victory in that confrontation, he calculated, with his proud, icy Machiavellianism, that France could now afford to pursue his grand design. He sought to use detente to bring about a European settlement based on the combination of a Western Europe under the primary influence of France, a Soviet Union tolerant of liberalization in Eastern Europe, and a reunited but weak Germany, plus Western security guarantees to Moscow regarding the feared growth of Chinese power.

De Gaulle's conception was fundamentally flawed, however. He underestimated Soviet power and overestimated that of the Chinese and the Americans. He also overestimated his ability to carry Bonn along with this plan. While it lasted, however—until the Soviet invasion of Czechoslovakia in 1968—a rapprochement between France and China seemed to him a desirable way of pushing the Soviets in the direction of his grand design.

With these parallel interests, Paris and Peking reestablished relations in 1964. (Great Britain had established diplomatic relations with the People's Republic of China in 1950, but Peking was only willing to maintain them at the chargé d'affaires level because the British sustained consular relations at a provincial level with Taiwan. The British and Chinese finally exchanged ambassadors in 1972, when London withdrew its consul from Taipei.) France's trade with China gradually increased, but this was soon outstripped by West Germany's, as facilitated by a West German trade mission in Peking. In any case, the breakout of the Cultural Revolution in late 1965 undercut progress in relations with Western Europe until the domestic political convulsion abated at the end of the decade.

For China, as for the Soviet Union, France had been only the prelude: both Moscow and Peking knew well that West Germany was becoming the most important power in Western Europe. It was economically and technologically the more powerful; and its geographic location, its previous military tradition, and its potential territorial irredentism made it a potential threat to Moscow—a point not lost on Peking. PRC interest in establishing contact with Bonn became evident early on. In 1955, after Konrad Adenauer had reestablished relations with Moscow (in large part to reinsure himself against the Soviet-American condominium he saw developing at the first Geneva summit conference that same year), the Chinese hinted to Bonn they would like relations as well. Adenauer held off, however, anticipating a Sino-Soviet split; but in 1957 informal trade relations were established. In 1960, after the public outbreak of the Moscow-Peking feud, China renewed its feelers. Bonn finally reciprocated in 1964, but Adenauer's successor, Ludwig Erhard, gave in to American pressure and declared that diplomatic relations would not be resumed. The Chinese broke off negotiations. However, in that summer Mao Zedong made quite clear in a published interview with some Japanese Socialists that he supported territorial irredentism on the part of Japan, West Germany, Poland, and Romania—the clearest bid he had yet made to nationalist sentiment in these four countries.

Nothing more of significance occurred in West German–Chinese contacts until 1969. This was the year of the first major Sino-Soviet border clashes, the initial one occurring on the Ussuri River frontier in Manchuria on March 2. The first incident—probably initiated by the Chinese, with the second and third precipitated by the Soviets—globalized the Sino-Soviet dispute, making Europe's relations with Moscow and Peking a matter of the strategic balance. This was also the year in which newly elected President Nixon began to prepare to pull out of the Vietnam War; in which the Cultural Revolution ended (in part because of the border clashes); in which Nixon and Kissinger decided to improve relations with China in order to help extricate the United States from the Vietnam War and to put pressure on the Soviet Union; and when in China conflict among a divided leadership about relations with the Soviet Union and the United States raged in full fury.

Ever since World War II and their withdrawal from their colonial possessions, the West European powers—with the exception of Gaullist France—have abstained from conducting anything like a global foreign policy, or indeed even from viewing their own policies from a global standpoint. This has been particularly true of the two great powers defeated in

World War II, West Germany and Japan. This attitude was encouraged by their relative military weakness, their reliance upon American military support, and their consequent vulnerability to political pressures from Washington. In the case of West Germany, this abstention from foreign policy initiatives was further encouraged by the massive Soviet nuclear and conventional military superiority on its eastern border.

Although it was little realized at the time, the impact on the German questions of the first Ussuri River border clash foreshadowed much of what was to come during the 1970s in East-West relations: a Soviet effort to achieve detente with the West in order to cope with its growing China problem. In February 1969, East Germany, acting with Soviet approval if not instigation, began to harass West German autobahn traffic into West Berlin, ostensibly because of the forthcoming election there of Bonn's Federal President. On March 3, the day of the election and the day after the first Ussuri River incident, the harassment ceased; and on March 11 the Soviet ambassador in Bonn unprecedentedly briefed Chancellor Kurt Kiesinger about the Soviet version of the border clash. Thus did Moscow make clear, however reluctantly, that it wanted to keep its western flank quiet while preoccupied with the heightened tensions along its eastern frontier.

In October of that same year the Brandt-Scheel political coalition, made up of the Social Democrats (the SPD) and the Free Democrats (FDP) came to power in Bonn. Willy Brandt was determined to normalize relations with the Soviet Union and thereafter with Eastern Europe in order, as he put it, to "maintain the substance of the German nation" through increased contacts with East Germany. Brandt and his associates were convinced that, given Sino-Soviet hostility, they had to postpone normalization with China until after they had improved relations with the Soviet Union and its East European allies.

Hence, although in the early 1970s Peking began to publicly endorse NATO, the European Economic Community (EEC), and even West European (including West German!) nuclear rearmament as it moved closer to Bonn's main ally, Washington, Brandt remained convinced (as has his successor, Helmut

Schmidt) that China is too weak and far away, and West Germany too weak and too near the Soviet Union, for Bonn to "play the Chinese card" against Moscow. Peking reciprocated by strongly attacking Brandt's new *Ostpolitik,* as it did detente in general. Nevertheless, diplomatic relations between Bonn and Peking were resumed in 1972, but not until Bonn had signed treaties with Moscow, Warsaw, and East Berlin giving de facto recognition to the postwar borders of Central and Eastern Europe. West German trade with the PRC increased rapidly, and for some years West Germany has led all other West European countries in commerce with China.

Indeed, as Helmut Sonnenfeldt of the Brookings Institution has pointed out, West Germany's (and Western Europe's) capital investments in technology transfers to the Soviet Union, for reasons of trade diversification and detente, affect China's security interests in Asia. Conversely, Moscow feels that the prospect of an eventual Chinese menace to the Soviet Far East is so great that it must build up a military-industrial base there largely independent of European Russia. The proposed Soviet–West European natural gas deal (in which the West Germans have a major role) would contribute significantly to Moscow's industrial development of Siberia. The Chinese resent this, but Peking is unlikely to dissuade the West Germans from proceeding. The United States could attempt to discourage the Federal Republic of Germany from pursuing its large economic investments in the USSR, but its capacity to do so—given German determination to diversify sources of energy supply—is limited.

Finally, one should mention Peking's attempts to cultivate the West European political right on the basis of a common anti-Sovietism. These attempts have been frequent throughout Western Europe, but from China's viewpoint the most important ones have been with the West German Christian Democratic Union and even more the Christian Social Union, led by China's favorite West European statesman, Franz Joseph Strauss. He and other conservative European political figures have been tempted to "play the China card" against the Soviet Union. Yet one should be careful not to overestimate China's possibilities in this respect. The PRC is indeed weak and far away from Europe. Perhaps more importantly, Western Europe, and particularly West Germany, is intensely fearful of war and the growth of Soviet military power. It is thus very doubtful, even if Strauss had been elected Chancellor in 1980, that he would have pursued an active China policy against the Soviet Union.

China's Relations with the European Communist Parties

Until Khrushchev's de-Stalinization program and the Sino-Soviet split, relations between the Chinese and the major West European Communist Parties (the French, Italian, and Spanish) had been uneventful. But Mao's opposition to de-Stalinization and then his break with Khrushchev initially left the West European Communist Parties on the Soviet side: some entirely, like the French; and some, notably the Italian, even farther to the right than was Khrushchev. This was particularly true with respect to policy toward Yugoslavia, with which Palmiro Togliatti, the Italian Party leader, had been cultivating good relations since the Tito-Khrushchev meeting at Belgrade in 1955. The fierce Chinese attack on the Yugoslavs in 1958 was reinforced by their direct criticism of Togliatti in the early 1960s. The Italian Communists were a favorite target of Maoist propaganda, not only for their refusal to break with the Soviets, but even more because of their domestic reformist ("revisionist") tendencies. In the 1960s Peking tried, as had Belgrade for a brief period in the early 1950s, to set up its own "Communist International," with China as its center. If it could not displace Moscow as the predominant influence within the established Communist Parties, it would try to split them or even set up new "Marxist-Leninist" ones. This Chinese attempt had hardly any success—in Europe only Albania supported Mao's efforts—and Peking abandoned the strategy in the 1970s after it decided to move toward Washington.

As the 1960s progressed, Togliatti and his successors intensified their revisionist tendencies. For the Chinese a far more important development, however, was their intensification of autonomist policies vis-à-vis the Soviet Union. Indeed, it was on this basis—the common desire for a pluralistic, i.e., a multinational, rather than a Soviet-centered International Communist and Workers Movement—that the Chinese and the Italian

Communists were led to reestablish Party relations at the end
of the 1970s.

In order for this to happen, the Chinese had to abandon their
global claims to Communist primacy on an extreme radical
platform. This required that Peking's hatred and fear of Moscow intensify and its commitment to radical ideology decline.
The former began with the Soviet invasion of Czechoslovakia
in 1968. This event, not the 1969 Ussuri River border incidents, was the real beginning of Peking's move toward the
United States—as demonstrated by the fact that the Chinese
ceased all their anti-Yugoslav propaganda on the day after the
invasion. Concurrently, the Italian, Spanish, and French Communists condemned the Soviet invasion—the first time that any
of these Parties had publicly attacked any Soviet foreign policy
moves.

They did so primarily for domestic electoral reasons. Having
long since given up their hopes for revolution, they increasingly realized that only by electoral victories could they hope
to participate in, and eventually hold, power. Success in this
strategy required that they gain votes to their right. This they
could do only by modifying their domestic and foreign policy
programs and actions so as to appeal to left wing Socialists and
Catholics.

The Italian and Spanish Communists, both anxious to avoid
domination by the French or Germans, were not, like their
countries, predisposed to an anti-American position. The
French Communists were the most nationalist, and Jacobin
as well, but they so hated the West Germans and Americans,
and their party organization was so neo-Stalinist, that their
turn toward reformism was shallow and brief. As soon as they
realized, in the summer of 1968, that if the Left came to power
in France the Socialists would be the senior partner in a left
coalition, they broke away from the Socialists, thus guarantee-
ing Giscard d'Estaing's victory, and they returned to a pro-
Soviet position. The Italians were so frightened by the
anti-Allende coup in Chile that they decided to support the
compromesso storico ("historic compromise")—the establishment of a coalition with the Christian Democrats in which
initially they would be the junior partner. The Spanish Communists were so weak, compared to the strong Socialist Party,

that they had to follow a "super-electoral" policy, an even greater stress on elections and a reformist domestic program than that promoted by the Italians. They were also the most strongly opposed to the Soviet Union, and their Spanish pride led them to express this more directly than did the supple Italians.

In 1971 the Spanish Communist leader Santiago Carrillo made a trip to China at the invitation of the Chinese Communist Party. It was probably not by accident that this occurred in the same year that Kissinger first arrived in Peking. We learned only much later that Carrillo carried a letter from the Italian Communist leadership proposing the resumption of Party relations with Peking. The Chinese at that time refused the offer, presumably as a result of the factional struggles going on in anticipation of the succession to Mao. Elements within the Chinese leadership were reluctant to abandon support of the pro-Peking "Marxist-Leninist" Parties in Western Europe; others probably resisted any dilution of the "anti-revisionist" policies of the Cultural Revolution period; and some may have feared that resumption of relations with the Italian and Spanish Parties might so offend Moscow as to limit still further whatever possibilities existed for a Sino-Soviet detente. (Some may also have feared that such a move would offend the United States and its European allies—although this is less likely to have been a matter of concern.)

Thereafter, nothing much happened in relations between the Chinese and the West European Communist Parties until the death of Mao Zedong and the return to power of Deng Xiaoping. In the interim, Sino-American relations had been strengthened and China itself was moving far away from Maoist radical revolutionary ideology and in the direction of a pragmatic reformism. Moreover, in this same period—the second half of the 1970s—the Soviet Union became the dominant foreign power in Angola, Ethiopia, and Afghanistan. Most important for the Chinese, Moscow had benefited substantially from the Vietnamese invasion of Cambodia—in part by gaining use of the American-built naval and air bases at Danang and Cam Ranh Bay on the Vietnamese coast. Thus Chinese fear of the Soviet Union deepened as Moscow enhanced its encirclement of the PRC.

Beginning with Moscow's invasion of Czechoslovakia in 1968, Soviet attractiveness to the political Left in Western Europe rapidly collapsed. The invasion of Afghanistan a decade later, and the Soviet repression of its own dissidents, destroyed any residual appeal that the Soviet model held for West European leftists. All that remained was the fear of growing Soviet military power. These developments have made the leaders of the West European Communist Parties even more likely to differ with Moscow in the 1980s than they were in the 1970s.

Finally, and here we return to Eastern Europe, the Italian and Spanish Communists gradually formed an axis with the Yugoslav and Romanian Parties during the 1970s to combat Soviet hegemony in what little remained of the "International Communist and Workers Movement." Yugoslavia and Romania had felt directly menaced by Moscow's intervention into Czechoslovakia, and they banded together to try to deter a Soviet invasion of themselves. Italian-Romanian and Italian-Yugoslav relations were strengthened, and all four parties resisted the frequent Soviet attempts to stage a "collective mobilization" to excommunicate the Chinese and thereby force all Communist Parties to abandon any tendencies toward neutralism in the Sino-Soviet conflict.

This is not to say that the Yugoslavs and Romanians on the one hand, and the Italians and Spanish on the other, agreed on programs of domestic reform: the former two were against it; and the latter two increasingly in favor. (And the Chinese did not come to support reformist policies until after Mao's death in 1976.) But joint opposition to Soviet hegemony was enough to give life to this loose coalition, and it successfully functioned in the four years of preparation for the 1976 East Berlin European Communist conference. The result was the refusal of the conference, despite Soviet pressures, to condemn the Chinese—just as the international Communist conference in Moscow in 1969 had refused to do.

Once Deng Xiaoping came to power, moreover, the Chinese internal situation changed rapidly in a direction favorable to closer relations with Eastern Europe. Yugoslav President Tito traveled to Peking in the fall of 1977, and Party relations were reestablished during his visit. Mao's successor, Hua Guofeng, visited Yugoslavia and Romania a year later. (There are now even signs that the Chinese are beginning to imitate the Yugoslav workers councils.) Tito reportedly urged Hua Guofeng to resume Party relations with the Italian and Spanish Parties. (By this time the French Communists had abandoned their joint front with the Socialists and returned to a largely pro-Soviet policy line.) The Italian Communist leader Enrico Berlinguer visited China in 1979 and Party relations were resumed. The Soviet Union criticized the Italian move, but by then there was nothing that Moscow could do to prevent it from happening. The same occurred with the Spanish Communists when Carrillo visited Peking in 1980. During the latter visit the Chinese made explicit their support of independence for all Communist Parties (i.e., their abandonment of any claim to a "leading role" in an international Communist movement) and of the doctrine of the noninevitability of war (i.e., their rejection of Mao's view that nuclear war would not necessarily be a disaster for humankind).

Thus by the end of the 1970s the organizational implications of the Sino-Soviet split—Sino-American normalization and the Sino-Italian-Spanish-Yugoslav-Romanian Communist rapprochement—had all taken place. Indeed, in early 1981 it seemed likely that, should the Soviets invade Poland, the Italian and Spanish Communist Parties would break off relations with the Soviet Communist Party. Thus, after two decades of effort the Chinese have made some significant progress in their desire to encircle the Soviet Union with the West European Communists, but much less progress in relations with the West European governments. Peking was also able to maintain modest gains in dealings with the Romanians and greatly improved ties with Yugoslavia.

Conclusion: "Weak and Far Away"

Since the breakdown in Sino-Soviet relations in 1959, and even more so since the Sino-American rapprochement of 1971, the principal objective of China's foreign policy has been to resist Soviet pressures through a global encirclement of the Soviet Union by way of an entente composed of itself, Japan, the United States, and Western Europe. From the Chinese viewpoint, Western Europe is the weakest link in this strategy because it is militarily weak and so fearful of the Soviet Union. China criticizes West European efforts to sustain an island of detente even in the face of Moscow's occupation of Afghanistan and the threatened invasion of Poland. The West European Communist Parties, such as the Italian and the Spanish, with whom Peking has reestablished Party relations, have thus far been unwilling to break with the Soviet Party. And, even worse from the Chinese point of view, after the Soviet invasion of Afghanistan, French and West German leaders Giscard and Schmidt came close to trying to mediate between Brezhnev and President Carter instead of finally joining in a global united front against Soviet hegemony.

This mood of detente at any price is particularly dangerous, the Chinese must feel, in the case of West Germany. Instead of striving to acquire its own nuclear weapons and following the American lead in policies toward Peking and Moscow, Bonn is becoming even more involved with the Soviet Union. For example, a projected natural gas deal would make the Federal Republic dependent on the Soviet Union for more than 30 percent of its natural gas supply. Moreover, Bonn has refused to fulfill the NATO guidelines in increasing defense expenditures and to cut off, or even cut back on, trade with the Soviet Union and Eastern Europe. France, except for its high level of military expenditures, has pursued essentially the same set of policies. The Chinese leaders, in short, see Europe in much the same light as does America's extreme right wing: a group of weak, fearful states being beguiled and driven by the Soviet Union toward "self-Finlandization."

For the Europeans, in contrast, China remains essentially irrelevant to their principal problems: the Soviet Union, about which China can do little; and the energy crisis and inflation, about which it can do nothing at all. They see China as China sees them: weak and far away. Moreover, the excesses of the Cultural Revolution—vividly communicated to the world by the television trial in 1980 of Mao's wife and other members of the Gang of Four—destroyed most of the little prestige that China had remaining in Europe, even in radical circles. Only trade with the PRC is important for the Europeans, but trade with the Soviet Union is much more significant.

It follows, therefore, that there is little prospect in the near future that Western Europe (much less Yugoslavia or Romania) will become a part of a global united front against the Soviet Union based on a quadruple entente of China, Japan, the United States, and America's NATO allies. The Western Europeans, above all the British and French, may well sell some arms to China, but probably in very modest numbers in the face of likely Soviet pressures. China is likely to have little influence over Soviet policy in Eastern Europe, although Moscow's concern about the effects of another Chinese incursion into Vietnam may help to swing the balance of opinion in the Kremlin against a Soviet invasion of Poland. Western Europe, notably West Germany, will continue to contribute somewhat to China's economic modernization, but certainly less than Japan, and quite possibly less than the United States as well. Thus, while Western Europe will have a modest economic interest in China, its political and security interests will remain severely limited because of its fear of the Soviet Union—much more limited than those of the United States.

There is no prospect in the near future, therefore, of significant relations between China and Europe, East or West, except in the realm of trade. The only possible exception to this judgment, and this is a very partial one, is Romania; but Peking can do little or nothing in a crisis to help Bucharest. For the Chinese and the Europeans it is true, in the last analysis, what Neville Chamberlain said about Czechoslovakia: "a far-away country of which we know little."

Robert A. Scalapino

7

China and Northeast Asia

For the People's Republic of China, Northeast Asia is of critical importance since it relates directly to the two primary concerns of this vast nation and its leaders: security and development. To many Chinese, moreover, the region represents an extension of their own cultural heritage, comprising societies that belong to the Sinic world, whatever the socioeconomic and political diversities of recent times.

China and the Threat from the North

We may define Northeast Asia as encompassing the Mongolian People's Republic (MPR), the Siberian portions of the USSR, the Korean Peninsula, Japan, and Taiwan in addition to the PRC itself. Issues of security dominate China's relations

ROBERT A. SCALAPINO *is director of the Institute of East Asian Studies, Robson Research Professor of Government, and editor of* Asian Survey *at the University of California at Berkeley. Professor Scalapino has written innumerable articles and more than fourteen books on Asian politics and U.S.–Asian policy.*

with its neighbors to the north and, from all current indications, will continue to do so in the years immediately ahead. Today, the Soviet Union has approximately forty-six divisions on the northern and western borders of the PRC, including its units in the People's Republic of Mongolia. These forces total about 400–500,000 men and are armed with the most modern military weapons, including a full nuclear arsenal. Additional Soviet contingents exist in rear areas. The Chinese use higher figures in estimating these Soviet forces, although the extent to which they include rear-area divisions is not clear. Vice Premier Deng Xiaoping, in a November 15, 1980 interview with Editor in Chief of the *Christian Science Monitor* Earl Foell, asserted, "If during the Khrushchev era there were only ten Soviet divisions stationed along the Sino-Soviet border, then in the Brezhnev era there are fifty-four divisions numbering one million men."

Throughout China's modern history, the primary security threat has come from the east, from the sea. First, the nations of Europe and subsequently Japan challenged China's independence and territorial integrity, establishing enclaves of power in coastal regions and in Manchuria. The other frontiers harbored less powerful "barbarians" who constituted periodic threats (especially in the north) when China's internal political decay had progressed to a crisis point, but they did not represent a steady or progressive challenge.

Today, the situation is radically different. The primary military pressure on the PRC comes from the north and west, impacting upon China's fragile interior border regions and the Manchurian industrial complex. A new "barbarian" has emerged, the Soviet Union, and it is armed with nuclear teeth. Nor is the Russian threat confined to these regions. With its Pacific Fleet gradually being augmented, the Soviet Union's containment policy toward China is vastly more complete than that attempted by the United States a few decades ago. The USSR today is underwriting a Vietnamese empire to the south and is in the process of acquiring new basing facilities for its Pacific naval and air forces. It is occupying Afghanistan and is aligned with India, the most formidable state on the Asian subcontinent. It is in full command of its Central Asian and

Siberian territories; and it is vying for influence in North Korea. In short, from whatever direction, the Soviet Union looms large on the Chinese horizon.

Chinese leaders probably do not fear an overt Soviet attack, although their caution in the Vietnam campaign of early 1979 indicates the realization that under certain circumstances a Sino-Soviet military conflict could erupt. From China's perspective, however, the more immediate and the more serious problem lies in a combination of the continuous pressures that the Soviet Union itself can exercise upon the PRC via its close-in, formidable military presence short of war, and the attitudes and actions of Asian neighbors aligned with the USSR. Indeed, the latter problem has become more serious as exemplified by Vietnam and Afghanistan in the south and west, Mongolia in the north, and with North Korea now contested.

Thus, the issue of security occupies a crucial position in every aspect of Chinese policy toward Northeast Asia. Broadly speaking, only two strategic alternatives exist: either a united front must be promoted, one serving to deter Soviet "social imperialism" and provide a shield for Chinese weakness; or some accommodation to the USSR, reducing the current level of tension, must be undertaken. The first of these alternatives, as is well known, is presently the one governing Chinese thought and policy. The strategy, with its emphasis upon a rearmed Japan, a strong NATO, and an alert Third World, rests in the final analysis upon the capacity and the will of the United States to play the role of a global countervailing power to the Soviet Union.

There is no current indication that a shift to the second strategy is being contemplated. Again, one may cite Deng Xiaoping as the most authoritative spokesman for present policies. In the interview noted above, the vice premier stated: "I have told my foreign friends many times that if the Soviet Union changes its global strategy and social-imperialist policy, then Sino-Soviet relations will improve immediately." After proceeding to give examples of what would constitute "proof" of such a shift—decreasing its troops on the PRC border to the level of the Khrushchev era, withdrawing its troops from Afghanistan, the Mongolian People's Republic, and Southeast Asia—Deng ended the subject by stating: "Today is the 15th of November. If today the Soviet Union does all this, then tomorrow, the 16th of November, our relations will improve. Otherwise, Sino-Soviet relations will not change even in ten to twenty years."

In the Sino-Soviet negotiations which were briefly renewed in 1979, the Chinese terms for serious discussions were stiff: a withdrawal of Soviet troops from disputed border regions, the removal of the Soviet military presence from the People's Republic of Mongolia, and the cessation of military assistance to Vietnam. There is no likelihood that Moscow would accept these conditions or ones similar to them. Hence, whatever the middle- and long-term future may hold with respect to Sino-Soviet relations (and one can make a cogent case for limited detente from a Chinese point of view—or conceive of leadership changes that might alter the picture), the immediate future contains no such prospects.

Despite this fact, however, Chinese defense policy is not currently based upon the rapid expansion and modernization of conventional forces. The classical "Maoist" defense strategy is being pursued, with certain modifications: the effort to achieve deterrence capability via the sustained development of nuclear weapons is coupled with a reliance upon "people's war," trusting the sheer mass of the Chinese population to give any potential aggressor cause for caution. Thus, large numbers of Chinese soldiers along with people's militia stand guard at the frontiers, with equipment that scarcely could be considered adequate, quite probably producing unhappiness in certain professional military circles over the priorities now in effect.

The Issue of Mongolia

It is from this perspective that one must view China's relations with the People's Republic of Mongolia (Outer Mongolia) and the Democratic People's Republic of Korea (North Korea), two small continental states that fly communist banners. Outer Mongolia quite as much as the USSR epitomizes the obstacles confronting China's desire to create a buffer system of "friendly states" on its borders. Even in the years before the Bolshevik Revolution, Russia had become deeply

involved in Outer Mongolia, cultivating the religious and political Mongol leaders in an effort to create an autonomous
region that could serve to protect Russian territory from massive Chinese migrations. With the founding of the USSR,
Soviet policies evolved in the same basic direction, gathering
momentum as a result of the use of Mongolian soil by anti-red
Russian bands and inept Chinese policies. In the early 1920s
a separate Mongolian state emerged, one wholly dependent
upon Soviet support.

After more than half a century, that situation continues to
prevail. With a population of only one and one-half million—
representing far less than the number of Mongols now living
in the PRC—Outer Mongolia has extremely limited choices.
The alternative to dependence upon the Soviet Union almost
certainly would be incorporation in some form within the Chinese empire. There is no indication that this is desired by any
significant number of MPR citizens. Meanwhile, the key
Mongolian political leaders have been heavily Russianized,
with their higher education generally taking place in the USSR,
their associations primarily with Russians, and with men like
Yumjaagyn Tsendenbal, first secretary of the Mongolian People's Revolutionary Party and long-time supreme leader, mar-
ried to a Russian.

In all of their political pronouncements and policies, the
Outer Mongolian leaders echo perfectly contemporary Soviet
positions, as might be expected. Never is there the slightest deviation. Thus, in recent years, a drum-fire attack upon China
has been maintained by the key Party and state organs of Ulan
Bator, the MPR capital. The Chinese are accused of having
frequently intimated that Outer Mongolia legitimately belongs
to China, notwithstanding earlier treaties. China's "reactionary" and "hegemonistic" policies toward Southeast Asia, "in
collusion with the USA," are credited with being the key
source of tension in the region. Peking's support for "a mili-
tarist Japan" is termed a threat to the peace of Northeast Asia,
particularly when coupled with "American imperialism."

Nor do MPR organs desist from comments on PRC internal
matters. Special attention is given to "the plight" of compatriots living in Inner Mongolia. A recent Outer Mongolian
broadcast claimed that Chinese statistics revealed that 40 percent

of all agricultural production brigades in Inner Mongolia were classified as "poor."

Generally, Chinese sources ignore Outer Mongolian attacks, privately dismissing them as "the barking of dogs at the master's command." Yet some apprehension may well be felt. The policies pursued during the Cultural Revolution, including the purges of a very sizable number of high Mongol CCP members on charges of "local nationalism" must have done great damage to Han-Mongol relations in Inner Mongolia. In recent years Chinese leaders have admitted that serious mistakes were made, and individuals have been rehabilitated and placed once again in prestigious party and state posts. The most effective policy, however, probably has been the ever greater numerical superiority of Chinese over Mongols in Inner Mongolia, now reportedly at least six to one.

Do present PRC leaders still regard Outer Mongolia, along with portions of Siberia, as legitimate parts of the Greater China, notwithstanding the events of the nineteenth and twentieth centuries? Such claims have not been set forth in official PRC statements, but the Russians and Outer Mongolians have some grounds for suspicion. On occasion, Chinese leaders have referred to the Mongols as one of the races making up the "great fraternal family" of China and emphasized the historical linkage through leaders like Genghis Khan. The Mongols also claim that in 1949 Mao Zedong inquired whether Soviet leaders would be amenable to a union between Outer Mongolia and China. Mao is said to have raised the same issue in conversations with a Japanese Socialist Party delegation in 1964. The Russians are acutely aware of the Chinese demand that they acknowledge the "illegal" seizure of vast tracts of Siberian land, with the pledge that if this were admitted, China would not press its claims. Snow will fall in the steamy jungles of New Guinea before the Russians make any such admission.

The Chinese position may even have hardened in the recent past. An article by Mao Hanying of the Geography Research Institute of the China Academy of Sciences, cited by Peking's domestic radio on November 25, 1980, asserted:

> The present Soviet domain was formed by Czarist Russia's continuous aggression and expansion for some three hundred to four hundred years. Beginning from the 1850s, Czarist Russia used armed force to compel

the authorities of China's Qing Dynasty to sign a series of unequal treaties and thus seized and occupied more than 1.5 million square kilometers of Chinese territory.

Mao's article ends with some data which Soviet leaders can only regard as ominous. After the October Revolution, it is noted, the USSR gave up part of the territory seized by the Czars in the West—but again, during and after World War II, the Soviet Union "seized some 700,000 square kilometers from neighboring countries." One possible conclusion: should it not give up its earlier ill-gotten gains, east and west, in accordance with the precedent set by the early Bolsheviks?

Boundaries and territorial claims were not an original cause of the Sino-Soviet cleavage, but at this point they have been woven into that conflict so tightly that it can never be fully resolved unless they are renegotiated. It is the destiny of the USSR and the PRC to live cheek-by-jowl with each other, with only Outer Mongolia—and to a much more limited extent North Korea—serving as buffer states. This greatly complicates the possibility of a Sino-Soviet rapprochement, particularly since Siberia is likely to remain lightly populated for many years despite the premium which the USSR has placed upon its development. A politically stable, economically developing, and militarily powerful China (the Soviet Union's nightmare) almost surely would demand a change in the political behavior of Outer Mongolia at a minimum.

Korea and Sino-Soviet Rivalry

The issues with respect to Chinese and Russian influence in North Korea are somewhat different than those related to Mongolia, at least for the present. The Democratic People's Republic of Korea (DPRK) and the Himalayan states (Nepal and Bhutan) remain the areas on China's borders where the Soviet Union has less than complete authority or a clear primacy of influence. Indeed, while North Korea began its existence as a creation of the USSR, after the Korean War, in the context of a significant Chinese presence, Korean Workers Party Chairman Kim Il-song seized upon *chuché* ("self-reliance")—first, as a club with which to beat his internal opponents, particularly those closely identified with Moscow or

Peking. Subsequently, *chuché* has become a constantly invoked fetish, to be invoked on all occasions.

Since 1956, when both Russians and Chinese attempted to intervene in internal DPRK politics in order to prevent the purge of their partisans, North Korea's relations with the major communist powers have been marked by a degree of suspicion and aloofness that has persisted to the present. In the course of events, however, perfect equidistance between the USSR and the PRC was rarely if ever possible, and in the years that followed, Soviet–North Korean relations suffered the greater slippage. Indeed, on issues like de-Stalinization and criticism of Albania, Pyongyang sided with Peking, indicating an ideological and political affinity. China, after all, had a geographic, cultural, and historical proximity to Korea which never could be matched by the Soviet Union.

Thus, by the end of the Khrushchev era, relations between the USSR and the DPRK were extremely bad. For a time, the Russians cut off economic and military assistance, presenting the North Koreans with a serious crisis by 1965. With the advent to power of Brezhnev and Kosygin, limited improvements were achieved, but Kim Il-song by this time had acquired a deep distrust of the Russians, a sentiment that was mutually shared.

In contrast, relations with China were warm until the height of the Cultural Revolution. During the "leftist" seizure of power in China, however, an anti-Kim note was struck, with wall posters in Peking referring to the North Korean leader as a "fat dictator" who lived in luxury while his people starved. A border dispute was also rumored. For several years, North Korea stood more aloof from both the USSR and the PRC than at any previous time. But when Zhou Enlai returned to the control of Chinese foreign policy at the end of the 1960s, one of his first acts was to visit Pyongyang; and one can be certain that he apologized for earlier Chinese transgressions.

Thus, beginning in 1970, Sino–North Korean relations were characterized by increasing warmth and cooperation. The landmarks were plainly visible: ideological-political pronouncements closely paralleling each other; numerous cultural exchanges and periodic state visits by top leaders; and increasing trade, with the Chinese supplying an ever-growing quantity of economic and military needs to the DPRK. In contrast, relations with the USSR remained cool despite North Korean dependence upon Russia for certain industrial and military items. The DPRK alignment with China was not total. North Korean leaders refrained from open criticism of the USSR by name. And the Chinese insisted privately that their leverage upon the Koreans was limited. On occasion, moreover, as when the Chinese took on the role of mediator in connection with the annual debates in the U.N. General Assembly on a Korean resolution, Pyongyang seemed miffed at Peking's policies.

Yet in general, it was the Soviet Union that received Kim's ire. The strong North Korean condemnation of Vietnam's invasion of Kampuchea (Cambodia), Kim Il-song's hosting of Sihanouk, and the reluctance to endorse the Soviet invasion of Afghanistan are merely the more recent illustrations. And while Kim visited Peking and certain East European capitals in 1975, he did not go to Moscow—according to Russian sources, because he was not invited. The Russians, moreover, kept a tight rein on economic assistance despite the increasingly desperate economic situation in which the North Koreans found themselves, culminating in their default on international debt payments in the mid-1970s. Care also was taken to avoid transferring the most sophisticated military equipment to the North Koreans, a limitation matched by the United States in its military assistance toward the South.

The Chinese, meanwhile, were increasing their trade and assistance to the DPRK, as has been noted, and also their public support for North Korean positions. When Kim visited Peking in April 1975, PRC leaders agreed to a joint communiqué stipulating that the DPRK was "the sole sovereign state" on the Korean Peninsula and, linking the Korean issue to that of Taiwan, thereby appearing to cement support for Kim Il-song's stand on reunification. In the years that followed, Deng Xiaoping and others regularly reiterated in public their support for the key DPRK proposals: a demand for the withdrawal of U.S. forces from South Korea; reunification via the Kim Il-song formula; nonrecognition of the "militarist-Fascist" government in Seoul; and a refusal to support the admission of the two Koreas to the United Nations. These verbal assurances, moreover, often were delivered at a high decibel level.

Deng Xiaoping's speech in August 1978 in Hamhung on the occasion of the thirtieth anniversary of the founding of the DPRK, for example, stood out in striking contrast to the very low-key statement of the Soviet delegation. Words were accompanied by some actions. Peking promised to increase its oil shipments, and by 1978 the flow of oil from China to North Korea matched that coming from the USSR.

Some Americans looked for signs of Chinese interest in reducing tension on the Korean Peninsula. They pointed to the fact (as did the Chinese privately) that Chinese leaders had urged *peaceful* reunification, seeking to dampen any North Korean aggressive plans. It is undoubtedly true that China and the Soviet Union have no desire to see another war erupt on the Korean Peninsula. This is one critical interest which all of the major powers have in common. However, in connection with China's emphasis upon peaceful reunification, it should be pointed out that Kim Il-song himself has long referred to his policy in precisely such terms, even applying that label to one of his published works.

It is also frequently asserted that despite their oft-stated public demands for a withdrawal of American troops from South Korea, Chinese leaders do not actually desire such a development, preferring the status quo to the hazards of unimpeded South-North confrontation on the Korean Peninsula, and possibly heightened Soviet involvement. This is conceivable, and indeed, individual Chinese give such hints on occasion in private conversations. The Chinese may take their official stance on an American troop withdrawal tongue-in-cheek, realizing that their protests will not alter American policy and, hence, that they can have the best of two political/strategic positions by keeping in step with Pyongyang on the one hand and relying upon a continued American presence on the other. In any case, Peking has never deviated in public from adherence to the Pyongyang line—and even in private its position is usually voiced in the same terms.

The Chinese have always had great confidence in their ability to understand and deal with the Koreans more satisfactorily than other external powers. It can be argued that they had a similar confidence with respect to the Vietnamese—a confidence which now has been rudely shaken. Nevertheless, historic

Chinese influence on the Korean Peninsula was much greater than that in Vietnam, and the ethnic ties are closer. Yet the nationalist tides sweeping through both North and South Korea do not exempt China, a fact of which Peking is aware.

To propitiate Kim Il-song, indeed, Chinese overtures to South Korea have been considerably more limited than those of the USSR. In contrast to Russian permission granted to South Korean citizens to visit the Soviet Union in connection with international athletic, academic, and professional conferences—including a government minister and journalists—to date no citizen of the Republic of Korea has been allowed to enter the PRC. There has been some Chinese–South Korean contact, however, via international meetings in third countries, and, according to one account, a discussion recently took place concerning the possibility of an athletic meet. One elderly Korean living in Manchuria was allowed to migrate to South Korea via Hong Kong. More importantly, the Chinese have displayed an interest in trade with the Republic of Korea, although such a development is in an embryonic stage compared to ROK trade with Eastern Europe. To summarize, in the past PRC authorities have been reluctant to offend the North Koreans by taking any action that might connote a movement toward a "two Koreas" policy.

Nevertheless, certain Chinese now privately express concern over trends in their relations with the DPRK. Beginning in 1979, the Soviet Union commenced an effort to improve its relations with North Korea and reverse the DPRK tilt toward China. The campaign has included a distinct upgrading of verbal support for North Korea on critical issues and greatly heightened praise for DPRK accomplishments. While certain statements are not new, recent Soviet pronouncements regarding North Korean successes and the skill of Pyongyang leaders are considerably more positive than prior to 1979. In place of the tepid statements of earlier years, moreover, Soviet spokesmen today publicly express unswerving support for Kim Il-song's reunification proposals. Their language is more explicit and their words more strident than those issued as late as mid-1978. Kim's three principles and five points relating to reunification are "realistic proposals, reflecting the will of the entire Korean people," according to Soviet media. The main responsibility for the current impasse in North–South Korean negotiations, moreover, is said to lie "with the Seoul regime and U.S. imperialism." These forces, harboring "militarist-Fascist policies," are creating a dangerous, provocative atmosphere which could burst forth in violence at any time, according to a recent *Izvestia* article.

As might be expected, Russian spokesmen seek to tie the Chinese into American plans as they define them. The *Izvestia* writer put it thus: "The Peking leaders, who intend to sacrifice the interests of other nations in fulfilling their anti-Soviet hegemonist aims, are sympathizing with this attempt of the U.S. imperialists."

Have Soviet words been matched by actions? The evidence thus far is cloudy. Efforts of the DPRK during the 1970s to obtain significant increases in Soviet economic aid seem to have achieved meager results. In January 1980, Kang Chin-t'ae, vice premier for economic affairs, went to the USSR, and there has been some speculation—without hard evidence as yet—that his mission met with greater success. Military assistance also has been a critical factor in Soviet–North Korean relations, and a matter of dispute in the past, although the DPRK is now dependent upon the USSR for only the most sophisticated equipment. One current question is whether the North Koreans will get MIG-23 fighter aircraft, long desired. One may assume that Kim Il-song and his colleagues are pressing the USSR for economic and military assistance to match the more supportive words coming from Moscow. The next several years should provide us with sufficient evidence to determine whether this in fact is taking place.

Meanwhile, the effect of stepped-up Soviet efforts upon North Korean attitudes and policies remains uncertain. On the issue of Indochina, the North Korean and Russian positions still appear to be widely separated. Pyongyang continues to take a critical view of Hanoi's invasion of Kampuchea. Sihanouk, moreover, has been a frequent guest of Kim Il-song, and gets truly royal treatment despite the fact that he is anathema both to the Russians and to the Vietnamese. And as recently as late August 1980, DPRK Vice Premier Kim Kyong-ryon asserted during a visit to Kuala Lumpur that North Korea supports the ASEAN demand that Vietnamese troops be withdrawn from Kampuchea.

The DPRK position on Afghanistan is somewhat more complex. In February 1980, North Korea—together with Rumania—refused to adhere to a joint statement defending Soviet actions in Afghanistan put forth at a Sofia parliamentary conference of twelve socialist countries. In mid-August, however, on the occasion of the anniversary of Afghanistan's independence, *Nodong Sinmun,* the leading North Korean Party newspaper, praised the 1978 revolution as "an event of great significance in the struggle of the Afghan people for consolidating national independence and achieving the independent development of the country." This article appeared to support the Babrak Karmal regime and praised its accomplishments to date, thereby separating Pyongyang's position dramatically from that of Peking. At the same time, the emphasis upon the linkage between the Afghan and the Korean people's "common struggle against imperialism and for independence" probably discomfitted, if not angered, the Russians.

Meanwhile, Kim Il-song finally set foot on Russian soil again, albeit not in Moscow. In May 1980 enroute to Tito's funeral, the North Korean leader made a brief stopover in Kiev. Moreover, he met with Brezhnev in Belgrade, with the meeting described officially in Pyongyang as "an important occasion for further developing and strengthening Korean-Soviet friendship." Soviet–North Korean political and cultural exchanges in general have increased and are being given somewhat more publicity in both countries.

Pyongyang also has made efforts to strengthen its ties with states aligned in some degree with the USSR, notably India and Cuba. In July 1980, for example, a high-level North Korean delegation visited New Delhi, even as Sino-Indian relations were troubled by Mrs. Gandhi's recognition of the Heng Samrin regime in Kampuchea. On the twentieth anniversary of the establishment of DPRK–Cuban relations in late August, moreover, *Nodong Sinmun* praised Havana and Fidel Castro unstintingly—in sharp contrast to the view of the Cubans prevailing in Peking. On September 1, Kim even sent Le Duan and other key Vietnamese leaders a telegram lauding the Vietnamese people for having become masters of their nation, and expressing the hope that relations between "our two peoples" would develop favorably. The theme here, as in the case of Afghanistan, was upon national independence; and Kim often proclaims that nonalignment in conformity with Third World interests constitutes the foundation of DPRK foreign policy. Thus, the Soviet Union probably remains less than satisfied with North Korea's response to its overtures. The Chinese, however, have good reason to be even more unhappy, given recent trends.

On the surface, to be sure, there are no strong indications that relations between the DPRK and the PRC have slipped. Yet there are persistent rumors and indirect documentary evidence that Pyongyang's leaders are disappointed with China's domestic and foreign policies. The new quotient of pragmatism in Chinese economic programs, the rapid turning outward to the advanced industrial world for assistance, the decline of ideology and the continuous attack on the cult of personality surrounding Mao Zedong all represent trends that stand in considerable contrast to Kim Il-songism. China's increasing identification with the United States and Japan on critical strategic issues also must be worrisome, despite Peking's constant reassurance that it will stand fast with respect to North Korean interests. It is true, of course, that the DPRK leadership wants to cultivate relations with both these nations, but for its own purposes and in its own way. There is also the suggestion in some quarters that Pyongyang is disappointed with the failure of China's economic support in the recent past to measure up to earlier promises.

In the light of the shadowy evidence on some of these matters at present, it is perhaps useful to note the contrasting key phrases used in official North Korean pronouncements dealing with China and Russia. With respect to the Chinese, the phrase is "to consolidate and develop" relations. In discussing trends in DPRK–USSR relations, the key phrase is "further to develop and strengthen" relations, suggesting that the task (and prospect?) is to induce improvement—where as in the Chinese case it is to hold the line, to prevent slippage. This, indeed, may be precisely how Kim and his supporters view the issue.

In summary, the Korean situation shows some signs of political fluidity. The Soviets, confronted with what they regard as a growing two-front threat, with a Sino-American-Japanese entente emerging in East Asia in company with NATO in the West, seem to be accelerating efforts to bolster their buffer state system and surround the PRC with a ring of steel. It is in this context that Soviet policies toward the DPRK have been altered, with a considerable effort now under way to strengthen ties to Pyongyang.

That effort, thus far, is most clearly seen in the increased verbal support being given the North Koreans on the reunification issue and on other matters of significance to Pyongyang. There also has been an upgrading, both quantitatively and qualitatively, in political and cultural exchanges. It is still unclear as to whether these have been accompanied by significant increases in Soviet economic and military assistance, but data on these programs should not be long in appearing. One must remember that there is a deep—and justified—legacy of mistrust between the Russians and the current North Korean leadership. This will not necessarily preclude an improvement in relations for reasons of perceived national interest, but it would be too much to expect the emergence of affection on either side.

On balance, however, it would appear that Pyongyang is responding positively to the new thrust of Soviet policy, albeit cautiously. At the same time, Pyongyang's fixation on "self-reliance" and "independence"—supreme testimony to the unsatisfactory nature of intracommunist relations over the past three and one-half decades—cannot but make the Russians uneasy and unhappy, especially when such themes are addressed to Soviet satellites or close allies. Moreover, in their efforts to induce greater American and Japanese interest in them, the North Koreans insist privately that they do not wish to be tied *merely* to their northern and western neighbors. It is not surprising that the Soviets continue to find the Koreans "difficult people."

If this analysis is correct, however, and if the present trends continue, problems in DPRK–PRC relations easily could be compounded. The evidence of North Korean disappointment with Chinese policies, domestic and foreign, is substantial, if indirect, as has been suggested. China, moreover, may be strong enough and close enough to exercise a certain veto power over North Korean actions, but it is too weak to substitute for the USSR in military terms, or to encourage any North Korean–Soviet confrontation. The very fact that the Chinese are trying so hard to please Pyongyang in their verbal reassurances at present, together with a certain reticence displayed by the North Koreans, suggests that this is a period of some fragility in the relationship.

One important variable in the Pyongyang-Peking-Moscow triangle relates to DPRK domestic politics. Kim Chong-il has now been designated heir-apparent to his father, but this first effort at communist monarchism could generate formidable opposition, possibly from within military ranks. And if there is a power struggle, there will be a great temptation for external intervention, especially if one or both of the quarreling factions request external support. There is no sign that Kim Il-song, the aging Great Leader, is likely to pass from the scene soon, but the uncertainties of the DPRK political future must trouble its communist neighbors as well as the ROK.

Strengthened Sino-Japanese Relations

Offsetting the current concern about North Korea, Chinese leaders have reason to take encouragement from the basic trends in Sino-Japanese relations, despite a few clouds on the horizon. Between December 3 and 5, 1980, the first Sino-Japanese governmental meeting took place in Peking, with six Japanese cabinet members present and thirteen PRC vice premiers, ministers, and vice ministers in attendance. Conference discussions ranged broadly over the present international situation, in addition to such specific topics as Sino-Japanese economic relations and exchanges of various types. At the conclusion of the meetings, an agreement was signed whereby Japan pledged 56 billion yuan ($270 million) in soft-term credits to China at an interest rate of 3 percent.

A long road had been traveled since 1972, just eight years earlier, when Japan first accorded diplomatic recognition to the People's Republic of China and broke diplomatic relations with the Republic of China on Taiwan. In that major decision, the Japanese business community played a significant role, a majority of its representatives having become convinced that it was in Japan's interest to assume the leading role in China's economic modernization. It is not difficult to understand Japanese hopes in this respect. Industrial capacities, geographic propinquity, and historic cultural ties combined to make Japan the logical front runner in any competition to interact with a resurgent Chinese industrial revolution.

Thus, from an early point in the post–Cultural Revolution era, Japan accounted for 20 to 25 percent of the PRC's expanding foreign trade. Nor did this interfere with continued gains in Japanese trade with Taiwan, conducted with the aid of "unofficial" government ties. By 1980, Japanese trade with the PRC had surpassed $8 billion per annum, an increase of sevenfold within eight years, and a 20 percent advance over 1979. Trade with Taiwan was at a level of approximately $8 billion, close to the Japan–PRC level. As was expected, Japanese exports to China were heavily oriented toward machinery and equipment, together with steel and chemicals. Imports consisted mainly of mineral products (with oil and coal key items) and agricultural products.

This economic intercourse was a natural and mutually beneficial one. Yet as the decade of the 1980s opened, problems had emerged. Whether they are of a temporary or a longer-term character remains to be determined. The roots of the difficulties were in the confusion and malaise affecting the Chinese economy. In a burst of enthusiasm after the overthrow of the Gang of Four and the return to power of Deng Xiaoping and the technocrats, China had hastily drawn up plans for rapid industrial expansion as well as vast increases in agricultural productivity. In its own way, Peking's ten-year plan promulgated in 1978 projected a Great Leap Forward, albeit one not as utopian as that set forth in 1958. The aim was to increase annual food production to 400 million tons and steel production to 60 million tons by the end of the plan period, to take two key elements. To meet these and other targets, a huge amount of foreign capital would be necessary, along with phenomenal improvements in managerial and labor skills.

Within a year, PRC leaders recognized that the ten-year plan was unrealistic. It was scrapped, and in the course of a series of experiments—some local, others province-wide—an effort was initiated to introduce some fundamental changes into the economic system. The new emphases were upon "market socialism" with various incentives aimed at increasing productivity introduced, decentralization in certain forms featured, and a sustained drive to improve skills at all levels initiated. A period of "readjustment" was announced, one that many now presume will continue into the mid-1980s. It also was indicated that in the period immediately ahead, the premium would be upon consumer industries as well as agriculture in an effort to improve living standards. Heavy industry is to be deemphasized for the present, as is defense spending.

Relatively serious problems in the Chinese economy were clearly discernible as 1980 drew to a close, both because of the misfortune of a bad harvest and, more fundamentally, because of overlapping or conflicting policies between the center and the provinces, leading to unnecessary duplication and a waste of capital and resources. There remained, moreover, the massive challenges of rebuilding a work ethic within the labor force, creating a new managerial class, training a new generation of scientific talent, and infusing the economy with modern technology.

Naturally, these problems impacted upon Sino-Japanese economic relations. When optimism was at its height, agreements had been reached on the importation of large numbers of plants from Japan, particularly in the heavy industrial category, with payment coming in major part in the form of rapidly increased Chinese oil shipments. In 1978 alone, Japan had contracted to export close to $4 billion worth of plants to China. By early 1979, however, warning signals were clearly visible, and by the end of 1980, substantial modifications of the original plans were under way.

The controversy within China which erupted over the massive Baoshan steel complex outside Shanghai was symptomatic of the difficulties. This plant, the costs of which steadily soared to over $5 billion, was being constructed with Japanese capital and the latest Japanese technology. Critics charged that it was far too costly, poorly located to take optimal advantage of China's iron ore deposits, too advanced for the level of China's technological skills, and premature in terms of the country's most immediate needs. By the fall of 1980, with attacks on

Baoshan emanating from National People's Congress delegates and appearing in the *People's Daily,* the national Party newspaper, it was clear that the government was signaling a basic change. Not long thereafter, it was announced that the second phase of Baoshan plant building had been halted. At this point, "leftist excesses" were blamed for the overenthusiastic rush toward heavy industry marking earlier programs. This charge seemed directed at a sizable faction within the Party and governmental bureaucracy, probably including Premier and Party Chairman Hua Guofeng.

In the light of these developments, Japanese expectations of trade with the PRC have been scaled down, at least for the immediate future. It is most unlikely that heavy industrial plant importations from Japan will be resumed by the Chinese on a significant scale in the near term. The experiences of recent years, moreover, have caused the initial romanticism about the China market in certain Japanese business circles to be replaced by a sober realism. However, sharp divisions of opinion concerning future prospects for China trade continue to exist in Japan. The pessimists believe that Sino-Japanese trade for at least the next few years will be held to an annual growth rate of about 4 percent, reaching only $10 billion by 1985. The optimists (including JETRO, the government-sponsored Japan External Trade Organization) believe that such trade can reach $20 billion by 1985, arguing that the slowdown in plant exports will be more than compensated for by increased exports of consumer goods.

Whatever the ultimate outcome, there can be no doubt that the health of the Chinese economy will have a major impact upon Sino-Japanese relations in the years ahead. The Japanese recognize, moreover, that any major political upheaval within China might lead to a dramatic change in economic policies. Despite the "trial-and-error" policies, replete with confusion and sudden shifts, that have characterized the recent past, the broad thrust has been toward pragmatic, market-oriented policies, with a strong commitment toward turning outward for advanced Japanese and Western technology and the training of scientists/engineers, managers, and economists.

There is a basic alternative, however, in case present policies appear to fail, one representing another and powerful side of the Chinese psyche, namely, withdrawal based upon "self-reliance." Whatever its economic flaws, "self-reliance," even in extreme form, has a deep appeal to a people in whom the strains of exclusiveness and xenophobia run deep. Even in this era, self-reliance has not been abandoned, either as a concept or as a practice, and in degree, of course, it is appropriate. Yet in the hands of new or old ultranationalist ideologues, it might come back in virulent form, although that possibility does not seem strong at present. In the past, there has often been a pendulum-like swing toward and away from intensive external contacts, not merely on the part of China, but among other Sinic societies as well. As a continental state with a massive population, moreover, China shares certain tendencies and habits of thought characteristic of other such states, including Russia and the United States—deeply implanted concepts of moral self-righteousness and self-sufficiency.

If present trends hold, however, Japan is likely to build an economic relationship with China that fulfills the Japanese hopes of the 1930s, yet without its political and military costs. In this light, it is perhaps ironic that today China looks to Japan not merely for economic assistance but increasingly for support in the security realm. Within less than a decade a dramatic change has taken place in the attitudes and policies of PRC leaders regarding the strategic role of Japan. For some two decades after the Communist advent to power in China, Peking's position on Japanese rearmament was entirely hostile. The basic themes were akin to those of Soviet leaders: Japanese militarism, cultivated by American imperialism, threatened to become a menace to Asia and the world. Finding natural allies among the Japanese Communists and left Socialists, PRC spokesmen loaned their support to various campaigns against the U.S.–Japan Mutual Security Treaty, the Japanese Self-Defense Forces, and the American military presence in Northeast Asia.

As the Sino-Soviet cleavage widened and deepened, and particularly after the Ussuri River military clashes on China's northern border in 1969, such attacks dribbled off into silence, and then from silence into an increasingly active stance of support for the U.S.–Japan defense relationship and, most recently, encouragement of Japan's rearmament. By the early

1970s, Chinese organs were asserting that Japan had every right to defend itself against Soviet "social imperialism." Issues between Japan and the USSR such as the rights of Japanese fishermen, and particularly the controversy over the four northern islands off the coast of Hokkaido held by the Russians, were featured in Chinese media and in the speeches of leading PRC spokesmen. Those Japanese who took a firm stand against the Russians were lauded, and Japanese nationalism was given approval as completely warranted in view of the Soviet threat.

As in the case of Western Europe, this shift of position by the Chinese produced new political alignments. A serious split had occurred earlier between the Chinese and Japanese Communist Parties, stemming from Mao's refusal to join in a united front with the Russians to aid Vietnam in 1966, a proposal forwarded by a Japanese mission headed by Miyamoto Kenji, Chairman of the JCP. This split has never been healed. After the new Chinese stance on Japanese defense, ties with the left Socialists also were weakened, although Socialist missions continued to make the pilgrimage to Peking and reiterate their general sympathy for the PRC. Yet a major change had occurred since the days of Asanuma Inejiro when the Japanese Socialist Party and the CCP had jointly proclaimed that the United States (later corrected to read "U.S. imperialism") was the common enemy of the Chinese and Japanese peoples. Even before formal diplomatic relations were established in 1972, Chinese leaders had discovered that the national interests of China lay in cultivating relations with those in power, namely, the leaders of the Liberal Democratic Party. Increasingly, moreover, in the late 1970s, PRC contacts in Japan were broadened to include key bureaucratic and defense figures, especially those individuals who held firmly to an anti-Soviet position.

With the return of Deng Xiaoping to authority in mid-1977, that which had been implicit was made explicit. First, after lengthy negotiations, Japan and China signed a Treaty of Peace and Friendship on August 12, 1978. At PRC insistence, the treaty included a clause of opposition to "hegemony" which, at least in the eyes of the Chinese, was directed against the USSR. In another section of the treaty, it was indicated that the document was not to affect the position of either contracting party regarding its relations with third countries. Soviet authorities did not accept this caveat, however, and vigorously denounced the treaty as yet another step in the direction of a Sino-American-Japanese alliance directed against the Soviet Union. Moscow was aware of the fact that Washington had quietly encouraged consummation of the treaty.

Soviet efforts to obtain a similar treaty were blocked because of the unresolved territorial dispute over the northern islands, as was a Japanese-Soviet peace treaty formally settling all matters relating to World War II. Prime Minister Takeo Fukuda spoke of an "omnidirectional diplomacy of peace" for Japan, by which he meant a policy of friendship toward all nations within the context of a special U.S.–Japan relationship. In fact, however, Japanese-Soviet relations continued to deteriorate, largely as a result of Russian policies both in East Asia and elsewhere in the world. Responding to the Vietnamese invasion of Kampuchea, Japan suspended its economic assistance to Hanoi; and after the Soviet invasion of Afghanistan, Tokyo supported the U.S.–initiated sanctions against Moscow more firmly than did certain Western European states.

Meanwhile, Chinese political-security policies aimed at Japan were not intended to reduce Soviet fears of a new strategic alliance. Shortly after the signing of the Sino-Japanese treaty, and apparently based on an initiative from Peking, a key Chinese military leader visited Japan. In early September 1978, Deputy Chief of the Chinese General Staff Zhang Caiqian arrived in Tokyo, spending six days there in discussions relating to security matters. Subsequently, such discussions have continued on an informal basis, in Peking as well as in Tokyo. Both Deng Xiaoping and Hua Guofeng, moreover, in the course of their visits to Japan in the past two years, have openly attacked Soviet policies and continued to call for a united effort against "hegemonism." The Chinese have also sustained their endorsement of the U.S.–Japan Mutual Security Treaty. Peking's initial official position was that "as a general principle, we do not favor the stationing of military forces abroad, but in the light of the prevailing threat, if the American and Japanese people favor the treaty, we accept it." Gradually, acceptance became support, and on several occasions Chinese leaders have informed the Japanese that they recognize the priority for Japan which relations with the United States must take over all other foreign ties.

The major shift in Chinese policy toward Japan—especially on security issues—unquestionably has helped to reduce domestic Japanese opposition to the Mutual Security Treaty and the Self-Defense Forces. This factor, together with Soviet actions and the gradual return of increased confidence in the American commitment, has resulted in greater support for alignment with the United States and the maintenance of defensive military units, as all recent public opinion polls indicate. One also should note that these same polls demonstrate that as the 1980s commenced the PRC had acquired very considerable popularity in Japan. When asked with which nations Japan should have closer ties, in a poll conducted in early 1980, the United States and the People's Republic of China scored almost evenly at the top of the list (34 and 33 percent respectively).

It would be incorrect, however, to assume that no complications exist with respect to political-security relations between China and Japan. When Chinese leaders visiting Japan castigate the USSR and call for a united front against Soviet "hegemony," many Japanese—not all of them leftists—wince. Since World War II, Japan has been enormously successful in pursuing a maximal gain/minimal risk foreign policy, one engendering a very high degree of internal support. In the broadest terms, Japan's foreign policy has attempted to separate politics and economics, making clear its affiliation with the United States (and benefiting greatly from the extensive American security guarantees) but doing business wherever the opportunity presented itself and in recent years seeking to maintain correct, relatively friendly relations with all parties. If this policy has not been wholly consummated, nor wholly successful, it still has represented the goal and, until recently, in increasing measure the reality of Japanese foreign policy.

Now, half-prodded, half-persuaded, Japan appears to be moving toward a more active political role, and one with heightened security requirements. In this connection, a great debate is gradually getting under way throughout the nation, with the most basic issues pertaining to political relations and security being aired. It now is increasingly recognized that the world of the 1980s is not that of the 1950s or the 1960s. The era of Pax

Americana for Asia—and for the world—is over, although the United States will remain a major Pacific-Asian power. Security must now be a collective, not a unilateral concern. A growing number of Japanese also see the Soviet Union as a long-term problem, although the nature and the extent of the threat remain hotly debated issues. Weak in its political, economic, cultural, and ideological appeals to Asians, will the USSR be tempted to use its expanding military power in order to enforce its will in an era when it has become a global power? Or will a combination of internal difficulties and external over-commitments act as severe restraints upon the exercise of Soviet military power abroad, especially against a politically stable, economically prosperous nation like Japan? And if the pressures from Moscow come in forms short of war, how can they best be met?

The answers to these questions will not be quickly or easily reached—in Tokyo or elsewhere. Meanwhile, in de facto terms, Japan has progressively moved toward involvement in a Sino-American-Japanese entente, albeit one with strict limits both of structure and of substance. In recent years, the Japanese tilt toward China as opposed to the USSR has been perceptible, and this trend has taken place with the acceptance—indeed, support—of the United States. It should be emphasized that bilateral relations between the three states involved in this entente are still vastly more important than the triangular relationship (and in each instance different in character), but it is clear that recent Soviet policies in Asia and in the world have promoted in embryonic form the united front of which the Chinese have been the chief spokesmen.

At the same time, various complexities mark the course of Japanese foreign policy today. If the dominant trend has been the one just described, Japan—in company with Western Europe—does not want to drift into an unmodulated confrontation with the Soviet Union. Thus there is evident resistance to the idea of a strategic alliance with China or arms sales to that nation, despite some voices favorable to the latter policy in industrial circles. Put simply, a majority of Japanese policy makers at present does not want to bear the costs and risks of being full-fledged participants in an overtly anti-Soviet alliance.

To understand the Japanese dilemma, some reference to

Soviet-Japanese relations is essential. Since World War II, Russia has followed unremittingly harsh policies toward Japan, commencing with the reluctance to return Japanese prisoners of war, the insistence that the Emperor be tried as a war criminal, and the demand for heavy reparations—and continuing down to the present on such issues as maritime jurisdiction and resolution of the four northern islands dispute. It is easy to argue that these policies have been short-sighted from the standpoint of Soviet national interests. Certainly, they have reaped a harvest of ill will in Japan, with the public and policy makers alike strongly "anti-Soviet," emotionally as well as in policy terms.

Some individuals within the USSR, cognizant of these facts, have argued for a more conciliatory policy. Indeed, a modest shift in that direction may be under way. The dominant theme, however, has been "one must treat the Japanese tough." The stick has been far more in evidence than the carrot. By confronting Japan with close-in military power, Moscow seems to aim at emphasizing the dangers for Tokyo of "anti-Soviet" policies. Recent Soviet fortifications on the disputed northern islands, moreover, represent an effort to add weight to the Russian insistence that there is no territorial dispute, the island question not being subject to negotiation.

While this position is unacceptable to Japanese authorities and, as noted earlier, they have refused thus far to move toward any treaty negotiations unless the territorial issue is placed on the agenda, Soviet policy makers firmly believe that economic considerations ultimately will bring Japan into a more compatible relationship with the USSR without the need to make any territorial or strategic concessions. According to their analysis, the Japanese desire to participate in the development of Siberia and to share in its rich resources will steadily grow, especially since the Russians believe that the China market will prove disappointing and that American-Japanese friction over economic issues will increase.

This is the carrot, and while it thus far has proven to be less than fully attractive to the Japanese, the Soviet gamble—with a little sweetening—may pay off. Japan has indicated a strong interest in Siberian lumber and coal. In an agreement reached in late 1980, the Japanese government agreed to provide additional short-term loans for the development of forestry and coal resources in Siberia in exchange for a Soviet commitment to supply both materials to Japan in specified amounts for six and twenty years respectively. Natural gas from Sakhalin is also being exploited for shipment to Japan. Japanese loans for these purposes now total over $1 billion, and this represents the second economic agreement between Japan and the USSR since Tokyo imposed selective economic sanctions against the Soviets following the intervention in Afghanistan, the first having related to a Japanese export of steel pipes.

Japanese-Soviet trade still amounts to a relatively modest $4 billion—only one-half that of Japan's trade with the PRC—but it is clear that the potential for increases is considerable if economic and strategic conditions were to improve. These are the reasons that the Tyumen oil and gas project, mammoth in its engineering and financial proportions, was set aside a few years ago. Japanese entrepreneurs did not regard the economic terms as favorable, and the Japanese government wanted American participation since the project had strategic overtones likely to disturb Peking. Such considerations will continue to be important, but if the Soviets choose to be flexible, the Japanese will likely accommodate them. Optimally, Japan would like to be the chief external agent in abetting the Chinese industrial revolution *and* in the development of the Soviet Far East.

Thus, neither a Sino-Japanese Pan-Asianism nor an Asian counterpart to NATO in the form of a Sino-American-Japanese military alliance is likely to take shape in the 1980s—unless Soviet expansion escalates. Ours is an age in which alliances are giving way to alignments. Coalitions are now less exclusive, less all-encompassing, and less demanding of those involved than the alliance patterns of the 1950s. Even the American-Japanese relationship increasingly partakes of alignment, and Sino-Japanese relations will surely reflect this trend toward more flexible international relationships. If China can get its own house in order, the economic interaction can be mutually beneficial; and on the strategic front, consultations may well become institutionalized in the period immediately ahead. It is also logical to send sizable numbers of Chinese students to Japan, there to acquire various skills. But the major differences that now exist between these two societies in their stages of economic development, political institutions, and important cultural-behavioral attributes are not likely to disappear or even to be significantly reduced in the decade ahead.

Chinese leaders are aware of these facts. Indeed, while they want economic assistance from Japan and the type of strategic relationship set forth above, as with the United States, they do not want a political alliance. For such purposes, China wishes to be identified primarily with the so-called Third World, the world of developing states. Having declared the socialist camp no longer in existence, destroyed by Soviet "fascism and social imperialism," PRC leaders seek their ideological outlet in identification with those societies having common developmental problems. Yet they have learned from experience that identification solely with the Third World—as was attempted during the 1960s and briefly in the 1970s (as Harry Harding details in chapter 9)—cannot satisfy China's economic and strategic interests.

The Taiwan Issue

There remains one additional state in Northeast Asia of special significance to China, namely, Taiwan or—to use its official designation—the Republic of China (ROC). Peking, to be sure, insists that Taiwan is a province of China, not a state, and vehemently opposes any developments which would strengthen the island's status as an independent political entity. And the Chinese government on Taiwan agrees, arguing that the issue is who has the moral and legal right to represent the Chinese people. But despite this abstract level of agreement on the part of the two governments, the fact is that two separate states exist, and have existed for more than thirty years. Peaceful unification, moreover, seems highly unlikely for the foreseeable future.

To PRC leaders, the Taiwan problem must seem most frustrating. Under present circumstances, the use of force to "liberate" the island is completely unfeasible. Taiwan has an exceptionally well-trained and well-equipped military force, quite capable of fending off an invasion from the mainland. The PRC lacks both the necessary air and sea power to undertake any large-scale operation of the type that would be necessary for a successful assault on Taiwan. It is true, of course, that nearly one-third of the ROC armed forces is kept on the offshore islands of Quemoy and Matsu, small dots of land within a few miles of the mainland. These could be captured in all probability if the PRC were prepared to pay a very high cost— or, more easily, they could be blockaded. But beyond the military costs of any type of attack, the political liabilities would be formidable. A successful campaign would contribute to, rather than hinder, the cause of one China/one Taiwan because it would create a clean geographic separation between the island and mainland. Moreover, it would risk the strong disapproval of both Japan and the United States, wrecking China's united front strategy. Thus, while Taiwan's commitment to these islands is foolish from a military standpoint, it is not likely to be challenged by the PRC, at least in the short term.

Yet if the military route does not seem promising for Peking, the political route is also yielding few returns at this point. After achieving diplomatic recognition from the United States, the PRC proffered what it regarded as most generous terms to Taipei. Urging the opening of all types of communications, including mail, exchanges of persons, and trade, PRC leaders announced that after reunification Taiwan could retain its economic system, its political autonomy, and—in some form— even its own military units. To be sure, promises of autonomy were flawed on occasion by references to Tibet and other "autonomous regions" within the PRC—involving peoples whose experiences with autonomy have been none too happy. The major problem, in any case, was all too obvious. Whatever degree of autonomy Peking granted, the PRC was naturally insistent that sovereignty must be abandoned, and that the ROC flag would have to come down. Taiwan, after all, was by common consent a province of China, not an independent nation.

To date, PRC overtures and requests for negotiation have been indignantly rejected by the ROC government with the assertion that the Nationalists will never again deal with the Chinese Communists, having learned from the bitter experiences of the Civil War years in the 1940s. Nor is there evidence

that a substantial number of people living in Taiwan are interested in union with the PRC on the terms advanced, or on any
terms likely to be put forth by Peking. The economic disparity
between the two states is huge. According to World Bank figures, in 1978 PRC per capita income was $300. In contrast,
per capita income in Taiwan stood at $1,420. Almost every
other economic indicator showed a comparable differential.

In addition, despite the strong cultural links between island
and mainland, the decades of separation and the contrasting
values and social systems under which the two peoples have
evolved have led to major variations in ways of life. For different reasons, this is as true for that 85 percent of the people on
the island who call themselves Taiwanese as it is for the more
recent refugees from the mainland's civil war. The former have
a limited identification with a land which neither they nor their
parents have ever seen. The latter lived in a radically different
China and have been witnesses to a transformation on the island
during the last thirty years which no one could have imagined
in 1949.

Despite these facts, however, the PRC's "soft" approach to
reunification has created certain problems for the Taiwan
authorities. First, they are acutely aware of the fact that a rigid
stance barring negotiations may cast Taiwan in an unfavorable
light internationally. Thus, statements from prominent Ameri
cans urging PRC–ROC discussions (such as that recently made
by Senator Robert Byrd) strike a very sensitive nerve in Taipei.
Off the record, the comment is: "You forced us into negotiations once, immediately after World War II, with disastrous
results. Never again!"

Yet it is impossible to prevent certain types of contacts between citizens of Taiwan and the PRC under prevailing circumstances, and the ROC government has had to adjust to this
fact. In 1980 the policy of total noncommunication with any
communist state was modified somewhat. Taiwan—moving in
the direction of South Korean policy—announced that trade
with Eastern Europe was permitted, and a Polish ship was the
first from this region to call at a Taiwan port. Closer to home,
indirect trade between China and Taiwan has begun to grow,
taking place via Hong Kong. JETRO, the Japanese trade organization, estimates that such trade has been growing at an average

rate of 15 percent per annum since 1976. While desirous of keeping the economic contacts indirect, Taipei authorities have officially acknowledged the existence of this trade and, on at least one occasion, seemed proud of the new market.

In addition to this indirect economic intercourse, PRC and ROC citizens are making contact with each other overseas on an expanding scale, and with the approval of both governments. The Taiwan government has authorized their students abroad to be "friendly and helpful" to classmates from the mainland. It also has sanctioned informal meetings among intellectuals and others attending international conferences or similar gatherings. Undoubtedly, intelligence from such contacts is flowing to both governments as well as to the parties immediately concerned. Nevertheless, the economic and personal interaction currently occurring stands in sharp contrast to the situation of only a few years ago.

There is no indication, however, that these activities are abetting unification efforts. Indeed, it may be that, in general, they are confirming ROC propaganda that economic and political conditions on the mainland are poor because of communism, and only an abandonment of the communist system can pave the way for unification. In the meanwhile, another process is gradually taking place in Taiwan itself, a process that may be termed "Taiwanization." Inevitably, as time passes, the Taiwanese are playing a larger role in their society. They always have been the dominant element in the private economic sector. They constitute the overwhelming majority within the armed forces, albeit with limited access to the officer ranks. And now they make up a majority of the membership of the Kuomintang, Taiwan's ruling Nationalist Party. While the independence movement is proscribed—and represents anathema both to the PRC and to the ROC leadership—a political evolution is under way in Taiwan which, whatever its ups and downs, ultimately will bring political dominance to those who consider themselves citizens of Taiwan, irrespective of their origins.

Such a development harbors a number of alternatives with respect to PRC–Taiwan relations, although it is difficult to envisage the amalgamation of Taiwan into China on terms acceptable to the present PRC leadership. Is a resort to force, therefore, an ultimate likelihood? No answer to this question is possible now, but one of the complexities of an American program of weapons transfers to the PRC (or the furnishing of sophisticated, "offensive" weapons to Taiwan) relates to this issue. Any U.S. weapons supplied to China would be more likely to strengthen the PRC vis-à-vis Southeast Asia (Hanoi) and Taiwan than to affect in any substantial manner the balance of power vis-à-vis the USSR. There are ways in which PRC actions could strike at Taiwan's security and, more particularly, its economic and political stability, short of all-out warfare. A blockade or a single attack upon a Taiwan merchant ship, for example, might have a serious effect on the island's morale or political stability.

The odds would appear to favor a continuance of Peking's "soft" policy for the present, assuming no dramatic changes in U.S. policies on this front—and equally, none on the part of Taiwan. Soviet spokesmen, it might be noted, recently have indicated informally that *if* Taiwan were to become officially independent, they might inaugurate relations with the island in some form. They have given similar unofficial support, incidentally, to the Tibetan independence movement. These may well be actions intended to stir up complexities in Sino-American and Sino-Indian relations, not true signals of Soviet policy intentions. Up to date, the USSR always has opted for aloofness from Taiwan, essentially because it did not wish to add a burden to its strained relations with Peking which might foreclose an eventual reconciliation.

In any case, despite their economic opening to Eastern Europe, the current authorities in Taiwan have given no indication that they desire to play a "Russian card." The hazards of moving in this direction, given Taiwan's economic and other postnormalization ties to the United States, are obvious. Another option for Taiwan would be that of developing nuclear weapons. This is probably feasible from a technical standpoint, especially if assistance could be obtained from one of the other pariah states (Israel or South Africa). But again, the reaction from the United States and Japan—not to mention the PRC— would be severe.

From all indications, the future of Taiwan is likely to remain an uncertain one, subject to many variables and potentially destabilizing developments both for PRC–Taiwan relations and China's dealings with the United States. It often has been argued that this is also an issue that could affect PRC internal politics as well as China's position in the Sino-American-Soviet triangle. Yet whatever the future may hold, there are far more important issues at present that relate to Chinese internal politics, starting with those pertaining to economic policies. Taiwan, to be sure, might become a weapon as some future power struggle unfolds, but it is unlikely to be the initial cause. Moreover, the cleavage between the PRC and the USSR exists because of very fundamental differences, as has been indicated, and it is very unlikely that the problem of Taiwan would in and of itself bring these two antagonists together.

Looking Ahead: A Continuing American Role in Asian Security

In looking toward the future, one must reiterate the fact that Northeast Asia is a region of critical importance to China—economically, politically, and strategically. It is also a region where Chinese policies can have an influence, in some instances a decisive influence. That is not the case with most other areas of the world. China, weak in almost every sense, including that of military capacity, is far from being a global power. Even its ability to influence regional events is limited—but here, at least, China's strategic policies can have an impact upon the USSR, its economic policies are of vital importance to Sino-Japanese relations, and its political policies will influence such diverse neighbors as North and South Korea, and Taiwan.

As is the case with its global policies, China's current actions in Northeast Asia are shaped in major degree by its hostility toward the Soviet Union. Indeed, Sino-Soviet relations have constituted one of the major variables of international relations in the second half of the twentieth century. After World War II, an alliance was consummated which united nearly a billion people and threatened to dominate the Eurasian continent. Yet in less than ten years that alliance broke apart, and a rising enmity ensued between the two Communist giants which has affected the policies of every nation in the world. What lies ahead? The likelihood of either a Sino-Soviet war or a restoration of the old alliance seems remote. War is very improbable because neither party could conceivably win such a conflict. Alliance is blocked by the fundamental differences that now mark each leadership's perceptions of its national interests. Vietnam and Afghanistan are only the most recent substantive issues which divide Peking and Moscow. The probable alternatives in Sino-Soviet relations are more limited: continuing hostility short of war, or a reduction of tension in the form of some limited, tactical detente. In the immediate future, the odds strongly favor the former alternative. There is nothing on the horizon to suggest that a Sino-Soviet rapprochement is imminent. In the longer run, some degree of accommodation—without love or trust—may be achieved, but that depends upon a host of variables, including China's relations with its Asian neighbors and with the United States.

As has been indicated, the USSR has a deep-seated fear of—some would say an obsession over—"the China problem." The Russian nightmare is that of an economically developed, politically unified, militarily strong nation of 1.3 billion, flexing its muscles in an expansionist manner and coveting the vast, underpopulated regions to the north and west. Such a vision may well be fanciful, but it has historic roots in the Russian experience, and it also reflects that combination of arrogance and inferiority, expansionism and defensiveness, that marks both Soviet policy and the Russian psyche. Nor is it an apprehension confined merely to the USSR. China's Asian neighbors also exhibit varying degrees of concern about the growth of a powerful and assertive China at some point in the future. And it is probably true that such a China would demand changes in relations with its border states and increased recognition of Peking as a regional, if not global, power.

Yet the immediate situation, as we have indicated, is not strength but weakness; and projections as to when or whether China will become a major power in the full sense of that term are hazardous indeed. Certainly, for the decade ahead PRC foreign policies will stem from China's fragility, not its power. From this fact flow several probabilities with respect to the Northeast Asian region. The status of the Mongolian People's Republic as a Soviet protectorate will not change. China will have a major stake in peace on the Korean Peninsula since any conflict would be seriously disruptive of Sino-Japanese and Sino-American relations.

It also seems likely that a period of time will elapse before any military threats could be mounted against Taiwan, thus enabling China-Taiwan relations to seek some regularized pattern. No one can predict with assurance what that pattern will be, but the chances of peaceful unification seem remote. One can hope that the chances of peaceful accommodation are much greater, and U.S. policy should be directed to that end.

Unfortunately, the Korean Peninsula will continue to represent a volatile region. Little help can be expected from Peking in resolving the Korean problem, since for China the first priority of this era lies in preventing the Soviet Union from completing its encirclement of the PRC by reestablishing its primacy in North Korea. Pyongyang is thus able to take advantage of the bitter Sino-Soviet quarrel by playing off one party against the other, at least up to a point. These circumstances suggest that the task for South Korea, the United States, and Japan is, first, to make North Korean aggression—particularly of the most likely Vietnam type—wholly unfeasible; second, to encourage South-North negotiations while standing firm on basic principles, rejecting any formula designed to abet communist domination; and finally, to insist that both the Soviet Union and China bear a responsibility for underwriting peace in this troubled region. In the final analysis, stability on the Korean Peninsula will come only when a modicum of agreement among the four major powers deeply concerned about Korea has been achieved, and when the Communist state in the North abandons efforts to achieve reunification of the Peninsula by force of arms.

China's relations with Japan will continue to be a critical aspect of any strategic equilibrium in Northeast Asia. In one sense, trends in Sino-Japanese relations fulfill a recurrent vision of earlier statesmen. Throughout the twentieth century, many Chinese—including Sun Yat-sen—saw Japan as the logical source of support for China's industrialization, and their dreams were matched by those of a diverse group of Japanese who held similar views. Earlier relations, however, were spoiled repeatedly by Japan's excesses and China's deficiencies of power. The clashes of rival nationalisms overwhelmed any potential for cooperation, leading to war and massive destruction. Ironically, as Mao Zedong himself once indicated, the Japanese—more than any other single factor—came to be responsible for the victory of communism in China. It is nevertheless ironic, if completely understandable, that today's Communist leaders are encouraging Japan to rebuild its military strength, confident that that strength will not be turned against China.

As we have indicated, it would be a grave mistake to assume that the new Sino-Japanese relationship signifies the advent of Pan-Asianism—the fulfillment of that goal of a relatively exclusivist, racially motivated regionalism which was the dream of certain Japanese and Chinese in the years before World War II. Asia today is much too diverse for such outmoded principles. Indeed, the Sino-Japanese tie will not even constitute an alliance of the conventional type. Rather, it will represent an alignment of states currently having certain economic and strategic interests in common. The relationship will not be without its difficulties, as recent events in the economic sphere have shown. China's modernization is bound to be a lengthy and painful process, replete with setbacks as well as successes. Nor is political stability assured at this point. Thus, there remains a tentativeness about the new interaction between China and Japan, and a series of tests lie ahead. Yet there is also a fundamental logic to the relationship, given the needs and capacities of these two highly diverse Sinic cultures.

In the new entente between Peking and Tokyo, one element is relatively weak, namely, military power. As we have indicated, the PRC's military forces are very antiquated for the most part, vastly inferior to those of the USSR, although probably serviceable for purely defensive purposes given China's geopolitical configuration. Japan, meanwhile, remains constrained in accepting any regional defense responsibilities by its constitution and the sentiments of a majority of its people.

Thus in the final analysis the issue of who will maintain a strategic balance in Northeast Asia still lies at the doorstep of the United States. The mutual security treaties with Japan and South Korea, combined with the growing "tilt" toward China, represent an American commitment of major proportions for which there is no immediate substitute, assuming the need to countervail a rising Soviet military presence in the region. U.S.

policies underwrite the emergence of two informal, unconnected regional "triangles" relating to military defense: the first, an American–Japanese–South Korean triangle; the second, an American–Japanese–Chinese triangle.

In addition to the question of burden sharing, current developments pose one critical strategic issue that is almost certain to preoccupy the Reagan administration as it did the Carter administration in its final years, namely, the question of how far the United States should go in consummating a de facto military alignment with the People's Republic of China. No American or Chinese leader currently is suggesting a formal military alliance, but the questions of whether the United States should sell military equipment and weaponry to the PRC, undertake some role in retraining the People's Liberation Army, and under some circumstances underwrite the security of China against the threat of Soviet attack have been and will be debated at many levels.

The arguments for a Sino-American—or, put more broadly, a Sino-American-Japanese—military alignment of substantial proportions are relatively simple. They relate first and foremost to Moscow's steady military expansion in Asia and elsewhere and to the perceived inability of any single nation—including the United States—to block such expansion effectively. If a meaningful balance of power is to be created in Asia, it is argued, it must include the two major nations of Northeast Asia as well as the United States. And there can be little doubt that if Soviet intrusions into the internal affairs of other nations continue—for example, in Poland—sentiment favorable to such a strategy will mount in the United States.

There are important considerations on the other side of the argument, however, that warrant attention. First, whatever our differences with the USSR—and they are both grave and likely to be long-standing—negotiations on global issues must continue if we are to avoid an unending series of catastrophes. Negotiations on such questions as strategic arms limitations and regional crises are inescapable unless we choose to pretend that the Soviet Union is not a global power. Such negotiations must be pursued by the United States from strength; but if the Russians perceive that we are committed to an anti-Soviet military alliance with China, the chances of meaningful negotiations in the near future are minimal, and the costs of the ensuing cold war are likely to be very high for all parties concerned, especially given the fragile nature of our economies.

Some advocates suggest that we can continue to "play the China card" as a means of inducing Soviet moderation, but in such a concept lies a serious deficiency. If we use military assistance to China as a lever upon Moscow, the implication is that should the Soviets moderate their policies, we would reduce or cease such aid. But in that case, the Chinese rightly would be angered, believing that they were being used as a pawn in a superpower game. The logic of military assistance is gradual escalation, with the implications for American-Soviet relations noted above.

There is an additional issue to be considered. Even if the commitment to defend China were indirect and only implicit in a military assistance program, it would add greatly to our military responsibilities without any requisite additions to our strategic capacities. Whatever the United States might do to assist China militarily, it certainly could not make it a match for the Soviet Union. The first effect, indeed, would be to strengthen the PRC against such states as Vietnam and Taiwan. The responsibility for meeting the Soviet Union would remain that of the United States.

Moreover, a military entente with China is not favored by any of America's major allies. Neither the states of Western Europe nor Japan want to see this development take place, under present circumstances at least. Hence, it would be a policy contributing more to disunity among allies than to unity.

There remains the issue of China's internal stability and, related to this, its future direction in foreign policy. As has been indicated, two basic alternatives would appear to exist, and it is possible to argue that unless China receives U.S. military assistance, the likelihood of Sino-Soviet rapprochement increases. But it can also be argued that it will be the capacity of the United States to serve as a global countervailing force to Soviet power—together with basic internal trends within the PRC and Soviet policies—that will play the major role in determining future Sino-Soviet relations. The truly critical determinant may well be the ability of the present leadership to make China's economic, social, and political policies work.

In the final analysis, the United States as well as Japan has a very considerable stake in an economically developing, politically stable China, and it is to this end that primary American attention should be devoted. China's current leadership has recognized that its first priority lies in raising agricultural and industrial productivity, not in a rapid military build-up. Such policies may well have their critics, particularly within military circles, and there are recurrent rumors that elements within the People's Liberation Army are not happy with many of the present-day policies. But these are eminently rational policies for China, and for the world. They deserve our support, since it is through these policies that China can contribute most to a peaceful, developing Asia.

Lucian W. Pye

8

The China Factor
in Southeast Asia

The former colonial countries of Southeast Asia gained independence and started their search for a place in the world scene at about the same time that the People's Republic of China (PRC) was established, a coincidence which leaders in Peking like to bring up with Southeast Asians, hinting that they, therefore, have much in common. Southeast Asians have generally rejected the further suggestion that China might properly be taken as a "model" for their development, or at least be recognized as their superior and, hence, natural leader. In the three decades since the establishment of the PRC, all the governments of Southeast Asia have had ambivalent and volatile feelings about their enormous neighbor to the north.

Indeed, the record of changing attitudes toward China by all the governments of Southeast Asia should be an embarrassment to geopolitical theorists who hold that geography and power

LUCIAN W. PYE *is Ford International Professor of Political Science at the Massachusetts Institute of Technology and a specialist in Asian political behavior. His numerous publications include* Guerrilla Communism in Malaya; Politics, Personality, and Nation-Building; The Spirit of Chinese Politics; *and* Mao Tse-tung: The Man in the Leader.

can provide guiding constants to world politics. The relations of geography and power have not changed, but nearly every country in the region has gone through a total reversal in their feelings of amity or enmity toward China. Indeed, those countries which were once the most suspicious and distrustful of China, such as Singapore, Thailand, and the Philippines, have now become Peking's strongest defenders in the region—which is not to say that they are particularly friendly, except for the fact that China's former close friends, such as Vietnam and its communist satellites which once professed to be as close to China as "lips to teeth," have become fighting enemies. And Indonesia, which was once Peking's leading noncommunist friend before the breakdown in relations in 1965, still refuses to reestablish diplomatic relations with the People's Republic of China.

As the PRC now enters its fourth decade it has three distinct patterns of relations with the different Southeast Asian countries. First, there is the bristly hatred between Peking and Hanoi and its puppet governments in Phnom Penh and Vientiane. Second, there are the complicated friend-foe relations with the five countries of the Association of Southeast Asian Nations (ASEAN)—Thailand, Malaysia, Indonesia, Singapore, and the Philippines. Each of these countries has its own particular views about China, but collectively ASEAN has been tilting increasingly toward greater, but still guarded, friendship with China. Finally, there is the separate pattern of Sino-Burmese relations, a case of tremulous protestation of friendship by the weak and haughty condescension, salted with acts of bullying, by the strong—in short, a modernized version of the ancient Chinese tribute system through which the Celestial Empire once sought to dominate Southeast Asia.

As is well known, the Chinese historically thought of themselves as the center of the civilized world and believed that all "barbarian" peoples were contending for the blessing of a suzerain relationship with their august imperial court, which was the hub of the tributary system. Southeast Asians, with the exception of the Sinified Vietnamese, saw the relationship in a somewhat different light. Although several of the principal kingdoms at one time or another periodically sent tribute missions to the Han court, Southeast Asian rulers were never as intimidated by China as the Chinese believed them to be. From earliest times the Southeast Asians, living on natural maritime crossroads, conceived of the world as multipolar. Indeed, they were far more sensitive to other civilizations than the Sinic: politically they modeled their governments after the Hindu concept of the state; in religion they embraced Buddhism, Islam, and Christianity; and culturally they borrowed very little from the Chinese—a fact which has punctured Chinese pretensions of superiority toward Southeast Asians. Emissaries involved in the tributary exchanges discovered that Chinese mandarins took themselves exceedingly seriously and hence could be easily disarmed by flattery.

During the colonial era China became even more irrelevant to Southeast Asians. They were, of course, aware of the tides of Chinese migrants, but China as a political factor barely existed for them. Thus, it was only after World War II that the complex and readily changeable relations began to take shape between a Communist-ruled China and the newly independent states of Southeast Asia.

Before we examine how the different patterns between them happened to evolve, we should take note of the peculiar perspective the United States brought to its understanding of the relations between China and Southeast Asia. Before World War II Americans stubbornly dissociated themselves from the problems of Southeast Asia as a region. In spite of, or maybe psychologically more correctly because of, our position in the Philippines, we would have nothing to do with the French, British, and Dutch colonial authorities. Consequently the birth of conscious American policy making toward Southeast Asia occurred in the context of the Communist victory in China and the emergence of independent states in Southeast Asia which were perceived to be fragile and vulnerable to subversion.

With this limited perspective of history, the United States adopted a new version of a "China-centered" Asia. The Korean War, followed by the prolonged tragedy of Vietnam, confirmed the American view that Southeast Asia should be understood largely in terms of our perceptions of China. As our relations with the PRC have changed, so we expect, from our ethnocentric perspective, that the orientations of the Southeast Asian states should also change. First, when we were seeking recruits for SEATO, we vigorously preached that China was more of a menace than Southeast Asians were inclined to believe; and now that Washington has opened relations with Peking we are equally active in trying to change the thinking of Southeast Asians and make them believe that the PRC is more benign than they suspect it to be.

Aside from this long record of rubbing many Southeast Asians the wrong way because of our tendency to make China the dominant factor in our approach to Southeast Asia, American policy, ironically, has worked against the Southeast Asian natural inclination for a multipolar world, the very diversified and pluralistic world which presumably has been the goal of America's foreign policy. Thus, the Southeast Asians would have welcomed the United States as a permanent major actor in the region, helping to bring balance in the relations of Southeast Asian states with their former colonial rulers, with a dynamic Japan, and, of course, with the two Communist powers, Peking and Moscow. But the Southeast Asians seem to feel that Washington has been too erratic and too absorbed with China to be an effective pole. At times we were too "involved" and domineering, and now we are seen as "abandoning" the region and losing interest in our relations there.

We are, however, getting ahead of our story even as we set down some of the themes which run through the role of the China factor in Southeast Asia and its consequences for American policy. We must now return to the early relationships between the countries of the region and the PRC.

Initial Fear and Awe of the People's Republic of China

Even before the People's Liberation Army had achieved victory in the Chinese civil war, most of the Communist Parties in Southeast Asia had attempted some form of "war of national liberation." Beginning in December 1945, the Viet Minh, under the leadership of Ho Chi Minh, had started fighting the French Expeditionary Force in Indochina. And in February 1948, at the Calcutta meeting of the Asian Youth Conference, the "Zhdanov line" of armed struggle was passed on to representatives of other Southeast Asian Parties. Shortly afterward came the prolonged Malayan Emergency, the short-lived uprising at Madiun of the Indonesian Communist Party (PKI), and the several-years-long uprising of the *Hukbalahap* movement in the Philippines. When Mao Zedong proclaimed the establishment of the PRC on October 1, 1949, the message sent to Southeast Asia was that the various Communist Parties should continue to follow Moscow's line of "armed struggle," and that this could best be done by copying the Chinese model of revolutionary warfare by first winning over the "countryside" and then seizing control of the "cities." By November of 1949, PRC Vice Chairman Liu Shaoqi was telling delegates attending the Asian and Australiasian Trade Union Conference in Peking that "armed struggle is the main form of struggle for the national liberation of many colonies and semicolonies."

During the period of the Korean War and until late 1952 Peking persisted in claiming that the newly independent countries of Southeast Asia were still under the control of their former masters and that armed struggle by local Communists was the only hope for liberation. At that time the Chinese leaders still refused to believe that there could be "neutrals" and asserted that everybody had to "lean to one side or the other." Thus, even though proudly neutralist Burma was the first noncommunist state to recognize the PRC, Peking remained hostile toward the new government in Rangoon and established ties with the Burmese Communist Party.

By 1954, largely as a result of the persistent pleading of New Delhi, the revolutionary leaders in Peking began to take a more positive view of "neutralism." In June of that year, the Chinese subscribed to the Indian concept of the "Five Principles of Peaceful Coexistence," and by the time of the Bandung Conference in April of the next year, the Chinese were enthusiastically calling for the strengthening of the nonaligned movement. Some of the Southeast Asian leaders, particularly the Indonesians, welcomed this softening of Chinese policies in favor of "peaceful coexistence," but the majority remained suspicious of Chinese intentions, particularly because Peking continued to call upon the Southeast Asian Communist Parties to overthrow their governments.

It was at this time that the Chinese, emulating the Soviets, began advancing the argument that friendly state-to-state relations should not preclude close Party-to-Party relations, even when the particular Party was trying to overthrow the government. To this day Peking clings to the peculiar notion that Party and state relations are separate matters, a view which has become one of the most serious obstacles to improving Chinese relations with Southeast Asian governments. When Vice Premier Deng Xiaoping visited Kuala Lumpur and Singapore in 1978, he found it necessary to preserve China's revolutionary credentials by saying, to the distress of his hosts, that China would continue to support the Malayan Communist Party which was still engaged in insurgency. In May of 1980 Foreign Minister Huang Hua upset Jakarta's plans for normalizing relations with the PRC by reenunciating in Bangkok the doctrine of the legitimacy of Peking's support for revolutionary movements in countries with whom China would like to have good state-to-state relations.

To this day the Chinese persist in three "revolutionary" practices which are profoundly disturbing to many Southeast Asian leaders who otherwise would welcome closer relations with the PRC. First, Peking continues to give at least lip service to the goal of communist insurgency in noncommunist Southeast Asia. Second, the Chinese maintain communications with Southeast Asian Communist Parties, including those in Burma and Malaysia which are engaged in fighting their governments; and Peking continues to broadcast revolutionary appeals in Southeast Asian languages. Third, Peking welcomes and gives sanctuary to revolutionary Southeast Asian leaders who are wanted by their governments.

During the 1950s and 1960s not all the governments in Southeast Asia were troubled by China's dual revolutionary and peaceful coexistence image. Although, as we shall shortly see, Hanoi was on occasion slightly miffed by Peking's policies, in the main North Vietnam was reassured by having an increasingly strong China as an immediate neighbor. In Kampuchea, Prince Norodom Sihanouk steadily became more confident about his ability to call upon Peking to balance off Washington and Saigon. The boldest attempt of any Southeast Asian leader to turn China's revolutionary pretensions to his advantage was unquestionably President Sukarno's policies, which eventually led to Indonesia's withdrawal from the United Nations of which

the PRC was not then a member. As an alternative to the
United Nations, Sukarno established the Newly Emerging
Forces which, while never capturing the imagination of the
Third World as intended, did stimulate talk of a "Peking–
Phnom Penh–Jakarta Axis." Sukarno's fanciful use of the image
of a revolutionary China stemmed partly from his foreign
policy ambitions, which took the form of asserting Indonesia's
leadership of Southeast Asia by engaging in "confrontation"
with Singapore and Malaysia which, he claimed, were not truly
independent of Britain. In addition, for domestic political reasons Sukarno sought to publicize his acceptability to Peking
as a way of trying to manage the Indonesian Communist Party.
The Communist-attempted coup of September 30, 1965, which
put Sukarno on the skids, was the decisive event which fundamentally changed Indonesia's feeling of friendship for the PRC
to those of a still-abiding distrust and hostility.

China was a factor in the domestic politics of most Southeast
Asian countries throughout the 1950s and 1960s because of
questions about the loyalties of the overseas Chinese. Even
before the period of European colonialism, Chinese had settled
in parts of Southeast Asia; and indeed the Chinese came to call
the region *Nan Yang* or "Southern Region" as though it were
a part of China proper comparable to what they call North
China, *Bei Yang*. During the colonial period, however, the
Chinese migrations expanded greatly and created problems in
race relations in several of the countries. The problem was
especially troublesome because Chinese monopolized much of
the local marketing and money lending operations, causing one
of the kings of Thailand to call them for the first time "the
Jews of the Orient." After independence it was easy for Europeans and Americans to return home, but the Chinese, divided
in their loyalties between the Communists, the Nationalists,
and the lands of their birth, generally had no realistic choice
but to stay where they were and become, in the words of a
thoughtful citizen of Singapore, "the last living remnants of
the colonial era."

Thus out of the crude intuitions of racial sentiments the
emerging nationalism of Southeast Asia found China to be the
targeted enemy, second only to their former colonial powers.
As China's prestige grew with the flood of propaganda about

Peking's new Communist regime, young overseas Chinese took manifest pride in the "mother country," and thereby convinced Southeast Asians that they were indeed potential fifth columns for the massive, revolutionary power to the north.

The experience of Burma during this period was most illuminating about the problems inherent for Southeast Asian countries in trying to get along with an increasingly powerful, self-assured, and revolutionary China. It is also important for understanding the apparent Chinese belief in the efficacy of intimidation toward smaller neighbors which surfaced as recently as in Peking's attempt to "teach a lesson" to Vietnam. The fact that Burma was the first noncommunist country to recognize the PRC did not bring it expected blessings, but rather seemed only to convince Peking that Rangoon was ripe for intimidation.

At every turn and in very imaginative ways the Chinese sought to drive home the point that Burma existed only at China's sufferance. Behind the high walls of its aloof embassy huge numbers of Chinese engaged in no recognizable diplomatic activities, but secretively flowed in and out as they made contacts with elements in the country who were not a part of the open political process. On occasion, when the Burmese would turn down an American request on the grounds that it would violate Burmese neutrality, as, for example, when they refused to allow a Rangoon University hall to be used for an American cultural exhibit, the Chinese would demand and get what the Americans had been refused because of their willingness to make explicit threats. When the Burmese and Chinese were negotiating their border differences, the Chinese chief negotiator, before the beginning of one of the sessions, asked his Burmese opposite number the population of Burma, and when told he commented, "We Chinese in one year can produce as many people as you have gotten after all of history."

Burma's relations with China have been exceedingly correct, wrapped in protestations of friendship, but basically filled with anxieties and the hopeless wish that China did not have to be such an omnipresent neighbor. General Ne Win, on eleven visits to Peking, has sought to soothe the Chinese with flattery.

In sum, during the first decade and a half of its existence, the PRC was seen by a majority of the leaders of Southeast

Asia as a rising menace. The exceptions were the men in Hanoi who spoke the language of world revolution, and Su-karno and Sihanouk in whose fervid minds glowed the illusion of manipulating China to their own interest. (The irony, of course, is that Vietnam and Indonesia were to become the fierc-est foes of China by the end of the next two decades, while Kampuchea was to be led into autogenocide by leaders who pro-fessed allegiance to Peking.) In the rest of Southeast Asia the PRC was seen in varying degrees as first, an ideological threat because of its espousal of revolution and its claim to having the secret of national development and economic miracles. Second, China was an insult to Southeast Asian nationalism because of its attractiveness to their ethnic Chinese who believed that an emerging, powerful China made it unnecessary for them to wholeheartedly support their countries of residence. Third, there was the basic geopolitical reality: the influence of a strong, united China had historically always spilled over its borders, and, therefore, the fragile, inchoate states neighboring the new China quite properly felt the need to take warning. Thailand, the Philippines, and South Vietnam responded by seeking closer ties with China's major antagonist, a perceived-to-be-powerful United States. Others sought security through nonalignment and a variety of ways of expressing their dis-tinctive degrees of neutralism.

This era of fear and awe of China came to an end as the result of two watershed events, the Cultural Revolution in China and the Vietnam War, especially its outcome.

The Watershed of the Cultural Revolution and the Vietnam War

The Great Proletarian Cultural Revolution—that season of unbridled madness for all China, when millions of possessed youths desecrated China's past greatness in their frenzy of idiocy, when the structures of government and Party were torn asunder and left near impotent, and which finally left a society permeated with abiding hatreds—destroyed throughout South-east Asia the image of China as either inspiring or fearsome. The monster that was China was suddenly absorbed in self-destruction of such a level that Vice Premier Deng Xiaoping was later to say that maybe Mao Zedong had killed more people than Stalin, and senior PRC officials were to claim that over three million Chinese had been killed and 100 million had suffered in the Cultural Revolution.

After a period of puzzled wonderment at such folly, China became a target of scorn for many Southeast Asians. It forfeited all claims of being a relevant "model," particularly after it had become clear that China's economic growth had been set back by decades, and that at least a generation of educated professionals had been destroyed. Only the most ideologically blinded of radicals could find merit in such revolutionary antics. Unlike in the United States, where a generation of parents unnerved by the drug culture and the antiwar protests of rebellious offspring felt the need to reach out to a youth culture that rejoiced in Maoist sentiments, in Southeast Asia adults felt no constraints in denouncing the absurdity of Mao's China. Consequently, even within the overseas Chinese communities, awe of the motherland evaporated.

Then in 1969 the *coup de grâce* to the image of a menacing China came with the news that Russian and Chinese troops were actually fighting each other. Southeast Asian leaders instantly recognized that unless China quickly sobered up it would have a permanent military problem on its northern borders and, hence, would no longer dare risk adventures to the south. For the next decade China ceased being a major factor in Southeast Asia.

As the threat of China receded, Southeast Asian leaders had to take more serious account of Vietnam, particularly after the United States withdrew from the war and Hanoi pushed on to victory. The immediate effect of the fall of Saigon in 1975 was the strengthening of ASEAN, even as all of the leaders of the five governments protested to the skies that they would never allow that association of peace-loving states to become a collective security arrangement, especially one directed against Hanoi, to whom all five signaled their desire for friendly relations. On the other hand, all the leaders in the region had to take note of the fact that Hanoi now possessed a huge arsenal of modern arms. Indeed, once the war booty taken with the collapse of the South was added to the generous Soviet supplies which had been massed for the final victory, Vietnam became one of the world's most heavily armed countries. Militarily it towered above the rest of Southeast Asia. The first response of the other countries of the region was prudence, if not timidity, and the avoidance of any provocations.

When by 1978 it had become clear that no effort to mollify the strongest country in the region would prevent it from trying, at the least, to consolidate control over the Indochina Peninsula, the ASEAN leaders rediscovered China as a factor in Southeast Asia, but this time a more positive one. As a consequence of its feud with Hanoi and its determination to "teach a lesson" to Vietnam for its internal policies and its reliance upon the Soviet Union in conquering China's only friend in the region, Kampuchea, the PRC was welcomed, more by some than by others, as a stabilizing force that could counter an aggressive Vietnam.

Before turning to the China factor in the current tensions between ASEAN and Vietnam over the latter's conquest of Kampuchea, we need to examine in some detail how the two Communist powers of China and Vietnam could so dramatically and completely dissolve their pledges of brotherhood and come to actual blows.

From Allies "As Close As Lips to Teeth" to "Teaching Lessons" by Warfare

Stalin's remarkable success in creating for a brief period the phenomenon of monolithic communism has caused most people to forget that the natural order among Marxists is ceaseless schisms, splits, and feuds which, since before the First International, have made a sham of the ideal of socialist solidarity. It should not be surprising, therefore, that communist governments are quick to fight each other, be it Russia and China, China and Vietnam, or Vietnam and Kampuchea. Yet the speed with which Peking and Hanoi went from profuse pledges of undying friendship to vituperation and mutual imprecations and then to actual conflict was astonishing even for Marxists.

Almost as surprising is the lack of serious Western analysis of how this conflict came about, a conflict which is likely to be second only to the Sino-Soviet feud in reshaping the Asian international system. An examination of published analyses in American papers and journals reveals that for all intents and purposes only two very simplistic theories have been advanced to explain this historic falling-out of Peking and Hanoi. The first theory, which implicitly puts the onus on Vietnam, holds that because of "history" there is an abiding hatred between Vietnamese and Chinese. The second theory sees the Chinese as the initiators of the feud because of their near "paranoid" suspicion of anyone on good terms with the Soviet Union. When the two theories are indiscriminately mixed, as they usually are, and treated as two aspects of a single "explanation," then there is, of course, no longer an unambiguous instigator of the difficulties, and thus the conflict can be said to have been "inevitable," which means that no further explanations are necessary.

One does not need to be a pesky skeptic of orthodoxies to flaw both theories. It is true that the Vietnamese make much of their heroic opposition to Chinese conquerors and of the stout-hearted resistance of such national heroines as the Trung sisters. Yet there is also the fact that the Vietnamese take profound pride in their Confucian and Mahayana Buddhist traditions, both of which came from China and which incline them to believe that they are superior to all other Southeast Asians. Oddly, many of the American writers who advance this "explanation" also argue that the United States should give aid to Hanoi in order to heal the wounds of the war. What strange psyches the Vietnamese must have if $12 billion in Chinese aid given during the war could not erase their ancient historic memories, but a much more modest American gift can make them forget more immediate hatreds. As for the second theory, is it really conceivable that the leaders in Peking are so witless as to throw away whatever influence they had in Hanoi just because of the intensity of their anti-Soviet feelings? If this is the logic of Chinese foreign policy, then any country wishing balanced relations with Peking and Moscow must expect the enmity of China.

We cannot hope to examine in these few pages all the factors which contributed to the Sino-Vietnamese conflict, but we can try to indicate their complexity and why the consequences of this confrontation are likely to be the dominant considerations affecting the China factor in Southeast Asia for the indefinite future.

In a Vietnamese "White Paper" published in 1978 that presents Hanoi's side of the case, it is argued that China first "betrayed" Vietnam at the 1954 Geneva Conference in Indochina. At that time Hanoi was unquestionably following the Chinese "model," for its policies in almost every field, including agriculture, were carbon copies of Peking's post-1949 practices. Yet according to the Vietnamese, Zhou Enlai at Geneva worked closely with the French to prevent a total Communist victory. Taking advantage of the fact that China was the main supplier of arms to the Viet Minh forces, Zhou pushed for a "Korean-type" solution which allowed for a South Vietnam regime. Zhou's professed concern was the danger of American involvement in Indochina, and he used this danger to pressure the Vietnamese into making concessions.

During the next decade Chinese aid and advice to Hanoi was extensive. The Vietnamese felt at times that the Chinese were heavy-handed, while the Chinese saw the Vietnamese as nipping the hand that fed them. Serious tensions began to build up as the North's involvement in the insurgency in the South mounted. The Chinese privately kept counseling caution and the need to avoid escalation above guerrilla operations, while publicly declaring that they would not fight in defense of Vietnam but only engage their forces if the United States attacked Chinese territory.

Indeed, throughout Hanoi's war the Chinese argued for strategies which the Vietnamese saw as demeaning and not what they wished to hear from a friend and ally. The Chinese basically did not want a turbulent situation on their borders which might throw them off course on their domestic development plans and prove to be exceedingly costly, as the Korean War had been. After the heavy American involvement in the war began, the Chinese continued to advise Hanoi not to increase the level of fighting in the South and to follow a more "protracted war" strategy. Taking to heart the American pledges given at the Warsaw ambassadorial talks, the Chinese leaders told Hanoi that the United States would not invade the North. China insisted that since the territory of North Vietnam was secure, Hanoi should avoid undue costs and impatient adventurism in seeking to win the South. In May 1966 Mao Zedong personally vetoed a proposal for a formal declaration of socialist solidarity in support of Hanoi and of opposition to the United States, an act which Hanoi believed to be inconsistent with being a loyal ally.

Mao's real blow to Hanoi's war effort, however, was the Cultural Revolution. At a moment when Hanoi believed itself to be engaged in a heroic struggle in the name of the proletariat of the world, Mao decreed that "revisionism" was a greater danger than "imperialism," and then by the self-destructive madness of the Cultural Revolution he made China *hors de combat* as far as even bluffing the threat of Chinese involvement in the Vietnam conflict. To add insult to injury, Peking subsequently engaged in all manner of harassments that impeded the flow of Soviet military supplies through China to Vietnam, while at the same time reducing Chinese aid. Indeed, between 1968 and 1970 there was a 50 percent decline in Chinese aid. Vietnam's sense of frustration and impotence reached a new high in 1969 when it could only haplessly look on with horror at Chinese and Russian troops shooting at each other along the Sino-Soviet frontier.

Yet for Hanoi the worst was yet to come. The ultimate act of Chinese betrayal of a beleaguered ally was Mao's decision to invite Dr. Henry Kissinger and President Richard Nixon to Peking while Vietnam was still fighting the war and stubbornly holding out in the peace negotiations. Peking could pretend that its policy of opening friendly relations with the United States was little different from Moscow's policy of seeking detente with Washington. But for Hanoi it was a profoundly different matter. Mao had allowed the United States to cover its impending failure in Vietnam with the aura of great success. The Vietnamese conflict, which had long commanded a central place in world politics, had suddenly been trivialized and in its place in shaping the international system was the new superpower triangle of Peking-Washington-Moscow. Peking had pulled the carpet out from under Hanoi and completely demoted the importance of Vietnam in world affairs.

Peking's self-righteous proclamation of the merits of expanding relations with Washington must have been especially galling to Hanoi because in 1968, when Hanoi had first agreed

to engage the United States in the Paris peace talks, it was
China who denounced the move by arguing that "the Vietnam
question can be solved only by completely defeating the U.S.
aggressor on the battlefield and driving it out of South
Vietnam."

Thus, when victory finally came for the Vietnamese they felt
isolated and no longer able to manage the Sino-Soviet dispute
to their advantage. Before 1965 China had provided more than
twice the amount of aid that the Soviet Union gave, and by
1966 China had over 40,000 technicians in Vietnam. In contrast, the Soviets were just beginning to go beyond their token
$35 million a year in military supplies. By the end of the war
Soviet aid was three times China's and had almost completely
replaced Chinese military assistance. This reversal of prime
supplier of military aid turned out to be critical for the success
of General Van Tien Dung's offensive in the spring of 1975
which captured Saigon, since only the Russians could provide
the requisite heavy equipment. Yet peace left Hanoi in a most
awkward situation because Hanoi was now more than ever
dependent upon Soviet generosity. But Vietnam was desperate
for precisely the kinds of economic aid which China rather than
Moscow could supply, such as half a million tons of rice a year,
substantial quantities of meat, vegetables, cooking oil, textiles,
and all the types of small consumer items which are so vital in
making an Asian population believe that its standard of living
is improving.

With the war won by a strategy contrary to China's advice,
Zhou Enlai felt it was appropriate to inform Le Duan that
China would have to look to improving the welfare of its own
needy population. Thus Peking would be scaling down its
assistance and thereafter providing only technical assistance on
joint venture projects. To drive home the point that China
would be looking after its own interests, Peking also informed
Hanoi that its victory would not alter China's claims to the
Paracel Islands which PLA troops had taken by force from the
Saigon government in January 1974. China's absolutely uncompromising position on the Paracels and the Spratleys was
more than an unneighborly attitude; it checkmated Hanoi's
hopes for a foreign exchange bonanza based on being able to
lease clear titles for offshore drilling in the South China Sea.

During 1976 and 1977 the two countries drifted further apart. China was absorbed with domestic problems relating to the succession struggle after Mao Zedong, while the Vietnamese were concentrating on postwar reconstruction. By 1977, however, it was inescapably apparent even to the most dedicated revolutionaries in Hanoi that they were flailing about with a program that could neither integrate North and South Vietnam nor revive the war-ravaged economy. With this awareness came an even deeper sense of isolation and, consequently, greater dependence upon the Soviet Union. A crisis of confidence spread throughout the leadership in Hanoi as increasing numbers of cadres discovered with their own eyes that the realities of South Vietnamese life were entirely unrelated to what they had been taught in their propaganda. At the Fourth Party Congress, in what must be one of history's most extreme examples of rulers losing all touch with reality, Vietnamese leaders proclaimed a five-year plan that called for $7 billion in foreign assistance. Vietnamese propaganda could joyfully proclaim that "we have friends everywhere"; yet where did they imagine they could get help on that scale? In a year's time, the plan was abandoned.

By early spring 1977 the regime had to acknowledge that lacking the wherewithal to procure fertilizers the country was permanently faced with an annual rice shortage of some two million tons; and as for the cities, there was neither the capital nor the managerial skills to produce the two to three million new jobs a year necessary to busy idle hands. It was in this context that the leaders first began to push their version of a "deurbanization policy" which was not as violent as the one promoted by Pol Pot's government in Kampuchea nor as large scale as the PRC's program of sending "educated" youth to the countryside. It involved little more than declaring the existence of "New Economic Zones" to which city people were deported and left largely to fend for themselves.

All of Vietnam's rehabilitation problems would have been much easier if the country could have received Chinese help. Instead, Peking continued to isolate Vietnam and to increase its support for the appallingly brutal regime of Pol Pot in Kampuchea. This was a government which had no need whatsoever for any form of economic aid or consumer goods, since it had a mind only for exterminating educated people, but which welcomed gifts of the small caliber military weapons which China had in abundance, now that they were not being sent to Vietnam.

As tensions developed between a defiant Kampuchea and a frustrated Vietnam, relations between Peking and Hanoi further deteriorated. Pol Pot, while visiting Peking, publicized Kampuchea's border problems with Vietnam. Vietnam responded with a dual campaign of domestically calling for "military preparedness" while in foreign affairs actively courting the ASEAN states. As we have already noted, this was a period in which all the ASEAN governments were holding out the olive branch to Vietnam. In addition, they were dumbfounded by the inhumanity of those who called themselves Kampucheans. The specter of Peking's power coming to the aid of the brutes of Phnom Penh made it easier for the Southeast Asian leaders to be gracious toward the Vietnamese.

In the meantime Pham Van Dong had prolonged his visit to Moscow; and almost immediately upon his and General Giap's return to Hanoi there were reports of clashes along the Kampuchean border. The pattern of "border incidents" soon spread to the north as Chinese and Vietnamese border guards became more aggressive in their dealings with each other. By the end of 1977 Hanoi was obviously more dependent upon the Soviets, who in turn were becoming bolder in Asia. In contrast, Washington was conspicuously more passive. The earlier maneuver of opening relations with Peking had not been followed up with normalization, and it was widely assumed that the Carter administration had decided that it should put normalization with China on a "back burner" while giving priority to the SALT negotiations and better relations with Moscow. At the time, a steady stream of Soviet officers was visiting Hanoi, including General Epishev who had played a major role in the invasion of Czechoslovakia in 1968. Soviet naval forces were also more actively patrolling Asian waters, raising concern among the Japanese public for their security.

At the end of 1977 Hanoi made the critical decision to give up any effort at balancing off Peking and Moscow and to throw in its lot with the richer, albeit more distant, Soviet Union. At this point the Chinese realized that instead of being able to dismiss Vietnam with a snub, it was they who were in danger of being isolated. For the moment the initiative seemed to lie with Hanoi and Moscow.

In January 1978, with considerable fanfare, Vietnamese forces poured into Kampuchea—but with no telling effect, since Pol Pot's troops merely dissolved into the jungles. The lack of any significant structure of government in this pathetic country meant that there was nothing to be shattered. It was like poking a pile of feathers. The purpose of the action, as was later revealed, was to test Chinese reactions—to see what risks Peking was prepared to take in support of its new-found friends in Phnom Penh. The Chinese demonstrated extraordinary self-restraint, a quality of character which was widely admired in American circles but which seemed to signal only opportunity to Moscow and Hanoi. There were no bitter denunciations from Peking but rather an even-handed appeal to both the Vietnamese and the Cambodians to settle their differences peacefully. To emphasize its pacific mood, Peking sent the widow of Zhou Enlai on an official visit to Hanoi. This measure was to be emphasized in the long list of self-justifying, if not self-pitying, items which became the grist of China's propaganda mill in the year ahead.

Hanoi and Moscow read the passiveness of the Chinese at the time to mean that they could push to the limit without fear of provoking serious counteractions. The Chinese, however, soon realized their mistake. Consequently, in March 1978, when the Vietnamese nationalized all remaining forms of small trade (thus ending the economic role long monopolized by people of Chinese extraction) and at the same time called for a more vigorous policy of sending urban residents to the New Economic Zones, Peking surprisingly unleashed a torrent of vitriolic denunciations of Hanoi. This Chinese outburst frightened the ASEAN governments, who were troubled at the prospect of Peking reversing its long-established policy toward overseas Chinese who were citizens of Southeast Asian countries. Peking's vigorous insistence that it had a legitimate right to protect the interests of Vietnamese of Chinese extraction meant that China might also intervene in support of overseas Chinese in other countries.

Hanoi angrily responded by pointing out that the Chinese government had long ago compelled all Chinese merchants within China to end their activities, and that Peking had also sent some twenty million of its urban residents to "rusticate" on communes and state farms. The Vietnamese insisted that it was ludicrous for Peking to complain that in practicing social-ism the Vietnamese were "taking away people's life savings." After all, what was communism supposed to be all about? To rub in the point, Hanoi's propaganda suggested that the Chi-nese were worse than unenlightened capitalists since they were complaining more than "Washington had when Cardenas took over American oil investments in Mexico." In any case Vietnam was only following the Chinese example in these domestic policies, and furthermore it was none of China's business what Vietnam did domestically.

Hypocritical or not, Peking's complaints became steadily shriller, thereby fueling the anxieties of the *Hoa Kieu,* "over-seas Chinese," who, in increasing numbers, were fleeing over-land into Yunnan, or were taking out to sea in the tragic drama of the "boat people." In the midst of a cacophony of Chinese propaganda, the voice of Deng Xiaoping soon took command, declaring first that Vietnam was the "Cuba of Asia" and what was happening was the work of the "Polar Bear," and that soon China would have to "take harsher measures" against Vietnam.

Thus Peking, in the spring of 1978, completely abandoned its passiveness toward Hanoi and dramatically raised the level of confrontation. On May 12 the Chinese withdrew all of their technicians from twenty-one projects in Vietnam; and on May 30 they closed the remaining fifty-one joint projects. On June 17 they ordered the Vietnamese to close their consulates in the PRC. The significance the Chinese attached to these actions can only be appreciated by recalling that when Nikita Khrush-chev withdrew Soviet technicians from China in 1960, the Chinese for more than a decade afterwards fumed about what they called the most despicable and shameless thing a stronger power could do to a weak and poor country. Next to the theme that the Soviets had become "revisionist"—a theme which in-cidently disappeared from Chinese propaganda after the enun-ciation of the Four Modernizations—the second most damning charge against the Russians was that they had departed China in the summer of 1960 taking with them the blueprints for over 160 unfinished projects. And now China was doing the

same thing to Hanoi. Unquestionably, Deng Xiaoping intended
to inflict severe and lasting damage on Vietnam.

As the tensions between China and Vietnam mounted, and
as the ASEAN countries took care to provoke neither side, the
two protagonists began looking over their shoulders to the two
superpowers to see what threats or advantages they might offer.
Even as Hanoi was moving closer to the Soviet Union, it also
sought to open a dialogue with the United States in the hope
of gaining diplomatic recognition and a substantial sum of
foreign aid. Again, an indication of the unrealistic state of
mind of the Vietnamese leaders was their bizarre notion that
in spite of their blatant violations of the Paris Accords the U.S.
Congress might still vote the aid which President Richard
Nixon had suggested would be forthcoming if Hanoi abided
by the cease-fire agreement. Even before the Chinese escalated
their pressures on Hanoi, the Vietnamese leaders seemingly took
heart from minor developments. A mission of American businessmen, largely based in Hong Kong, visited Hanoi and spoke
about the prospects of rapid growth of trade and aid if normalization took place; and then on April 21 President Carter took
an initiative which Hanoi must have welcomed when he publicly condemned the Pol Pot regime in Kampuchea as "the
worst violator of human rights in the world today."

In spite of Carter's criticism of its ally, Kampuchea, Peking
happily found that Washington was about to bestir itself in
Sino-American relations. Right in the midst of the two-phased
Chinese withdrawal of technicians from Vietnam, but more
obviously following upon the first Marxist coup in Afghanistan,
the President's national security adviser, Zbigniew Brzezinski,
visited Peking and caused something of a stir at the Great Wall
when he threw out the challenge, "The last one to the top of
the wall takes on the Polar Bear." (The woman who was the
object of the challenge has since been purged and sent to the
countryside for "reeducation.") Brzezinski's trip was followed
by a succession of pilgrimages to Peking by high American
officials, each of whom was anxious to claim greater accomplishments than his predecessors in building U.S.–China
relations.

At that time Washington was, like Gaul, divided into three
parts. Secretary of State Cyrus Vance was giving primacy to

improving relations with Moscow and completing negotiations of the SALT II Treaty. He was thus very hesitant to annoy the Soviets by dealing with Peking. At the National Security Council, Brzezinski was more convinced than ever after his first visit to Peking that the best way to raise the level of civility in Soviet-American relations was to have cordial dealings with China. And in the State Department's Bureau of East Asian and Pacific Affairs, Assistant Secretary Richard Holbrooke was seemingly committed to the well-intended but strategically questionable policy of achieving the early normalization of America's relations with Hanoi, or at least preventing those relations from falling into the deep freeze that had befallen American relations with China for twenty years. The President, as was his want, did not play the role of coordinator among these disparate positions, in part because he was immersed in the Middle East problem and working toward the Camp David accords. This extraordinary division of orientations in Washington invited activists in other capitals to exploit American uncertainty. Thus Peking set about to play the "Brzezinski card," while Moscow played the "Vance–SALT II card," and Hanoi assumed that it had a trick up its sleeve as it steadily reduced, in secret negotiation with Holbrooke, the terms it was demanding for normalization.

While the Americans were thus engaged in their separate explorations, the next move in world politics was initiated by Hanoi and Moscow. Acting clearly in response to Peking's efforts to sabotage their economy, the Vietnamese announced on July 1, 1978 that they wished to join CMEA, the Soviet–Eastern European version of the European Common Market. Amazingly, on the next day Moscow proclaimed the admission completed, although the process supposedly required time-consuming negotiations among all the member states. Next, the Vietnamese floated rumors that they had dropped all demands that the United States would have to provide economic aid as a precondition to normalization.

Thus in midsummer of 1978 it appeared as though Moscow and Hanoi were holding their own as far as commanding the attention of the appropriate leadership circles in Washington, while the Chinese had still not figured out how to turn their expanding relations with Washington to tactical advantage in their feud with Hanoi. In various ways they sought to attract attention to what they considered to be the evils of the Vietnamese. In July, with great fanfare and to the cheers of 150,000 people in Canton, PRC leaders—in an astonishing Oriental version of gunboat diplomacy—dispatched two boats to bring back "victimized and ostracized" ethnic Chinese from Ho Chi Minh City (formerly Saigon). When the Vietnamese refused docking privileges, and after the boats had circled for two weeks in the Gulf of Tonkin, Peking recalled them out of "compassion for the seasick crews." In August the Chinese closed down the flow of refugees at the now unfelicitously named "Friendship Gate" by insisting that everyone seeking to flee Vietnam would have to return to Hanoi and get "proper papers" from the Chinese embassy. Apparently there had been a command decision by China's leaders that the 150,000 refugees who had already poured into China were the limit, and it was left to lower-level bureaucrats to figure out how to justify a stop in the flow. The decision helped China's propaganda effort by instantly increasing the flow of "boat people" and thereby directing world attention to Hanoi's brutality toward its citizens. In Southeast Asia, however, the Chinese actions of the summer of 1978 were viewed with alarm because they seemed to verge again on the irrational. Furthermore, the ASEAN leaders were perplexed about what to do about the "boat people" and panicked at the prospect of absorbing huge numbers of Vietnamese, whether or not of Chinese ethnic origin.

All of the Southeast Asian countries were profoundly troubled by Peking's revival of the concept that all ethnic Chinese, no matter how many generations their families had lived abroad, could be the legitimate concern of China. Deng Xiaoping on June 5 explicitly stated that China would protect "victimized Chinese nationals," an unambiguous return to the older Chinese doctrine of *jus sanguinis*.

In the summer of 1978 Chinese intelligence must have picked up the signs of impending coordinated moves by Moscow and Hanoi. With great vigor Peking orchestrated a broadfronted diplomatic campaign aimed at preventing the isolation of China. By early July Peking's propaganda became conspicuously less provocative toward the Soviet Union; yet at the same time Chinese officials stirred up diplomatic initiatives with Japan, India, Eastern Europe, the United States, and the ASEAN countries, all of which had strong anti-Soviet as well as anti-Vietnamese implications.

On their eastern flank the Chinese brought new life to negotiations with Japan over a Treaty of Peace and Friendship which had been long stalled by the Chinese insistence that the treaty contain an "antihegemony" clause—their anti-Soviet code word. On August 12 agreement was reached when the Chinese, still holding to the inclusion of the clause, accepted the Japanese demand that there be a clarifying clause stating that the treaty was not directed against any specific power. However, when Vice Premier Deng went to Tokyo in September for the ceremonial signing of the treaty, he caused general consternation by discarding all subtlety and code words and publicly warning about the Soviet threat.

Toward South Asia the Chinese sent out signals that they were ready to repair relations with New Delhi. They soon got an agreement that the Indian foreign minister would visit Peking, a visit which did take place—much to the embarrassment and anger of the Indians—just as Peking launched its February 1979 invasion of Vietnam.

During the last two weeks of August, Chairman Hua Guofeng made state visits to Romania, Yugoslavia, and Iran. At every stop he sought to convey in none too subtle a fashion the idea that if Moscow wished to meddle in "China's back yard"— that is, Vietnam—then China would retaliate in Russia's back yard. Whether Peking's gesture succeeded in intimidating Moscow, or only made the Kremlin more determined to consolidate relations with Hanoi, is a matter for historical judgment.

During the summer the Chinese also arranged for Prime Minister Deng to visit Bangkok, Kuala Lumpur, and Singapore in a move designed to offset Hanoi's diplomacy toward ASEAN. The trip, however, came too late to intimidate the Vietnamese and, as we shall see, only added to Peking's frustrations.

The ace in the hole of Chinese diplomacy was their success in stimulating Washington to move toward normalization and thus balance the growing intimacy between Moscow and Hanoi.

Following Brzezinski's May visit to Peking, the head of the American Liaison Office in the Chinese capital, Leonard Woodcock, began to spell out to senior PRC officials Washington's concept of how normalization of U.S.–China relations might be completed. The Chinese must have been gratified when on September 19, two days after his Camp David triumph in bringing together Egypt and Israel, President Carter received the new head of the Chinese Liaison Office in the White House to urge full normalization. Ever since Watergate and the break in continuity with a new administration, it had been the Americans who had dragged their feet in carrying out what was implicit in the Shanghai Communiqué.

Now confident that Washington was committed to formalizing relations, Peking, on September 26 (one week after Carter's initiative), unilaterally terminated negotiations with the Vietnamese and mounted a ferocious campaign of vituperation against Hanoi while raising somewhat their criticism of Moscow. Hanoi responded two days later by informing Assistant Secretary Holbrooke that all was in order for the normalization of relations between the United States and Vietnam. They wished this fact to be instantly publicized, an event which would have left Peking isolated. Brzezinski was quick to recognize the absurdity of normalizing with Hanoi before normalizing with Peking, and the White House ordered that nothing more should be done in talks with the Vietnamese.

Hanoi, however, was not paralyzed. The Vietnamese found that Moscow had become increasingly exasperated with what they considered the blatant anti-Soviet character of the normalization negotiations between Washington and Peking. On November 1, Le Duan and Pham Van Dong arrived in Moscow, and two days later it was announced that Vietnam and the Soviet Union had signed a twenty-five year Treaty of Friendship, essentially identical to the treaties signed by the Soviets with India just before the Bangladesh war of 1971 and Afghanistan in 1978 (a treaty subsequently used by Moscow to justify its invasion of that country in 1980).

Two days after the open acknowledgment of the alliance between Vietnam and the Soviet Union, Deng Xiaoping began his Southeast Asian trip. In spite of the disturbing news of Moscow's backing of Hanoi, Deng's reception in Kuala Lumpur and Singapore was surprisingly cool. At no stop were there public displays of welcome. He used words to describe Hanoi which had not been heard since American diplomats a decade earlier had also tried to cajole the region into united opposition to North Vietnam. As we have already noted, he felt compelled to repeat China's absurd thesis about her right to support insurgents against states with whom Peking wished to maintain friendly relations; and to make matters worse he was disturbingly equivocal about protecting the rights of ethnic Chinese citizens. For Southeast Asians, the only positive result of Deng's visit was his visible astonishment that Southeast Asia was so very much more advanced economically than the PRC and his admission that China had much to learn from Southeast Asia. At last there seemed to be a consensus that the PRC was not a "model" for the development of other societies.

When Deng got back to Peking, the final steps were taken to reach agreement on normalization with Washington as a counter to Hanoi's newly formed treaty relationship with Moscow. The announcement on December 15 that U.S.–PRC normalization would take place on January 1, 1979 and that Deng would visit Washington later that month had the effect in the United States of submerging public concern about the Vietnamese-Soviet Treaty. In Southeast Asia, however, there was considerable reaction and manifest anxiety that the region would soon again be the battlefield of great-power competition. Indeed, ten days after the announcement by Washington and Peking of the decision to normalize, on December 25, Vietnam countered with its decisive invasion of Kampuchea. Although Pol Pot's regime was effectively dispersed, Deng could confidently warn Hanoi of inevitable Chinese counteractions, knowing that Washington would not want to spoil American euphoria about China by criticizing Peking for whatever it might do. The Vietnamese were in an equally self-assured state of mind because of their treaty with the Soviets. They also legitimized their increased dependency upon Moscow by citing to all concerned the abruptness with which Washington had ended negotiations with them and had instead normalized relations with China. Diplomatically the stage was set for Chinese forces to cross the border into Vietnam on February

17, 1979, thus making good on Deng Xiaoping's threat to "teach a lesson" to the leadership in Hanoi.

For Washington the pedagogical war created an awkward situation. The enthusiasts of the new friendship with Peking were somewhat embarrassed by the PRC's use of force, but hoped the conflict would pass quickly; while the critics of normalization, who were mostly concerned about breaking official relations with Taiwan, were generally of the belief that anyone who would beat up on the North Vietnamese could not be all bad. In the excitement over normalization, Washington wished to soft-pedal the idea that United States diplomacy might have contributed to either the initial Vietnamese invasion of Kampuchea or the Chinese invasion of Vietnam; yet Washington was aware of the danger of war. On November 5, two days after the announcement of the Soviet-Vietnamese Treaty, the United States notified all members of the U.N. Security Council that American intelligence believed a Vietnamese attack on Kampuchea was imminent. U.S. officials asked each country to do what it could to prevent such a conflict. This could be seen as an ineffectual attempt to elicit Soviet help in restraining Vietnam, a move which Southeast Asian leaders interpreted as a sign of Washington's impotence in the emerging crisis.

Indeed, the leaders of the ASEAN countries had increasingly mixed feelings about Washington's enthusiasm for normalization with Peking. They welcomed, as did the Japanese, any move that reduced tensions in East Asia, but they were deeply concerned that Washington's focus was almost entirely upon the "triangular" diplomacy involving Moscow-Peking-Washington and the issue of Taiwan. Washington seemed blind to the issues between Peking and Hanoi and to the prospect that the PRC might use its new relationship with the United States not to challenge the Soviet Union but to expand its influence in Southeast Asia, a region the United States seemed all too anxious to forget.

Historians will have great difficulties with the crucial year of 1978 as they attempt to distinguish reactions from provocative initiatives in the complex interactions of Hanoi, Peking, Moscow, Washington, and the ASEAN capitals. Nearly every move by each of the parties can be seen as either a thrust or a parry, and in each instance it is debatable whether actions were appropriate or provocative, whether they signaled intended purposes or only confused matters. The problem of judgment is made even more complex because behind the chronology of manifest actions there are the far more critical but also impenetrable questions of the precise times when decisions for action were taken in the various capitals. To what extent did each actor have foreknowledge about what the others were planning to do? How good were the various intelligence services, and how ignorant were the various decision makers?

Elizabeth Becker of the *Washington Post* reports, for example, that high Vietnamese officials informed her that Hanoi's decision to conquer Kampuchea was made at a Politburo meeting in July. If this indeed was the case, then it would seem that Peking's attempts at intimidation in the spring failed to deter and only drove Hanoi and Moscow closer. But then there is also the question of when did Peking, and for that matter Washington, first know of Hanoi's decision. This opens such further lines of questioning as to whether Washington might not have been able to deter Hanoi if it had managed its normalization moves with Vietnam, and with Peking, in a different manner. This is not the place to speculate on these important questions, but eventually the full story will come out, and only then will it be possible to evaluate the precise weight of the China factor in creating the Kampuchean crisis.

ASEAN Confronts the Kampuchean Crisis

Among the ASEAN countries there was general consternation and some confusion over Vietnam's conquest of Kampuchea and China's attempt to "teach a lesson" to Hanoi. The blatant Vietnamese aggression and Hanoi's establishment of a puppet government in Phnom Penh under Heng Samrin suggested that the "domino theory" was valid at least for Indochina. Thailand now confronted directly on its borders the battle-tested and well-armed Vietnamese army. China's limited penetration of Vietnam's northern border elicited mixed reactions. All of the ASEAN leaders quickly appreciated that China's conflict with Vietnam might give Thailand and the rest of

Southeast Asia some insurance against Vietnamese aggressiveness. Yet at the same time none welcomed the idea of China's armies crossing a neighbor's borders and becoming such an active factor in the affairs of Southeast Asia. Furthermore, there was anxious speculation over whether the Soviet Union would honor its new treaty obligation with Vietnam. There was thus considerable relief when Peking withdrew its forces from Vietnamese territory, even though the Chinese had failed to force Vietnam to reduce the numbers of its troops in either Kampuchea or Laos.

During 1979 the ASEAN governments increasingly coordinated their policies for dealing with the Kampuchean crisis. Hence, when the United Nations General Assembly met in the fall it was ASEAN diplomats, and not those of China or the superpowers, who overcame the opposition of the Soviet Union and its allies and mobilized world support for a formula which would resolve the Kampuchean war. ASEAN's approach, which also became the policy of the United States, called for (1) Vietnam to withdraw all of its forces from Kampuchea, (2) the establishment of a neutral and independent Kampuchea, (3) the nonrecognition of the Heng Samrin puppet regime, and (4) the continued seating in international bodies of the Democratic Kampuchean government, that is, the Pol Pot regime. This last item has made it somewhat awkward for the United States to claim to be in complete agreement with ASEAN since Washington had never recognized that barbaric government which may have exterminated nearly a quarter of the Cambodian people (indeed, perhaps a third, if it is held accountable for the full toll of the famine of the years 1979 and 1980).

Chinese policy toward Kampuchea and Vietnam is significantly different from both ASEAN's and Washington's. Broadly speaking, Peking is committed to a war of attrition against Hanoi. At very low cost to itself it is able to keep the Vietnamese on a war footing. The two-pronged Chinese approach involves, first, a low-level flow of arms to the remnant Pol Pot forces operating near the Thai border, a strategy that requires the tacit cooperation of Bangkok; and second, a continuous series of border incidents along the Sino-Vietnamese frontier, involving the PLA firing into Vietnam, so as to keep the Vietnamese fully mobilized for an indefinite period.

Peking's goal is very simple: it wishes immediately to punish Hanoi severely for its close reliance upon the Soviet Union, and in the longer run it aspires to bring Hanoi to its knees. The Chinese argue that if their pressure is maintained, the Vietnamese will sooner or later have to withdraw from Kampuchea and then the Chinese-supported Khmer Rouge (i.e., Pol Pot's forces) or a coalition government will replace the Heng Samrin government. Eventually, however, Peking would like to see the Soviets pull out completely from Vietnam; and to the extent that Hanoi must look abroad for security, it should develop a dependency upon China. Given the conspicuous and frustrating failure of U.S. armed forces to wear down the fighting will of the Vietnamese, Americans can only question the hubris of the Chinese and wonder whether they too will not in time be driven to greater anger and greater acts of violence against Vietnam.

Since the Vietnamese conquest of Kampuchea, the Chinese have been embarrassed by the reputation of the fanatical Pol Pot. In a search for cosmetic respectability, Peking apparently insisted that he be replaced as formal leader of "Democratic Kampuchea" by Khieu Sampan. In the summer of 1980, in a further effort to broaden its base of popular support, the Khmer Rouge made the astonishing announcement that it was prepared to abandon its Marxist ideology in the name of which it had committed some of the worst atrocities since Hitler. The Cambodian people apparently find all who would rule them abominable in as much as wherever the Khmer Rouge forces operate the population generally welcomes the Vietnamese conquerors; but once order is established by the Vietnamese, Cambodian nationalism revives and there is widespread opposition to the puppet Phnom Penh regime. For the United States and ASEAN it is unseemly that the non-Communist forces opposing the Vietnamese are the Khmer Serei whose leaders are little better than thugs and scheming bandits.

In the spring of 1980 strains developed in the ASEAN consensus about Kampuchea, largely because of different views about the China factor in Southeast Asia.

Specifically, Thailand and Singapore had become increasingly "hawkish." Bangkok could no longer close its eyes to the dangers of having Vietnamese forces on its border at a time when it was maintaining on its territory camps for Kampuchean refugees, within which Khmer Rouge and Khmer Serei elements operated. Thai attitudes had gone through significant change since 1978 when Bangkok was a leader in ASEAN's friendship campaign toward Hanoi. Until the Vietnamese conquest of Kampuchea made the policy absurd, the Thais went to great lengths to avoid provoking Vietnam. They clung to the wishful hope that after thirty years of warfare the Vietnamese might be inclined at last to concentrate on peaceful economic development. Even when Peking set out to "teach a lesson" to Vietnam, the Thais remained skeptical of Chinese intentions, in part because the Chinese were still supporting the illegal Thai Communist Party, composed of ethnic Chinese, and also because of China's earlier penetration into Laos during the Vietnam War. Gradually, however, Bangkok found that in order to prevent the consolidation of the Vietnamese puppet government of Heng Samrin it was necessary, step by step, to cooperate more openly in allowing Chinese aid to reach the Pol Pot remnants.

Most important of all, the new government of Prime Minister Prem Tinsulanond recognized in May 1980 that China's repeated threats to "teach another lesson" to Vietnam provided significant security for Thailand. The very fact that Hanoi was complaining that China had staged over five hundred attacks against Vietnamese territory in the six months following the withdrawal of Chinese forces made it clear that nearly 250,000 Vietnamese troops would have to be permanently stationed along the Chinese border. With another 250,000 necessary for the occupation of South Vietnam and 50,000 in Laos, this left only about 300,000 for the occupation of Kampuchea—an overall situation which would bleed the Vietnamese economy and society, thus making the Thais feel secure against the menacing Vietnamese.

Singapore also became more vociferously hard-line in opposing Hanoi's conquest of Kampuchea, but for somewhat different reasons. Above all, in 1976—soon after Hanoi's conquest of Saigon—Prime Minister Lee Kuan Yew discovered that he was no longer terrorized by the thought of the PRC subverting his country. Rather, he saw a new threat in the conspicuously growing Soviet naval presence in the region, which was certain to become worse as the Soviets gradually worked toward permanent basing arrangements in Vietnam. Previously Lee had worried about the appeals of PRC propaganda among the 85 percent of his people who are ethnically Chinese; and he had vigorously egged on the United States in its Vietnam War effort, as he hoped to gain more time to build a stronger sense of Singaporean national identity. However, after President Nixon's visit to China, Lee went there himself and found the country backward, lacking in potential appeal for affluent Singaporeans, and, above all, gratifyingly passionate in its condemnation of all forms of radicalism.

Prime Minister Lee not only concluded that Singapore had little to fear from such a hapless giant, but he realized that his population of industrious and skilled people of Chinese origin constituted not a potential target of PRC penetration but a great comparative advantage in the race among capitalists to penetrate the China market and exploit Peking's need for foreign assistance in its Four Modernizations. He thus blessed the efforts of Singapore businessmen to establish joint ventures in China, while at the same time jailing anyone who succumbed to the lure of communism.

Singapore interpreted the Vietnamese invasion of Kampuchea to mean that Hanoi and Moscow were now working hand in glove with each other and that American influence no longer existed in the situation. Lee worked hard for the ASEAN consensus against any international legitimization of the Heng Samrin government. While welcoming Chinese blows against Hanoi, Lee remained concerned that a Vietnamese collapse would result in a precipitous withdrawal from Kampuchea, leading to a Khmer Rouge takeover. This would bring Chinese influence to power in Phnom Penh, an eventuality that would cause panic in Kuala Lumpur and Jakarta. Lee, therefore, has called for the building up of some alternative leadership among the Kampuchean refugees. His appeals seem completely unrealistic, however, in view of the weaknesses of the two possible sources of that leadership, the Khmer Serei and Prince Sihanouk.

In the meantime, Lee has been pushing a strategem which the other ASEAN leaders see as a risky ploy. He wants to isolate Hanoi as much as possible on the assumption that Moscow's ultimate objective is to obtain access to the ASEAN countries, and that therefore the Soviets will not want to become completely isolated with Hanoi. Consequently, Lee expects that in time Moscow will pressure Hanoi to make concessions which would reduce the confrontation between Vietnam and ASEAN. The danger, of course, is that long before Moscow moves toward such a moderating role the Soviet tie with Vietnam will have become both enduring and legitimized in world politics.

The view from Jakarta is quite different from Bangkok and Singapore since the Indonesian leaders have no doubts in their minds that the one unambiguous external threat to the region is and will long be China. Their memories of Peking's support for the Indonesian Communists have not faded, and their suspicions about the loyalties of their own ethnic Chinese were confirmed when the majority of them quickly changed their citizenship in response to changes in the law. During President Sukarno's rule, PRC Premier Zhou Enlai negotiated an agreement with Foreign Minister Subandrio which required all Chinese in Indonesia to make a citizenship decision including the option of "Chinese citizenship, but resident in Indonesia." Over two million of the three million overseas Chinese in Indonesia chose this alternative since it gave them the best of both worlds. Then when this category was eliminated in 1980, almost all of the two million declared for Indonesian citizenship, suggesting to many Indonesians that their loyalties might not be very strong.

The intensity of the Indonesian leaders' distrust of Peking and of their country's ethnic Chinese was so great that Jakarta did not react strongly to Hanoi's invasion of Kampuchea. In the councils of ASEAN the Indonesians argued that the Vietnamese had made a "mistake," not an immoral act of aggression, and that great care should be taken not to unduly polarize relations or to force Vietnam into a corner. Although Jakarta accepted the need to have a common ASEAN position against the legitimacy of the Heng Samrin government, one of the key Indonesian decision makers described in 1980 the need for a viable Vietnam to balance Chinese power by saying, "Vietnam is like a cork in an upside-down bottle. If the cork is pulled out, the Chinese will flow down into all of Southeast Asia."

The Indonesians have steadfastly turned a deaf ear to Singapore's warnings about Soviet penetration in the region. Indeed, they have tolerated the dissemination of Soviet propaganda attacking the Chinese, a tolerance which has been influenced by the fact that the remaining Indonesian Communists are almost entirely ethnic Chinese.

With some reluctance, the Indonesian leadership decided in the spring of 1980 that once the reregistration of ethnic Chinese in the country was completed, certainly by August 1980, Jakarta would recognize Peking. Anti-Chinese elements in the leadership had little difficulty in getting a postponement of the decision in the wake of Chinese Foreign Minister Huang Hua's clumsy statements during his visit to Kuala Lumpur and Singapore about China's right to have Party-to-Party relations with revolutionary movements. In contrast, Vietnamese Foreign Minister Nguyen Co Thach was extraordinarily understanding and reassuring during his visit to Jakarta in June 1980. The postponement of recognition was awkward for Singapore in that Lee Kuan Yew has committed Singapore to being the last of the ASEAN countries that will recognize the PRC. (The Indonesian public was further put off about recognizing Peking and had their suspicions about the clannishness of the Chinese reconfirmed in the spring of 1980 when they saw on television in every *kampong* in the country their national badminton team play the PRC national team in Singapore before an audience which deliriously cheered the Chinese and booed Singapore's Indonesian "allies.")

Kuala Lumpur's views of the Kampuchean war and of the China factor in Southeast Asia have generally been quite similar to Indonesia's. The Malaysians, like the Indonesians, enjoy extolling the virtues of nonalignment. They are most insistent that ASEAN must never become a security arrangement. They have gone more than the extra mile in denying the possibility that Vietnam might become a threat to the peace of the region. Faced with an explosive domestic problem because of its huge Chinese minority and the long history of its Chinese community's support for the Malayan Communist Party, the Malaysian government has taken exceptional care not to provoke the PRC. Indeed, Malaysia was the first ASEAN country to recognize Peking.

Furthermore, the "neutralist" proclivities of the Malaysians have long made them want to hear Hanoi's side of every story, first during the Vietnam War when they saw Saigon and Bangkok as too closely tied to the United States, and then after the fall of Saigon they continued to believe that their relations with their strong Thai neighbor would be smoother if Bangkok had to worry a bit about Hanoi.

Malaysia has substantive reasons for being more than just annoyed by China's protestations about the legitimacy of Party-to-Party relations: the secretary-general of the Malayan Communist Party (MCP), Chin Peng, has been operating out of Peking since 1961, and the Voice of the Malaysian Revolution radio broadcasting from China continues to attack the Malayan government and supports the MCP's policy of armed insurrection which has strained the country since 1948. In November 1980, Musa Ahmad, chairman of the MCP, mysteriously left China after being there for 25 years and appeared on Malaysian national television to denounce China for managing the MCP.

These strains within ASEAN between hard-line Singapore and Thailand and the more accommodating Kuala Lumpur and Jakarta might have led to a break in the consensus about the Kampuchean war were it not for the harmonizing role of the Philippines and the crude and erratic aggressiveness of Hanoi.

Manila has performed a vital function in maintaining consensus within ASEAN, a task made easier because the political culture of most ASEAN countries places exceptional importance on consensus itself. Manila's task has also been made easier because each of the other ASEAN countries believes it has a special relationship with the Philippines: both Indonesia and Malaysia think of the Philippines as being especially close to them because of their common racial bonds; Bangkok feels that it has a special relationship with Manila because of their long intimacy as the two Asian powers within SEATO; and as for Singapore, Prime Minister Lee Kuan Yew and President Ferdinand Marcos have personally struck it off very well, each finding a bit of himself in the other. (In addition, the Singapore Air Force, lacking adequate air space over its small island, has become dependent upon Philippine bases for training its pilots.) The Philippines developed an early distrust of Vietnam at the time they supported the American war effort there. As for China, President Marcos made a brief move toward warm relations with Peking when, as a bargaining ploy against the United States in the negotiations to renew the agreements on Clark Field and Subic Bay, he sought to play his own "China card." Marcos was embarrassed when Peking told him that he should be more gracious toward the Americans, a development which cooled his ardor for relations with the PRC and left Manila's policy toward the Sino-Vietnamese conflict somewhere between the position of Singapore and Bangkok on the one hand and Jakarta and Kuala Lumpur on the other.

Since 1975, and even more strikingly since 1979, Hanoi's actions, with certain notable exceptions, have been peculiarly clumsy toward ASEAN. This development in Hanoi's diplomacy was striking because historically the Vietnamese, in contrast to all other Asian Communists and especially the Chinese and Koreans (who long ago made a virtue of self-reliance), have been remarkably skilled in soliciting foreign help and influencing foreign opinion. Yet since 1979 Hanoi has repeatedly damaged itself and caused ASEAN to consolidate against it, thereby making China seem to be an increasingly positive factor in Southeast Asia.

The incomprehensible stupidity in Hanoi's management of its relations with ASEAN was well illustrated in June 1980. Early in that month the Thais felt bold enough to ignore Vietnamese protests and to send some 36,000 Kampuchean refugees in Thai camps back across the border into their own country. Hanoi's claim that Khmer Rouge fighting men would be among those returned probably was correct, but what was absolutely certain was that the Vietnamese military attack across the Thai border and into a refugee camp on June 25 was maladroit and produced a reaction precisely the opposite of what the Vietnamese wanted. The timing of the attack was inept, if not totally irrational, since it actually caught Vietnamese Foreign Minister Thach in Bangkok as he was returning from his surprisingly successful six-day visit to Indonesia. Worse, the attack came on the eve of a three-day meeting of the ASEAN foreign ministers in Kuala Lumpur to which Secretary of State Edmund Muskie had been especially invited. As anyone except the Vietnamese would have predicted, the action instantly dissipated the strains building up within ASEAN and produced a substantial spirit of consensus against

Vietnam. Apparently the Vietnamese believed that they could readily intimidate the ASEAN leaders and gain concessions from them.

Hanoi's actions have thus made the PRC into a less threatening factor in Southeast Asia. Peking's promise not to stand idly by should Thailand be attacked has the ring of authority of a now increasingly legitimate actor in maintaining a balance of power in Southeast Asia.

The Uncertain Future

Two years after Hanoi's attempt to dominate all of Indochina it might seem that the policies of ASEAN (and the United States with respect to Kampuchea) were prevailing. The only trouble with such a conclusion is that there is a fundamental flaw in the goals of that policy: it is quite inconceivable that Kampuchea can in the near future become "an independent and neutral country"—the autogenocide which Pol Pot so effectively carried out in Kampuchea having destroyed educated Cambodians to a point where Kampuchea, for some time, will have to depend upon external aid from some source.

If that source of support for an "independent" Kampuchea were to be China, it would be unacceptable to not only Hanoi and Moscow but also Jakarta, Kuala Lumpur, and probably even Singapore. Support by Bangkok would be unacceptable to the Vietnamese. The British have suggested international support, but neither ASEAN nor Hanoi trusts the United Nations Secretariat and especially the current secretary-general. Washington has encouraged consideration of the name of Prince Norodom Sihanouk; but the Prince has double-crossed too many of those involved, including Thailand and China, to be trusted to be truly neutral.

Eventually order is most likely to come to Indochina through a process in which the Vietnamese military presence will recede but Vietnamese civilian cadres will help administer the country. The issue for the early 1980s is whether the ASEAN countries will be able to maintain consensus over the question of an acceptable degree of Vietnamese withdrawal.

Should there be an improvement in relations between Vietnam and the ASEAN countries, then Peking would no longer be seen in quite the same positive light as a tacit protector of ASEAN. (It was, of course, precisely this prospect that stability in Kampuchea could eventually lead to a cooling of Chinese-ASEAN relations which caused India to help its ally, the Soviet Union, and Moscow's ally Vietnam, by being the first noncommunist country to recognize the Heng Samrin government.) Any reduction in Hanoi's isolation would probably also make it easier for the Soviet Union to improve relations with at least some of the ASEAN countries. Such a development would in turn further reduce the need of ASEAN for better relations with China. At the same time, however, in varying degrees, all of the ASEAN governments would like to have the insurance that in the long run Peking will remain an enduring deterrent to the assertion of Vietnamese ambitions in Southeast Asia.

In short, the strategic dimension of the China factor in Southeast Asia is likely to involve a delicate balance in which good relations will depend upon Peking being seen as not unduly interested in the region nor too threateningly strong, but interested enough and strong enough to restrain Vietnam.

Aside from the consequences that would follow from any settlement of the Kampuchean war, future Southeast Asian attitudes toward China are most likely to be affected by economic developments, and especially the degree of success of China's Four Modernizations. Whereas Singapore and Hong Kong can foresee possible roles for their Chinese entrepreneurs in Peking's modernization program, in the rest of Southeast Asia it is more likely that China will become a strong economic competitor. This will be particularly the case if China succeeds in exploiting its cheap labor market and attracts foreign capital in joint ventures to export light consumer products, electronics, and textiles—the very fields which Indonesia, Malaysia, and the Philippines are trying to establish as the bases for their growing industrialization. Whereas South Korea, Taiwan, Hong Kong, and Singapore, the "East Asian Gang of Four," are likely to stay well ahead of China by moving to more advanced levels of technology, the rest of Southeast Asia may soon find China a threatening economic rival.

Thus, just as in the past, the Southeast Asian countries have been ambivalent about the PRC. Nearly all have radically changed from friendship to animosity or the other way around; hence, in the future there are likely to be further changes and uncertainties in their relations with the one billion Chinese to the north. As of 1980, Southeast Asians tend to be wary about the PRC, for it does not seem natural to them that any country should go through such extreme changes in political orientation in such a brief period of time as has China. Their suspicion is that any country which can make the radical changes that China has done since the mid-1960s is all too likely to make further changes.

Moreover, most Southeast Asia leaders are bemused, but also somewhat irritated, by Washington's efforts since the 1950s to influence their views of China—first to turn them against the PRC, and now to urge them to develop warmer relations than they are prepared for. None of the Southeast Asian countries shares America's current enthusiasm for the PRC, and all are concerned that Washington's idealization of Peking will soon yield imprudent attempts to build up China's military capabilities. It seems self-evident to Southeast Asians that long before China can be made into a meaningful military balance against the Soviet Union it will have obtained enough power to become a disturbing threat to Southeast Asia. Indeed, Southeast Asians know that guns can be pointed in all directions, and they worry that the United States will be unable to guarantee that any newly acquired Chinese weapons will only be aimed to the north. After all, the first Chinese adventure immediately after the establishment of the new relations with the United States was to the south. In Southeast Asian eyes, the pedagogical war against Vietnam suggested that China's power was about right as it is, enough to menace but not overpower Hanoi.

Those Southeast Asian leaders who have long seen merit in the doctrines of nonalignment are now being joined by those who see American power receding from the region in pressing the view that all should cooperate to keep Sino-Soviet competition out of the region. Thus even those who might be inclined to become more tolerant of the PRC are inhibited by fears that welcoming Peking would cause Moscow to knock on their doors.

Neither the PRC nor the USSR is currently seen as a legitimate principal actor in Southeast Asia, and a major uncertainty for the future is the question of which, if either, is going to become the more accepted. This question will determine the future of the China factor in Southeast Asia.

In the meantime, these trends point to the need for the United States to take a more activist role as a balancing force capable of giving greater stability to a region prone to volatile changes. The Southeast Asians complain that since the Vietnam War Washington has withdrawn from the region and its security commitments lack credibility; yet this stems in no small measure, as we noted at the outset, from their belief that American policy has been unduly China-centered. In spite of America's dramatic humanitarian support for both the "boat people" and the Cambodian refugees, there is a feeling of abandonment as Washington seems excessively fascinated by its new relationship with Peking.

According to this view, the United States has failed in the post-Vietnam situation to define, as a world power should, its relationship and responsibilities toward Southeast Asia. Consequently it has not just failed to limit the destructive impact in the region of the Sino-Soviet feud, it has actually exacerbated those tensions. Certain Southeast Asian statesmen are profoundly worried that Washington has mortgaged its Southeast Asian policies to Peking, whether by cavalierly playing a "China card" against Moscow or by being excessively timid about offending Chinese sensibilities. Even the leaders of the ASEAN countries who now welcome PRC pressures on Vietnam believe that Peking's mistakes helped produce the situation in which Moscow has been the sole winner of the Vietnam-Kampuchean crisis.

Before 1978 there were less than one thousand Russians in Vietnam; a year after China's attempt to "teach a lesson" to Hanoi there were over six thousand Russians. This development, in spite of Chinese protestations about their fears of Soviet encirclement, may not be contrary to Peking's wishes. Just as during the Vietnam War the Chinese blocked the transit of Soviet arms through China, in part because they hoped to force a Soviet naval confrontation with the Seventh Fleet, so now it may again be in China's interest to have Soviet naval forces at Cam Ranh Bay and Soviet air power at Danang confront American forces at Subic Bay and Clark Field. For as Singapore's elder statesman Goh Keng Swee has written, "The Chinese would regard the effect of the Soviet presence [at Cam Ranh Bay] on American and Japanese attitudes toward regional and global security to be a salutory one." Such a confrontation, however, does not serve U.S. interests, and therefore it becomes essential to differentiate America's objectives from those of the PRC in Southeast Asia.

Although ASEAN leaders call for greater United States leadership, particularly with respect to the intractable Kampuchean problem, Washington's practice of encouraging ASEAN to assume leadership, especially in the United Nations, has helped to strengthen the association. Yet Washington will have to take greater initiatives in the early 1980s to seek an easing of the polarization between Hanoi and ASEAN if it is to prevent a further expansion of either PRC or Soviet influence in the region. ASEAN efforts to arrange for an international conference on Kampuchean problems correctly identify the need for a diplomatic solution. The visits to Peking of Prime Minister Prem of Thailand in October 1980 and of Prime Minister Lee of Singapore in December succeeded in drawing China away from its uncompromising hard-line commitment to the Khmer Rouge and moving PRC leaders toward the idea of a united front of all Cambodians. This change in Peking's attitude encouraged the ASEAN leaders to pressure the various Cambodian factions to unite under the leadership of Prince Norodom Sihanouk. The always Machiavellian Sihanouk decided to play coy, and by the spring of 1981 it was far from certain that an effective united front could be formed, particularly since all the non-Communist leaders feared that should the front succeed it would only pave the way for a return to power of the Khmer Rouge, who would still command the guns.

In the complex and delicate maneuvering between ASEAN and Hanoi which will be taking place over the next few years, the United States will have to play a key role. First, it must provide Thailand with further security reassurances, largely by demonstrating that it has the capability of projecting military power into the region. Second, it must demonstrate flexibility toward Hanoi to the extent of reassuring the Vietnamese that if their troops are withdrawn from Kampuchea it should still be possible to create a "neutralized" Kampuchea in which there will be some room for Vietnamese civilian concerns. There are, of course, many more problems of detail that would have to go into the solution of the Kampuchean problem, but these lie well beyond the scope of this chapter.

Our overall policy conclusion is a very simple one: the United States can and should have positive relations with both the Southeast Asian countries and the PRC, but this cannot be done if we persist, as we have in the past, in making our Southeast Asian policy a function of our China policy. A more balanced approach requires that we go beyond the negative problem of not allowing the China factor to dominate our relations with Southeast Asia and make the positive commitment to our allies and friends in the region that we will not damage their interests as we build our new relationship with China.

Harry Harding

9

China and the Third World

From Revolution to Containment

With the end of the "development decades" of the 1960s and 1970s, it has become fashionable in the West to proclaim the decline of the Third World as a powerful force in international affairs. As evidence, scholars and policy makers point to the growing competition among Third World countries for regional influence, tensions between oil-importing and oil-exporting states within the developing world, the rivalries among developing countries for markets in the West, the steady disintegration of the nonaligned movement of the 1950s, and the emergence of a group of newly industrialized states whose

HARRY HARDING *is associate professor of political science at Stanford University. Educated at Princeton and Stanford, he taught for a year at Swarthmore College before joining the Stanford faculty in 1971. He is the author of* Organizing China: the Problem of Bureaucracy, 1949–1976, *and a number of monographs and articles on Chinese domestic politics, foreign policy, Sino-American relations, Chinese strategic and military policy, and the social sciences in China. In 1979–80, he served as coordinator of the East Asia Program at the Woodrow Wilson International Center for Scholars in Washington, D.C. The author wishes to express appreciation to Tonya Creek of the Johns Hopkins School of Advanced International Studies for her assistance in the preparation of this chapter.*

economies more closely resemble those of the developed countries than those of the rest of the less developed world. The
Third World, we are told, no longer exists.

To the Chinese, however, there still is a Third World. In
the official Chinese analysis, the developing countries still constitute a united, relatively homogeneous bloc with common
economic and political interests. Ever since the Yenan period
of the mid-1940s, in fact, Chinese Communist leaders have
described the developing areas of Asia, Africa, and Latin
America as a major force in international affairs, opposing the
efforts of imperialist countries at economic exploitation and
political domination. Even before they came to power in 1949,
the Chinese Communists shared Lenin's view that the national
liberation struggle of colonies and semicolonies against European imperialism was the principal feature of international
politics in the first half of the twentieth century. By 1956 Mao
Zedong had concluded that the contradiction between American imperialism and the developing nations was at least as
important as the struggle between the United States and the
socialist camp. And in 1977 authoritative presentations of the
official Chinese world view again argued that the Third World
was the "main force" in the ongoing resistance to the Soviet
Union's bid for global hegemony.

Moreover, ever since the establishment of the People's Republic in 1949, Chinese leaders have tended to depict their
country as an integral part of the developing world. As they
see it, China is linked to the Third World by common bonds
of history and ethnicity. While never completely colonized by
the West, China was nonetheless a victim of foreign invasion,
economic penetration, and cultural humiliation in the late
nineteenth century, becoming what Chinese Communist doctrine describes as a "semicolony" of the Western powers. In
the Chinese view, their country's historical experience is, therefore, more comparable to that of the Third World than to the
experience of any European country. As a result, even though
China formally joined the socialist camp in 1950, and although
Chinese leaders claimed membership in that camp long after
the Sino-Soviet split in the early 1960s, China's self-identification
has been more with the Third World than with the socialist
states of Eastern Europe or the Soviet Union.

China's principal foreign policy concern over the past thirty years has been to ensure its own security against encirclement or attack, first by the United States, and then by the Soviet Union. But China has seen its relations with the Third World as an important part of that effort, as well as the key to its longer-range goal of promoting fundamental change in the international political and economic order. By encouraging the Third World to reject the overtures of the superpowers and to demand an international order more conducive to "peace" and "economic construction," China has sought to stem the advance of American and Russian influence. By seeking to develop diplomatic and economic relations with important developing countries, particularly in Asia, China has tried to break out of the isolation and encirclement which it believes each superpower has, in turn, sought to impose upon it. And by occasionally supporting revolutionary movements within Third World countries, China has attempted to weaken or overthrow governments which had established relations with its principal adversaries.

Chinese policy toward the Third World has, of course, undergone substantial change since the Cultural Revolution, and particularly since the death of Mao Zedong in 1976. With the end of the Cultural Revolution, China began to show less interest in revolutionary change within the developing countries, even though it retained some residual connections with insurgent and guerrilla movements, particularly in Southeast Asia. After the death of Mao, Peking also displayed less concern with a transformation of the international system, and less interest in the Third World's demands for a new international economic order. Increasingly, too, China's policy toward the Third World has become directed against the Soviet Union, emphasizing the danger of Soviet expansion and encouraging Third World resistance to Soviet overtures. As China has become a status quo power, interested above all in containment of the Soviet Union, its opposition to American policy in the Third World has become ever more muted.

China's changing policy toward the Third World and its strategic alignment with the United States against the Soviet Union add up to a net gain for the United States in dealing with the developing countries. China can no longer be expected automatically to oppose American initiatives on regional and economic issues, as it did in the past, and can actually be anticipated to give some American undertakings its active support. But China will be no panacea for the United States. Because Peking's influence in the Third World is limited and its economic and military resources are in short supply, the impact of the "China factor" on America's relations with the developing world must not be overestimated. Moreover, one should not assume a full coincidence of U.S. and Chinese interests in the Third World.

China's Changing Policy Toward the Third World, 1949–1971

The notion that the Third World is one of the main progressive forces in international affairs, and that it could help China break out of isolation and encirclement, has been a nearly constant feature of Chinese foreign policy since 1949. Despite this continuity, however, China's policy toward the Third World underwent significant variation and development between 1949 and the end of the Cultural Revolution. While any periodization is bound to be arbitrary, it is still possible to identify four relatively distinct stages in China's evolving relations with the developing world.

The first period, from the establishment of the People's Republic in 1949 to about 1953, had unique qualities when compared to all those that followed. In those years, China hewed closely to the Soviet view of international affairs—a view of international politics as a direct confrontation between the socialist camp and the capitalist bloc. Despite their earlier attention to the role of the colonies and the developing countries in international affairs, the Chinese accepted the Soviet position that Asia, Africa, and Latin America would play only a minor part in the conflict between East and West. Peking's position was that the main feature of politics in the Third World would be revolutionary struggle, not only against colonial governments but also against the "bourgeois" regimes in the newly independent states. Moreover, Chinese leaders also believed that their own revolutionary history was a more appropriate model for revolutionary movements in the Third

World than was the Soviet Union's October Revolution. In accordance with these assessments, the Chinese provided substantial amounts of military and economic assistance to the Viet Minh forces fighting the French in Indochina, and rhetorical support and lesser amounts of material aid to Communist Parties in Thailand, Burma, Malaya, and the Philippines.

By 1953, however, the Chinese had returned to their earlier position that the Third World was a growing force in international affairs with an identity distinct from either the socialist or the capitalist camps. During the second period of its Third World policy, from about 1953 to 1957, China sought to improve relations with virtually all independent Third World governments, particularly in Asia and the Middle East. Its goals were to weaken the diplomatic isolation, economic embargo, and military encirclement imposed upon it by the United States and to encourage the developing countries to adopt a position of benign neutrality in the struggle between East and West.

China's more positive assessment of the governments in newly independent developing countries was prompted by Indian efforts to mediate the Korean War and by Burmese and Indian refusals to participate in the San Francisco conference on peace with Japan. In Peking's eyes, these developments indicated that the smaller countries in Asia might not, in fact, be eager to join the United States in an anti-Chinese coalition and that other developing nations might similarly be encouraged to seek greater independence from the West. At the same time it was assumed that these countries were not prepared to align themselves closely with the Soviet Union, except on a tactical basis. China's position was that the developing countries' desire for political sovereignty and economic development would make them significant "forces for peace," but not necessarily members of the socialist camp.

Accordingly, in 1953–54 Peking developed the five principles of peaceful coexistence as a framework for its improving relations with India and Burma. And in 1955, at the first Afro-Asian summit meeting in Bandung, Indonesia, it extended those principles to the rest of the Third World as well. In this way China sought to link itself with the nonaligned movement led by Nasser of Egypt, Tito of Yugoslavia, and Nehru of India.

In late 1957 China began to depart from this "Bandung line" in its relations with the Third World. Peking's hopes for broadened diplomatic relations in Asia were disappointed when new governments came to power in Burma and Thailand that were seemingly uninterested in accommodation with China, when Peking's relations with Indonesia were strained by incidents involving overseas Chinese, and when disagreements emerged between Peking and New Delhi over the Sino-Indian border. In addition, China experienced serious differences with Nasser over his suppression of the Egyptian Communist Party and his hostility to the Iraqi revolution of 1958. To the Chinese, these developments raised the ominous possibility that, contrary to their original expectations, Third World "nonalignment" might prove more helpful to the West than to the socialist bloc. This disillusionment with "wavering" Third World leaders was reinforced by the disappointment that Chinese leaders felt in their own intellectuals, who had made sweeping criticisms of Party leadership and socialist policies during the Hundred Flowers movement of 1957. Both in China and abroad, "bourgeois" elites had revealed themselves to be unreliable partners of the Chinese Communist Party.

These considerations produced a more militant and more differentiated policy toward the Third World between the late 1950s and the mid-1960s. Prior to this period, Peking had welcomed Third World nonalignment as a way of breaking through the American encirclement of China. Now it began to prod developing countries to more actively assault the interests of both the United States and the Soviet Union. During the Bandung period China had invited good relations with virtually the entire Third World. Now it began drawing clear distinctions among the developing countries, choosing friendly ties with some, correct but cool contacts with others, and hostile relations with still others.

China reserved friendly relations for a relatively small group of countries that were willing to align themselves actively with Chinese interests and policies. In Asia, China forged close ties with countries like Pakistan, Vietnam, and (before the 1965 coup) Indonesia, which had indicated their friendship to China and their hostility to India or the United States. Elsewhere, particularly in Africa, China looked for countries which supported Chinese demands for a thorough restructuring of the United Nations, showed an interest in the Chinese development model, gave national liberation movements sanctuary in their territory, or maintained a clear distance from both the United States and the Soviet Union. These friendly nations, including Guinea, Algeria, Ghana, Tanzania, and the Congo (Brazzaville), received from China greater economic assistance, more extensive cultural and technical exchanges, and a warmer diplomatic relationship. Peking hoped that a second Afro-Asian summit meeting, scheduled for Algiers in 1965 as a sequel to the Bandung conference, could provide a forum for these more radical states to recruit even greater support from the rest of the Third World. Unfortunately for China, a coup in Algeria on the eve of the conference required the indefinite postponement of the meeting.

With a few exceptions, China was willing during this period to have correct relations with any Third World country which had extended diplomatic recognition to Peking or had voted for the PRC's admission to the United Nations. But China's more assertive foreign policy, together with its growing polemics with the Soviet Union, made it difficult for Peking to move beyond correctness with most of the developing world. In contrast to the Soviet line, Chinese doctrine held that most Third World countries were controlled by "bourgeois" elites, that peaceful transition to socialism in such countries was impossible, and that the developing countries were therefore prime candidates for armed proletarian revolution. While China usually refrained from active support of revolutionary movements in countries with whom it had correct relations, Chinese leaders made no secret of the fact that they believed there was an "excellent revolutionary situation" in much of the Third World, as Premier Zhou Enlai asserted during a tour of Africa in 1963–64.

Finally, a third group of developing countries experienced hostile relations with China during the early and mid-1960s. Some, like India and (after the 1965 coup) Indonesia, had disputes with China over territory or over the status of overseas Chinese. Others, like Thailand, the Philippines, and Malaysia, were closely tied to the West. Still others refused to recognize Peking or, as in the case of a number of smaller African countries, broke relations with the PRC after charging it with subversion. Together with the apartheid states and the remaining colonies in Africa, such countries were identified by China as targets of revolution, and their Peking-oriented Communist Parties and national liberation movements received verbal, and in some cases material, Chinese support.

The outbreak of the Cultural Revolution in mid-1966 brought this third period to an abrupt end. China's assessment of the Third World, once complex and differentiated, now became stark and foreboding. Together with the United States, the Soviet Union, and the developed countries, most Third World governments were regarded as hostile and reactionary. Peking remained on friendly terms with only a few governments, notably Albania, Vietnam, Tanzania, and Pakistan. Elsewhere in the Third World, China withdrew its ambassadors (except for its emissary to Cairo), drastically reduced its economic aid, and renewed its support for armed struggle by Maoist insurgent forces against their local governments. "In Asia, Africa, and Latin America, the storm centers of world revolution," Peking declared, "people in an increasing number of countries have come to see the truth that political power grows out of the barrel of a gun, and have taken the correct road of armed struggle." The Third World was still seen as the force that would cause the collapse of the West. The "peoples of the world," as PRC Defense Minister Lin Biao put it in September 1965, would surround the developed "cities" from the developing "countryside." Yet violent revolutionary change would be required inside most Third World countries before they could successfully undertake their historic mission.

Chinese policy toward the Third World, then, exhibited a complex mixture of change and continuity during the first twenty years of the People's Republic. The main continuities were China's self-identification with the developing countries of Asia, Africa, and Latin America; its belief that the Third World was the principal cockpit for revolutionary change in international affairs; and its assessment that dealings with the Third World could further its own national security vis-à-vis the United States.

But change was apparent as well—change that was more

cyclical than linear in character. First of all, China's policy toward the Third World between 1949 and 1971 can be described as an alternation between two sets of attitudes toward the governments of developing countries. In one orientation, established Third World governments were regarded as reactionary at home and as accomplices of imperialism in the conduct of their foreign relations. In the second orientation, in contrast, established Third World governments were depicted as a progressive force in international affairs, seeking greater political and economic independence from the major developed powers. The first orientation led China to favor relations with revolutionary and leftist forces within the developing countries (a "united front from below"), as in the early 1950s and during the Cultural Revolution. The second orientation encouraged Peking to stress good relations with virtually all established Third World governments regardless of their domestic characteristics (a "united front from above"), as in the mid-1950s.

The alternation between these two sets of policies was linked to a large degree with Chinese domestic developments. Periods of conciliation toward China's own "bourgeoisie" were usually periods in which Peking was equally conciliatory toward "bourgeois" leaders in the Third World; while times of intensified class struggle inside China witnessed a harsher stand toward established Third World governments. But domestic developments cannot explain all the change. The alternation between conciliation and confrontation was also related to China's perception of the willingness of Third World leaders to participate in the international united front that Peking was attempting to form.

China's policy toward the Third World can also be described as an alternation between simplicity and complexity—between periods when Third World countries were seen as an essentially homogeneous international force and periods when China was keenly aware of the differences among the developing nations. In periods of simplicity, as in the mid-1950s and during the Cultural Revolution, China tended to treat all Third World countries in the same manner, whether friendly (as in the mid-1950s) or hostile (as in the Cultural Revolution). In periods of complexity, such as between 1957 and 1966, Peking drew sharper distinctions between more "progressive" and more "reactionary" governments within the Third World and treated the former more favorably than the latter.

China and the Third World since the Cultural Revolution

Since the Cultural Revolution (1965–1969), China's foreign policy posture and its relations with the Third World have both changed considerably. As a result of the Soviet invasion of Czechoslovakia in 1968, the growing military confrontation along the long frontier between China and the Soviet Union, and the Sino-Soviet border clashes of 1969, Peking began increasingly to regard the USSR, rather than the United States, as its principal strategic adversary. This meant that China's policy toward the Third World came steadily to assume an anti-Soviet, rather than an anti-American, character. Moreover, compared with the 1960s, China's policy toward the developing world in the 1970s was much more accommodating toward established governments, less focused on insurrectionary movements, and founded on the assumption that the Third World was a homogeneous and progressive international force.

In the Chinese analysis, the United States had, through a combination of military alliances, political subversion, and economic penetration, occupied an "unprecedented overlord position" in international affairs during the twenty years between the end of World War II and the escalation of American participation in the Vietnam conflict. But America's defeat in Indochina, combined with the rise of the Soviet Union, Western Europe, and Japan, served to weaken the relative power and influence of the United States. As a result, by the mid-1970s Washington was "forced to concede that it could no longer have its own way in the world."

The Soviet Union, in contrast, was described not only as the first socialist state to have degenerated into a revisionist society, but also as the first socialist country to have become a full-fledged imperialist power, seeking—like England, France, Germany, and the United States before it—nothing less than full world hegemony. In the Chinese view, Moscow had taken advantage of the American quagmire in Vietnam to "develop its own strength [and] narrow the gap in economic development between itself and the United States" and to "immensely expand" its military power. According to Peking, Moscow's "aggressive ambitions" exceeded those of the United States, and the repressive character of the Soviet system enabled Moscow to develop military capabilities far beyond those of America.

In 1974, therefore, China announced its conclusion that international politics had undergone "great upheaval, great division, and great realignment" in the 1960s. The main features of this realignment were the disintegration of the socialist camp, largely as a result of the Sino-Soviet split; a comparable weakening of the Western alliance, primarily as a result of the decline in the relative power of the United States; the reorientation of American foreign policy from the offensive to the defensive; and the evolution of the Soviet Union into a "social-imperialist" power that could compete effectively with the United States for world hegemony.

The Chinese assessment, presented by Vice Premier Deng Xiaoping in a major address to the United Nations in April 1974, was that the world was now divided into three parts. The First World consisted of the two superpowers, the United States and the Soviet Union, which were contending with each other for world domination. The Second World was comprised of the developed states of Japan, Oceania, and Eastern and Western Europe, which were believed to be seeking greater autonomy from the two superpowers. And the Third World consisted of the developing countries of Asia, Africa, and Latin America, which were not only attempting to preserve their political independence, but were also struggling for changes in the international economic order that could facilitate their economic and social modernization. China, while still a socialist country, was said to belong to the Third World.

In this Chinese analysis, known as the "theory of the three worlds," the principal feature of international politics in the post-Vietnam era was the opposition of the Third World to the attempts of both superpowers at global hegemony. With this in mind the Chinese abandoned the position, adopted in 1965, that only a small number of friendly states, orthodox Maoist political parties, and revolutionary movements were worthy of inclusion in an antirevisionist and antiimperialist alignment. Instead, the Chinese now argued that the united front should include virtually all established Third World governments, regardless of their domestic economic policies and political orientation. In line with this assessment the Chinese sought, as in the Bandung period, to establish first diplomatic relations and then economic ties with almost all developing nations.

In such a united front, national liberation movements and revolutionary insurgencies were to play a relatively small role, in contrast with the Cultural Revolutionary period. Indeed, the 1970s witnessed a steady decline in Chinese support for revolutionary movements within Third World countries. In part, this was to avoid offending Third World governments with which China wished to forge closer relations and which Peking hoped would support the PRC's admission to the United Nations. In part, too, it reflected the fact that the more militant policy of the Cultural Revolution had produced few benefits, and had served only to strain China's relations with virtually all the developing states. This tendency was evident first in the early 1970s when China broke off its links with a left wing insurgency in Oman and when it denounced guerrilla activity in Sri Lanka as inspired by "Trotskyists." It was also reflected in an attenuation of Chinese ties with the Palestine Liberation Organization (PLO) so that Peking might improve its relations with the more conservative Arab governments in the Middle East. By 1973 China was not supporting revolutionary movements in any country in Africa with which it had normal diplomatic relations. The change was also visible in Chinese rhetoric. References to armed struggle, people's war, and national liberation movements steadily declined through the 1970s, and the very term "revolution" came increasingly to mean resistance by Third World governments against superpower "hegemonism."

There have been limits, however, on China's ability and willingness totally to terminate its support for revolutionary change in the Third World. Some countries, such as Israel, Southwest Africa, South Africa, and (until its formal independence) Rhodesia, remain beyond the pale, and China has continued support for such "national liberation" movements as the PLO and the Southwest Africa People's Organization (SWAPO). Even here, however, Peking has become ever more willing to support diplomatic solutions to such problems as Palestine, Rhodesia, and Southwest Africa as a way of minimizing Soviet involvement in the final outcome. In Southeast Asia, China has continued to provide low-level support—principally radio broadcasting facilities—to the Communist Parties of Indonesia, Burma, Thailand, the Philippines, and Malaysia. This support, which is a major irritant in China's relations with the ASEAN states, continued for a variety of reasons. In part, it reflects Peking's concern that a total break with these Communist Parties would encourage them to develop ties to Moscow—or to Hanoi; in part, too, it is the result of domestic pressure inside China not to abandon fellow Communist leaders with whom Peking has historical and ideological connections.

Chinese policy toward the Third World since the Cultural Revolution has been remarkably undifferentiated. While acknowledging differences in the level of economic development, in the domestic policies of political leaders, and even in the international orientation of Third World countries, Peking has sought to minimize their significance.

> "Whatever the differences in the Political conditions of the Third World countries," one major Chinese statement declared, "they cannot change the fundamental contradiction between imperialism and hegemonism on the one hand and the countries and people of the Third World on the other. . . . Judging from their deeds and general orientation in international political struggles over the last thirty years or so, the oppressed nations in Asia, Africa, and Latin America are revolutionary and progressive as far as their essence and main aspect are concerned."

Soviet analyses which separate developing countries into "progressive" and "reactionary" categories, or even American discussions of the differences between "newly industrialized countries" and the so-called Fourth World, are described by Peking as underhanded attempts to weaken the unity of the developing world.

These then have been the main features of Chinese policy toward the Third World since the end of the Cultural Revolution. While these aspects have remained constant, there have been some major changes in emphasis from the early 1970s to the early 1980s. In fact, these changes have been significant enough to suggest that China's relations with the developing world can be divided into two further periods since 1971: a period of international economic reform and a period of strategic containment. During the first period, from 1971 to the end of 1978, China's policy toward the developing countries centered around China's support of Third World demands for a "new international economic order." It was reflected in a major Chinese economic assistance program and in Peking's efforts to formulate and disseminate a model of social and economic change for adoption by the Third World. In 1978, in contrast, China entered a second period, in which its Third World policy centered on the creation of an international united front against the Soviet Union. As part of this shift in emphasis, China (1) showed less interest in the "new international economic order" and a growing preoccupation with the political and military threat posed by the Soviet Union to the security of the developing world; (2) reduced its foreign economic assistance program, while maintaining relatively constant levels of military aid to developing countries; and (3) virtually ended its attempts to portray itself as a model for economic development and social change in the Third World.

Let us consider each of these changes in turn.

FROM ECONOMICS TO SECURITY

In the Chinese analysis, the legacy of past American expansion had been a postwar international economic order that favored the interests of the developed capitalist countries of the West at the expense of the interests of the Third World. Almost every aspect of that system—from the law of the sea to the conduct of multinational corporations, from the international monetary system to the international commodities markets—enables the developed states to extract natural resources and commercial profit from the developing nations. In the 1960s, the Third World had begun to try to compel the developed states to reform the international economy in ways that would be more conducive to their own development and sovereignty. China described this movement as the "just struggle of Third World countries to safeguard state sovereignty, protect national economic rights and interests, [and] develop their national economy."

Beginning in the early 1970s, therefore, China showed considerable interest in, and support for, Third World demands for a new international economic order. In their own press, and in statements before the United Nations and its agencies, the Chinese spoke approvingly of the major U.N. resolutions on international economic reforms and the proposals presented by the developing nations for a redistribution of global economic resources. Specifically, Peking expressed support for the formation of producers' cartels such as OPEC, the restriction or nationalization of multinational corporations, greater control over territorial seas and seabed resources, regional economic cooperation among Third World countries, the creation of an integrated commodities program to ensure stable prices for Third World exports, and the renegotiation of the foreign debt of the developing countries.

It is important to emphasize that the Chinese supported such proposals at a distance. Peking never joined OPEC, even though it became a petroleum exporter in the late 1970s; nor did it become a member of the U.N. Group of 77, even though it identified itself as a developing nation. Peking also refrained from active participation in the technical discussions involved in drawing up the detailed proposals outlined above. But China did place its diplomatic resources behind the concept of a new international economic order and supported the principle that it should be achieved through negotiation rather than confrontation. Samuel Kim, author of the most detailed study of Chinese participation in the United Nations, *China, the United Nations, and World Order,* has concluded that China's support for the new international economic order was a process of "mutual legitimation." China provided the concept with greater visibility than might otherwise have been the case, while simultaneously demonstrating to the Third World—which still remembered the radical Chinese foreign policy of the Cultural Revolution—that it was interested in cooperative diplomacy in the pursuit of common economic interests.

Since 1978, however, China's interest in the new international economic order has declined noticeably, with the concept receiving substantially reduced attention in both the Chinese press and Chinese statements to international organizations. In fact some PRC officials now privately suggest that international economic reform is both infeasible and unnecessary. Instead Peking increasingly argues that the Third World should devote its attention to strategic rather than economic issues—to combatting Soviet attempts at world hegemony rather than to restructuring the international economy.

The Chinese believe the ultimate targets of Soviet expansion are China, Europe, Japan, and the United States. But Moscow is not yet powerful enough to take on these targets directly. It therefore seeks to isolate and weaken China and the West by expanding Soviet influence in the Third World. More specifically, the Soviet Union is described as trying to gain control of a number of strategic points in the developing world through a series of "southward thrusts": a drive into central and southern Africa which began in the mid-1970s; a thrust into the Horn of Africa and the Middle East which was launched later in the decade; and a push into Southeast Asia which began with the formation of the Soviet-Vietnamese alliance in 1978. The aim of these "thrusts to the south" is to gain control over major sources of raw materials, and over the sea lanes which carry these materials to the West.

Soviet tactics in the Third World have changed considerably since the late 1960s, the Chinese argue. Initially Moscow employed the rather standard instruments of economic and military assistance to friendly Third World governments to gain influence and control, with the occasional subversion of unfriendly governments. All the while the Soviet Union used the banners of "anticolonialism," "socialism," and "antiimperialism" to represent itself as the "natural ally" of the developing nations. Somewhat later the Soviet Union began to draw distinctions between "progressive" and "reactionary" forces in conflicts within or among Third World countries as a justification for selective intervention on the side of client governments and political movements. This intervention took the form, first, of the use of proxy forces in the mid-1970s—the Cubans in Africa and the Vietnamese in Southeast Asia—and then of the direct introduction of Soviet forces in the invasion of Afghanistan in 1979.

In the face of this Soviet strategy, the Chinese insist, it is necessary to form a broad international united front, to join together the Third World (the direct victims of Moscow's "southward thrusts"), the Second World nations of Europe and Japan (against whom Soviet expansionism is ultimately directed), and, increasingly, the United States. In this connection it has been Chinese policy:

1. to encourage individual and collective Third World resistance to intervention by the Soviet Union and its proxies, and provide assistance to resistance forces in countries that are the victims of Soviet intervention, as in the case of Angola (1975), Zaire (1977–78), Kampuchea (1978–), and Afghanistan (1979–);
2. to urge the Third World to block Soviet participation in negotiations aimed at resolving conflicts among developing countries (as in the Middle East);
3. to support Third World countries such as Egypt and Somalia that have sought to dissolve their military and political links with the Soviet Union; and
4. to support action by Europe and the United States that assists countries that have been attacked by the Soviet Union or its proxies.

As China's attention has focused more sharply on the Soviet threat to the developing countries it has tried to rechannel Third World interest from the new international economic order to containment of the Soviet Union. In discussing the 1980 special session of the United Nations General Assembly on development, for example, one Chinese press account argued that the interest of the Third World in economic development required, as a prerequisite, concerted action against the Soviet Union: "The general debate at the U.N. special session further demonstrates to the people that peace and development are inseparable. Without peace, there can be no talk of economic development. And only by fighting hegemonism can world peace be safeguarded."

THE DECLINE OF ECONOMIC ASSISTANCE

After having virtually terminated its foreign aid program during the Cultural Revolution, China undertook an ambitious program of economic assistance to developing countries in the early 1970s. New aid extensions rose from $16 million in 1969 to about $640 million per year over the next four years (Table 1). The new Chinese aid program was ambitious indeed. Within two years China extended more aid to the Third World

TABLE 1. CHINESE ECONOMIC AND MILITARY ASSISTANCE PROGRAMS, 1970–1978

Year	1 Economic aid extensions ($ million)	2 Economic aid deliveries ($ million)	3 Military assistance agreements ($ million)	4 Military assistance deliveries ($ million)	3 ÷ 1 Ratio of economic to military assistance
1970	781	70	65	30	.08
1971	563	190	80	60	.14
1972	607	260	80	75	.13
1973	600	240	25	80	.04
1974	282	255	85	25	.30
1975	366	180	40	85	.11
1976	150	315	145	80	.97
1977	182	225	50	70	.27
1978	185	215	90	55	.49
Average, 1970–73	638	190	62	61	.10
Average, 1974–75	324	203	62	55	.19
Average, 1976–78	172	252	95	68	.55

Source: U.S. Central Intelligence Agency, National Foreign Assessment Center, *Handbook of Economic Statistics*, August 1979.

than in the sixteen years between 1954 and 1969. New extensions were nearly ten times the annual level attained in the 1950s and 1960s.

To be sure, a substantial proportion of the $2.6 billion in aid extended by China between 1970 and 1973 was earmarked for a single showcase project: the Tanzam Railroad, designed to give Zambia a rail outlet to the sea that would not pass through the white regimes of southern Africa. But the remainder of the aid, some $2.2 billion in all, went to smaller projects in twenty-four African, five Asian, five Middle Eastern, and three Latin American countries. This increase in both the amount of aid and the number of recipients was linked to

China's desire to develop diplomatic relations with important Third World countries, establish its credentials as a leader of the developing nations, and—initially—to win support for its admission to the United Nations.

In the latter part of the 1970s, however, China's foreign aid extensions dropped drastically, from the $600 million per year mentioned above to an average of $324 million per year during 1974–75, and to an average of about $170 million per year in 1977–78. This decline in economic assistance appears to have been caused by several factors. For one thing, by the mid-1970s China had already achieved the goals that had prompted it to increase its foreign aid program in the first place: it was a member of the United Nations, it had diplomatic relations with most developing nations, and it was regarded as a major force in the Third World. For another, China itself was experiencing serious domestic economic problems in the mid-1970s, particularly in 1976 and 1977, which made it especially difficult to maintain the levels of foreign assistance that Peking had been providing earlier in the decade.

But the decline in Chinese economic aid programs may also have reflected the shift in Peking's overall foreign policy orientation at about this time: the change from the earlier identification with economic trends in the Third World to the later concern with the geopolitical problem of Soviet expansion. Thus, during the second half of the 1970s, military agreements and deliveries were largely exempt from the reductions which were imposed on the civilian assistance programs (Table 1). As a result, since military assistance was remaining relatively steady while economic aid was declining, it came to assume a much larger proportion of China's overall foreign aid program, rising from about 10 percent of the total value of aid in the early 1970s to about 50 percent by the end of the decade.

FROM TEACHER TO STUDENT

In the early 1970s China placed considerable emphasis on codifying and disseminating its own national experience as a model for Third World countries to emulate. This was not a model of people's war or armed revolution, as had been the case in the early 1960s and during the Cultural Revolution.

Rather, it was a model of economic and social development, embodying the familiar Chinese themes of self-reliance, labor-intensive industrialization, and agricultural modernization. Interestingly, however, the export version of the Chinese developmental model was not the Chinese experience unalloyed. Peking apparently concluded that it would not be feasible for other Third World countries to copy the Chinese example in its pure form. China's recommendation, therefore, was not that other developing nations reject foreign investment, as China had done, but rather that they regulate it and control it; not that they reject foreign aid, as China had done since its break with the Soviet Union, but rather that they accept only technology that was, in Peking's words, "practical, effective, cheap, and convenient for use"; not that they establish a socialist system, as the Chinese Communist Party insisted was necessary at home, but rather that they simply create more effective state controls over the national economy.

In the late 1970s, moreover, China made fewer and fewer claims to be a model for emulation by other developing countries. In part this was because China itself had come to believe that each country—including socialist countries—had to forge its own path, learning from the achievements and shortcomings of a number of other nations and not copying any single model. In part, too, this shift in emphasis reflected the fact that after the purge of the Gang of Four and the inauguration of the Four Modernizations, China was uncertain of its own course. China's post-Mao leaders, such as Deng Xiaoping and Zhao Ziyang, were not only repudiating the policies and programs of the past ten years, but were also questioning some of the basic assumptions about socialist development that dated back to the mid-1950s. At a time when China itself was experimenting with a wide range of economic reforms—from administrative decentralization to market socialism, from reducing the level of national investment to increasing the opportunities for consumer purchasing—Peking was hardly in a position to promulgate a model for other developing countries to follow.

These three changes—the shift from economic to security concerns, the decline in Chinese economic assistance programs, and the metamorphosis of China from teacher to student—are part of the broader transformation in Chinese foreign policy that occurred during the 1970s. In the early part of the decade, while China could no longer be regarded as a revolutionary power actively supporting revolutionary movements in other countries or disdainfully rejecting established international institutions and procedures, it still remained interested in promoting reforms of the international system. Moreover, in announcing the "theory of the three worlds" in 1974, Peking was also articulating, at least in theory, a "dual adversary policy"— a united front against both the United States and the Soviet Union. Even though the USSR was described as "the more ferocious, the more reckless, [and] the more treacherous" of the two superpowers, the Chinese still declared that "U.S. imperialism has not changed as far as its policies of aggression and hegemonism are concerned, nor has it lessened its exploitation and oppression of the people at home and abroad." China's own rapprochement with the United States was justified as a tactical maneuver to gain even a "temporary, vacillating, unstable, unreliable, and conditional ally" against the Soviet Union.

By the end of the decade, however, subtle but significant changes had occurred in the Chinese position. In the face of continuing Soviet expansion in such places as the Horn of Africa, Afghanistan, and Southeast Asia, Peking tilted even further toward the United States as a strategic partner against the Soviet Union's alleged quest for global hegemony. Normalization of Sino-American relations removed an important source of Chinese dissatisfaction with the United States. And growing Chinese interest in foreign capital and technology led Peking to strengthen its economic and scientific relations with Washington, as well as with the other advanced countries of Western Europe and Japan.

As a result of these three developments, Peking gradually redefined the international united front that it had been trying to form. PRC leaders made fewer and fewer references to the United States as an "imperialist" power, and the growing warmth in Sino-American relations suggested that, in fact if not in theory, China now regarded the United States as a member of the Second World rather than the First—that is, as a developed capitalist country which, like the former imperialist powers of Western Europe, had been forced by circumstance to abandon its hopes of global domination. China's relationship with the United States was no longer described merely as a tactical maneuver, but rather as a "strategic decision" that could bring Peking economic and technological benefits as well as greater national security. In effect, China moved from a "dual adversary" policy to a "single adversary" posture in which the Soviet Union was not simply China's *principal* enemy, but instead, together with such proxy states as Vietnam and Cuba, its *sole* enemy. It also ceased, to a large extent, acting as an international reformer and became increasingly a status quo power, concerned above all else with preventing the expansion of Soviet influence.

This broader transformation in Chinese foreign policy— from revolution to reform to containment—helps explain the changes in China's relations with the Third World between the early 1970s and the early 1980s. For one thing, it spurred China to downplay its former interest in economic issues and the new international economic order—a program which, after all, had been primarily directed against the United States—and to increase its advocacy of a strategic geopolitical alignment against the Soviet Union. For another, it has led China to assign the Third World a somewhat smaller role in its assessment of international politics. As China has become a status quo power rather than a revolutionary one, it has come to the conclusion that the developed countries—particularly the United States, Western Europe, and Japan—would be the most powerful and effective forces in an anti-Soviet united front. In the early 1970s China still regarded the developing countries as the main actors in the transformation of the international system. But by the early 1980s they had become, in Peking's analysis, merely the arena in which the global ambitions of the Soviet Union were being pursued.

An Evaluation of China's Policies toward the Third World

An evaluation of China's policy toward the Third World since the end of the Cultural Revolution requires attention to three sets of questions. First, what resources can Peking bring to its relations with the developing countries? Second, how skillfully has China applied its capabilities in pursuit of its objectives? And third, and most important, how successful has China been in achieving the goals of its Third World policy? In general, China's relations with the Third World have been characterized by the relatively skillful use of limited resources. This combination of skill and constraint has enabled China to achieve some, but not all, of its objectives in the developing countries.

LIMITED RESOURCES

Since the Cultural Revolution, Chinese leaders have repeatedly acknowledged that China remains a poor and backward nation, particularly in comparison with the two superpowers and with the more advanced and dynamic economies of East Asia. As such, despite its enormous size and population, China has relatively few material resources to devote to its policy toward the Third World.

These constraints are apparent, first of all, in China's military capabilities. The PRC's armed forces are large, but are plagued by limited mobility, obsolescent equipment, and lack of experience in combined air and ground operations. For countries bordering China, such as Vietnam and India, the People's Liberation Army, to be sure, has already proven itself to be a force to be reckoned with. And for other countries in East Asia the prospect of the eventual modernization of the PLA is grounds for concern about China's capabilities over the longer term. But unlike the Soviet Union or the United States, or even Britain or France, China lacks the ability to project military power far beyond its borders—unless, like Cuba, it were to become a military surrogate for a larger power willing to provide necessary logistical and financial support.

China can, of course, use military resources in more limited ways. It can provide weapons, training, and assistance to both established governments and insurgencies. Indeed, Chinese military support for Pakistan, Egypt, Tanzania, and the Pol Pot regime in Kampuchea has not been inconsiderable. But China's technological inferiority means that it has few sophisticated weapons available for sale to Third World governments and that it cannot be the principal source of supply for countries seeking a modern armed force. Accordingly, total Chinese arms exports between 1955 and 1978 totalled only $755 million, compared to about $5 billion each for Britain and France, $25 billion for the Soviet Union, and more than $50 billion for the United States. Even countries like Pakistan, which in the past had purchased substantial amounts of Chinese weaponry, have turned in recent years to other suppliers to obtain more sophisticated equipment. And given China's decreasing interest in supporting revolutionary and national liberation movements, fewer military resources have been channeled in those directions.

The constraints on China's capabilities are also evident in its foreign aid program. It is true that for a brief period in the early 1970s China was able to match or exceed new Soviet aid commitments. In general, however, China has not been able to compete with the major powers in terms of the total value of its economic assistance. China's foreign aid between 1954 and 1978 totalled about $2.5 billion, about one-quarter of that offered by Great Britain, one-third of that by the Soviet Union or by Japan, and about one-fortieth of that granted by the United States. The technological constraints on China's foreign assistance program are also significant, as reflected in the disappointing results of the Tanzam Railroad, China's showcase assistance project in East Africa.

Finally, constraints of a third kind have been apparent in Peking's diplomatic activities. As in the 1950s and 1960s, Chinese diplomacy remained focused on Southeast Asia, South Asia, and Africa, and, to a lesser degree, on the Middle East. Its activities in Latin America and the Caribbean, while increasing over the past decade, are still quite limited. Similarly, the PRC has not yet participated actively in detailed technical and functional international discussions, partly out of reticence, but partly because of its shortage of experienced diplomats and of knowledgeable professional personnel. Even in the diplomatic sphere, then, China still has not acquired a full global reach.

China's principal resources, therefore, are more rhetorical and symbolic than material. In the past, the appeal of its culture, the force of its ideology, the clarity of its world view, the size of its population, and the hospitality of its people have given China an influence in world affairs far beyond that which would have been predicted by an assessment of its material resources alone. One can argue, however, that China's advantages in these areas have been declining somewhat in recent years. China's history, culture, size, and future prospects will always give Peking a significant voice in international affairs. But some of its other symbolic resources have been dissipated. The process of de-Maoization has meant a repudiation of the ideology of self-reliance and revolution that some groups in the Third World (and in the West, as well) found so attractive in the late 1960s and early 1970s. At the same time, China's own uncertainty about its own social and economic programs and its search for ideas and assistance in Eastern Europe and the West have meant that Peking no longer has a coherent model of domestic development to export. In fact, as one observer has put it, "If [the Third World] continues to seek a 'Chinese model,' it might as well seek it in the West; going there via Peking makes little sense."

SKILLFUL STRATEGY—WITH SOME LAPSES OF JUDGMENT

Any Chinese strategist, however, would assume that his country's foreign policy would have to proceed on the basis of limited material resources. Indeed, the essence of Chinese statecraft has traditionally been the formulation of strategies by which the weak could overcome their material disadvantages and use available resources skillfully to defeat the strong. A second question, therefore, is how effectively Peking has used its limited capabilities to pursue its goals in the Third World. And the answer, paradoxically, is that China has been more skillful in employing the resources that are in short supply than the capabilities that are relatively more abundant. That is, Peking has used its limited military and economic resources more effectively in the Third World than its more abundant symbolic and rhetorical capabilities.

In its economic aid program, China has allocated its limited resources according to the principles of both dispersion and concentration. It has given relatively small amounts of aid to a large number of countries, but has concentrated the largest quantities in relatively few hands. As of the end of 1977, China had extended economic assistance to no fewer than fifty-five countries, including all but nine of the nations that had been recipients of Soviet aid. At the same time, the largest Chinese aid programs, comprising 27 percent of the total, were located in only three countries: Tanzania and Zambia, where the Tanzam Railroad was a symbol of China's emergence as a major international donor; and Pakistan, whose friendship has been a crucial element in China's efforts to ensure its security against both India and the Soviet Union. What is more, China has apparently avoided any head-to-head competition with Moscow in its aid programs. While Peking has given symbolic amounts of economic assistance to virtually all nations which have received aid from the Soviet Union, it has reserved its larger programs for those countries to which Moscow has given relatively less.

Similarly, China has focused its military assistance in relatively few countries, where it has been an effective symbol of its interest and support. Examples include Peking's provision of engines and spare parts for Soviet-built MIGs to Egypt shortly after Cairo's abrogation of the Soviet-Egyptian friendship treaty in 1976, and its extensive military assistance to Pakistan at times when the United States was reluctant to do so. In both cases, Chinese aid offered timely assistance to a strategically located country whose relations with its major ally were either broken or strained. But both Egypt and Pakistan later turned to the United States for the more sophisticated military equipment which, as mentioned above, Peking is unable to provide.

In both its civilian and military aid programs Peking has tried to maximize the impact of its limited resources by developing a style of behavior that could distinguish it from both the Soviet Union and the United States. The fact that China, itself a poor country, gave any economic assistance at all—and the fact that more than half of the recipients have had per capita gross national products higher than China's—may be more impressive than the limited amounts of aid China has been able to provide. Moreover, China has always emphasized the attractive and distinctive features of its aid program, as embodied in the "Eight Principles" of Chinese economic assistance formulated in 1963–64. According to these principles, the PRC would attach no strings to its economic aid, provide attractive financial terms, help the recipients become as self-reliant as possible, support labor-intensive projects, provide high quality equipment, and ensure that Chinese technical specialists would have the same standards of living as their counterparts in the recipient country. These characteristics also guided Peking's assistance program in the 1970s. They gave China a unique reputation, as Colin Legum, African specialist and editor of *Communism in Africa,* has put it, for "generosity and disinterest" in the Third World.

Intriguingly, it is in the area of rhetoric and symbolism that Chinese policy toward the Third World has been somewhat less effective, particularly after Peking began to demonstrate single-minded concern with containing the Soviet Union. This is not a new problem for the Chinese, who have often found it difficult to identify issues that are of real relevance to developing countries and to formulate positions on those issues that would attract Third World support. In the mid-1960s, for instance, China found that few developing countries shared its opposition to the United Nations and to arms control negotiations; few supported China in its border dispute with India and its ideological confrontation with the Soviet Union; and even fewer joined China in backing Indonesia's policy of "confrontation" against Malaysia. And yet these were the issues around which Peking sought to gain support from the Third World at the abortive "second Bandung" conference in 1965.

The same gap between Chinese policy and Third World concerns is also evident today, although to a lesser degree. China's problems in this regard are fourfold. First, Peking's world view, which stresses containment of the Soviet Union, is of only partial relevance to the Third World. In the eyes of many developing countries, China has overstated the danger of Soviet expansionism, and has exaggerated the degree to which united action against the Soviet Union is the principal task facing the Third World. China's tendency automatically to oppose forces in the Third World that it believes to be associated with Moscow has alienated a number of countries, most notably Mozambique and even Tanzania, which have tilted away from Peking as a result of Chinese policy in Angola. Indeed, China runs the risk of being perceived as highly manipulative—of seeking to inveigle other nations into joining the Chinese side in what is seen as essentially a bilateral dispute between Peking and Moscow. At the same time, China's declining interest in issues related to the new international economic order, however understandable it might be from a Chinese perspective, can only serve to make Chinese foreign policy less attractive to some developing states. In Samuel Kim's words, "China's moral and symbolic authority in the Third World geopolitics of nonalignment has been weakened by its almost blind ideological warfare against the Soviet Union, on the one hand, and by its growing political-strategic ties with the United States, on the other." As China becomes a status quo power, in short, it may find itself losing, rather than gaining, influence in the Third World.

Second, whatever the attractiveness of China's world view, many Third World leaders find gaps between Peking's rhetoric and its actual foreign policy behavior. The theory of the three worlds, still the official theoretical basis of PRC foreign policy, cannot explain China's growing strategic alignment with the United States, or its decreasing interest in a new international economic order. China's progressive rhetoric clashes with its close diplomatic and economic relations with Pinochet's Chile, Mobutu's Zaire, and, in the past, with the Iran of the Shah. China's talk of self-determination and national liberation contradicts its opposition to the independence of Bangladesh in 1971 and its initial veto of that country's membership in the United Nations. And given its repeated denunciations of racism and apartheid, China has been embarrassed by its support, along with South Africa, of the National Union for Total Independence of Angola (UNITA) movement.

Third, China's self-identification as a Third World country is questioned by a number of developing nations. China insists, as we have seen, that it is a "developing country belonging to the Third World" and that it will "never become a superpower." But such claims are not universally accepted by the developing countries. As Lucian Pye's contribution to this volume indicates, suspicions of China's longer-term intentions and capabilities are particularly prevalent in Southeast Asia, where the PRC continues to give at least rhetorical support to insurrectionary Communist Parties, where China has a long tradition of cultural and political influence, and where large numbers of overseas Chinese have been a frequent irritant in

Peking's relations with its neighbors. The Chinese invasion of Vietnam in early 1979 served to increase this apprehension. But suspicions doubtless exist elsewhere, too, among Third World countries who perceive that China's real affiliation—and, increasingly, its self-identification—lies more with the developed countries of the West than with the Third World. Such doubts are fueled by China's size and population, its possession of nuclear weapons, its permanent membership on the U.N. Security Council, its refusal to join other developing countries in the Group of 77, and by Western discussion of a strategic partnership with China.

Finally, Peking tends to treat the Third World as an abstraction, ignoring, or at least downplaying, the divisions that distinguish some developing countries from others. China had, for example, steadfastly opposed the tendency to divide the less developed countries into a "Third World," comprising those nations which are experiencing substantial economic growth, and a "Fourth World," made up of those countries enjoying little or no economic development. It has devoted little attention to the differences between oil-exporting and oil-importing countries within the Third World, or explained how developing countries which must import petroleum can meet the challenge of rising energy prices. Nor has Peking shown a deep interest in the causes of local and regional conflict within the Third World, such as that between Iran and Iraq, or between Ethiopia and Somalia. In each case, China's position has been to warn that the "two superpowers," or, more recently, the Soviet Union alone, were attempting to create artificial distinctions within the Third World or were trying to manipulate local conflicts among the developing states as part of a strategy of global hegemonism.

MIXED RESULTS

Given the relatively limited resources it has to devote to foreign policy, and its occasional lapses in strategic judgment, it is not surprising that China has achieved only mixed results in its relations with the Third World. As a general rule, China has been much better able to achieve its bilateral goals in the Third World—the development of good working relations with a large number of developing nations—than to attain its broader strategic objective of limiting the expansion of Soviet influence.

In bilateral terms, China's main objectives have been to achieve formal diplomatic relations with Third World countries; to obtain, in the early 1970s, support for its admission to the United Nations; and to develop beneficial economic and technical ties with the Third World. These objectives have largely been achieved. China is now, thanks in large part to support from the Third World, a member of the United Nations. It has diplomatic relations with all but a handful of Third World states, largely in Latin America, the area that traditionally has been of lowest priority to Peking. The surplus China earns regularly in its trade with the Third World has, until recently, been able to offset the deficits it runs in its trade with more developed states. And in the mid-1970s China was buying about one-half of its imported crude materials (including most of its imported crude rubber and all of its imported petroleum), between one-third and one-half of its imported nonferrous metals, and between one-fifth and one-fourth of its imported food stuffs from the Third World.

And yet despite the dramatic improvement in China's relations with most Third World countries since the Cultural Revolution, there remain a number of developing countries with whom Peking's relations remain strained. These include countries in Latin America and Africa which still recognize Taipei, largely for ideological reasons. There are developing countries which are aligned with the Soviet Union, particularly Cuba, Vietnam, Angola, Mozambique, Ethiopia, and South Yemen. And, above all, there are important countries in Asia, particularly India and Indonesia, whose past confrontations with China still hamper the improvement of bilateral relations with Peking.

Moreover, as Alan Hutchison, author of *China's African Revolution,* has pointed out, there have been no "Third World Albanias"—no Third World countries that have chosen to align themselves as closely to China as has Cuba to the Soviet Union, or South Korea to the United States. A few developing countries have had close relations with Peking—Pakistan and Tanzania are probably the best examples—but even they have sought to diversify their diplomatic and economic options, somewhat at the expense of their relationships with China. Indeed, the failure of Tanzania to side with China in opposing Moscow's involvement in the Zaire crisis of 1977–78 demonstrates the limited rewards that China reaped from its largest economic investment in the Third World, the Tanzam Railroad. And the current vulnerability of Pakistan, the recipient of the bulk of China's military aid, to Soviet pressure in Southwest Asia also reveals the limitations on Peking's ability to maintain close alliances in the Third World. Given China's economic and military weakness, this situation should not be surprising. But it is still true that while China may have "friends all over the world," as Peking liked to boast in the 1970s, it has no allies, and few quasi-allies, among the developing nations. Few countries have been willing to take the Chinese side in the Sino-Soviet dispute.

Although Peking's relations with most Third World countries are relatively good, it is difficult to see comparable signs of success in the multilateral aspects of China's Third World diplomacy. China's influence upon the restructuring of the international economy and Soviet expansion in the Third World has in each case been minimal. While supporting the concept of a new international economic order, Peking has made few concrete proposals on international economic issues, and has not played a decisive role in international conferences and negotiations on "world order" questions. And while China has given diplomatic support and some military assistance to the anti-Soviet side in the crises involving Bangladesh, Angola, Zaire, Ethiopia and Somalia, and Afghanistan, the effect of China's involvement has been small. In the Bangladesh and Angolan affairs, China not only chose the losing side, but also took a position that lost it popularity with the Third World. When East Pakistan, with Indian support, sought to declare its independence from West Pakistan, China not only was unable to prevent the disintegration of its South Asian ally, but was also placed in the awkward position of opposing a clear instance of national self-determination. Similarly, during the Angolan civil war, China was not only unable to prevent the victory of the Soviet-supported Popular Movement for the Liberation of

Angola (MPLA), but also found itself supporting the same faction as South Africa. In each case, China's actions were both unpopular and ineffective.

Indeed, China's failures in Bangladesh and Angola may have encouraged Peking to take a more cautious role in later crises. In the Angolan and Cuban attacks on Zaire in 1977–78, the Ethiopian-Somali war of 1977–78, and the Soviet invasion of Afghanistan in 1979, China's position was less to intervene directly than to encourage Western countries, particularly the United States, to provide material support to the anti-Soviet side. In this sense, direct Chinese involvement in resisting Soviet advances in the Third World has been declining, not increasing.

Moreover, while China has provided moral encouragement and limited material aid to countries which have broken off relations with the Soviet Union, it is difficult to argue that the prospects of Chinese assistance were a major factor in their decisions. In 1976, for example, China was able to provide Egypt with military assistance following Cairo's abrogation of its friendship treaty with Moscow; and in the following year Peking assumed some of the Russian aid projects in Somalia after that country's break with the Soviet Union. Both countries later turned to closer cooperation with the United States, and their "China connection" turned out to be relatively short-lived.

To this general pattern, however, there is an important exception. Chinese military assistance to Pol Pot's forces in Kampuchea, channeled through Thailand, has played a significant role in sustaining Cambodian resistance to the Heng Samrin government, just as Chinese diplomatic support, together with that of the ASEAN countries, has enabled the Pol Pot regime to retain its seat in the United Nations. China has not been able to cause the collapse of the Heng Samrin government or to force the withdrawal of Vietnamese forces from Kampuchea, but it has been able to obstruct the consolidation of Hanoi's control over Indochina and demonstrate its determination to influence events in Southeast Asia even in the face of Soviet military pressures.

Outside Southeast Asia, then, China's direct role in resisting Soviet expansion in the Third World has been minimal. The

PRC has been a spectator—or, even more, a cheerleader—but not a major participant. But Peking's *indirect* role may well be greater than such an analysis would indicate. Through its persistent warnings about Soviet intentions and capabilities, and through effective contacts with anti-Soviet leaders in both the Third World and the West, China may well be helping create an informal united front against the Soviet Union. The strength and durability of that united front depend, of course, on many factors other than Chinese policy. But while Peking's direct participation in the anti-Soviet alignment may be limited, it may be playing a catalytic role of no small significance.

Implications for the United States

Peking's policy toward the Third World, in short, underwent substantial change during the 1970s. China, in essence, became a status quo power, concerned not with promoting a new vision of the international order, but rather with organizing opposition to what it regards as Soviet expansionism. China's interest in internal revolutions, or even in a new international economic order, declined markedly, although it has not completely disappeared. China's relations with most Third World governments are reasonably good, even though there remains some doubt about the validity of Peking's world view, and some suspicion about China's longer-term intentions. China's effect on developments within the Third World, particularly those conflicts reflecting the global competition between the Soviet Union and the United States, remains limited, however, largely because of the constraints on Peking's economic and military capabilities.

These developments in China's relations with the Third World must also be seen in the context of the broader reorientation of Chinese foreign policy during the same period. Throughout the 1970s China turned increasingly to the West, first as a counterweight against the Soviet Union, and then as a source of capital, technology, and assistance. While China still refuses to speak of an alliance with the United States, it is willing to talk of *alignment*—an intensive relationship, with both economic and security components, in which the two countries would jointly pursue their common strategic interests and in which the United States would contribute to China's economic, scientific, and possibly even its military modernization.

What are the consequences of these developments for American relations with the Third World? And conversely, how might current trends in the Third World affect U.S. relations with China? The effect of the "China factor" is mixed, but the positive implications appear to far outweigh the negative ones.

ECONOMIC PROBLEMS

China's interest in gaining access to Western capital, markets, and technical assistance will pose some problems for American policy toward the Third World. All three of these commodities are in short supply, and the United States will have to weigh the new requests made by China against the longer-standing demands of other developing countries. Chinese exports of labor-intensive manufactured goods will encounter not only growing protectionist sentiment within the United States, but also competition from other developing countries, particularly the industrializing states of Southeast Asia, but also some of the "newly industrialized states" such as South Korea. In the long run, many economists hold, such competition will be a healthy development. But the United States may also face the more immediate problem of determining what constitutes a fair share of the American market for Chinese products, particularly in areas covered by orderly marketing agreements. The dissatisfaction of both China and other textile exporting countries with the Sino-American textile agreement of 1980 illustrates the problem clearly.

Similar difficulties exist in the areas of technical assistance and development capital. China has had little difficulty in obtaining loans, on commercial terms, from American and foreign banks. But China's desire for concessionary interest rates and development assistance will be more difficult to meet. China's membership in the World Bank has already produced concern in other large developing countries, particularly India and Indonesia, that their access to low-cost loans from the International Development Association (IDA), the "soft window" of the World Bank, will be reduced. Unless the more developed states can agree to increase their contributions to IDA, the World Bank makes loans beyond the total of its capital and reserves, or IDA changes its present policy of allocating its funds proportionately to the population of the developing states, there is a strong possibility that China's share of IDA loans will come at the expense of other members of the Third World. Wahington's attitudes toward China's claims on World Bank resources and its willingness to support larger contributions to IDA in the Sixth and Seventh Replenishments, which will cover loans through the mid-1980s, will be important factors in resolving these issues.

Just as international financial institutions may be strained by China's opening to the West, so too will American foreign assistance programs. As of this writing, the United States appears unlikely to extend formal economic or technical assistance to China, except on a reimbursable basis or as part of ad hoc agency-to-agency exchange programs. Should the United States decide to do so, however, it would have to decide whether to accommodate China by increasing its total foreign assistance program, or by reducing the share allocated to other developing states. Given the lack of domestic support for foreign aid, and the steady decline in American foreign assistance programs as a proportion of GNP since 1960, the latter course is more likely than the former.

STRATEGIC ADVANTAGES

The likelihood that China will compete with other Third World countries for scarce American resources and for access to an increasingly protectionist American marketplace should be of some concern to those in the United States who are interested in maintaining good relations with both China and the other developing nations. On balance, however, China's new relationships with the Third World and the United States tend to reinforce, rather than undermine, American policy toward the less-developed countries.

In essence, the United States now enjoys the *end of Chinese opposition* to most of its initiatives in the Third World. Until the Sino-American rapprochement of the early 1970s, Peking consistently denounced American policy as exploitative and oppressive, urged Third World countries to loosen their political and military ties to the United States, and often supported insurgencies in developing countries that were closely aligned with Washington. Even in the late 1970s, China still emphasized, as part of the "theory of the three worlds," the conflicts of interest between the United States and the Third World, charging that Washington sought to maintain its "hegemony" in the developing areas and was unreasonably resisting Third World demands for a new international economic order.

More recently, however, China's opposition to American policy toward the Third World has virtually come to an end. China now refrains from actively supporting revolution in developing countries aligned with the United States. With the exception of South Korea, Peking no longer opposes an American military presence in the Third World, but actually encourages its expansion, so long as it can be justified as helping to stem Soviet expansion. China has supported Third World countries, like Pakistan, Thailand, Egypt, and Somalia, which have forged relatively close economic and political ties with Washington. And by its own actions Peking is demonstrating that it now recognizes and accepts the role that American capital and technology, both public and private, can play in promoting economic development in the Third World.

Thus on a wide range of specific Third World issues, China has become much more supportive than obstructive of U.S. foreign policy actions and objectives. While critical of American policy toward the Palestinian problem, Peking has been sympathetic toward the American attempt to mediate the negotiations between Israel and Egypt, symbolized by the Camp David summit of September 1978. Although China disapproved of the sanctions imposed by the United States against Iran in late 1979 and the abortive attempt to rescue the hostages in 1980, it also criticized Iran for its violation of international law and the principles of diplomatic conduct. Peking has supported the strengthening of ASEAN, the deployment of an American rapid deployment force in the Middle East, Western assistance to Zaire in 1978, and American aid to Somalia. It has, at least tacitly, approved of Western initiatives to secure the independence of Namibia and to solve the Rhodesian crisis.

And it has refrained from vigorous criticism of American policy toward South Africa or Washington's position on international economic issues.

In short, the changes in Sino-American relations and in Chinese policy toward the Third World since 1977 have led to increased Chinese sympathy, and even support, for American policy toward the developing countries. China no longer works against American initiatives in the Third World and has ceased trying to build an anti-American coalition of poorer states. China's anti-Soviet posture reinforces that of the United States. And as Sino-American relations develop further, it might well be possible for Peking to act in tandem with Washington in dealing with crises in the Third World. In some cases China can serve as an intermediary, conveying American interests and opinions to countries where it enjoys greater entrée than does the United States. In other instances Peking could act as an active partner, coordinating its policy with that of Washington. And in still other cases China could provide an alternative source of diplomatic, economic, and military support for countries which want to distance themselves from the Soviet Union but do not want to align themselves with the United States.

LIMITED BENEFITS FOR THE UNITED STATES

Despite this positive assessment, however, it is necessary not to overestimate the impact of the China factor on American relations with the Third World. For one thing, China cannot be expected to act as a surrogate for, or a client of, the United States. China will continue to hold views that diverge from those of the United States on a number of critical issues, including international economics, South Africa, and the Palestinian problem. Peking will seek to maintain some distance from Washington on still other issues, so as to preserve its reputation in the Third World as an autonomous international actor. And China may have learned, in the case of Angola, that it may pay a serious price if it is associated with unsuccessful American policy initiatives. For all these reasons, then, Peking will wish to demonstrate its independence from American policy toward the Third World. Such independence should be welcomed by Washington, however, for it will make Chinese support for American initiatives, when it is forthcoming, all the more meaningful and credible.

A second ground for caution is the possibility that the parallels between the two countries' policies toward the Third World could diminish, or even vanish, if domestic changes in either China or the United States produce major foreign policy consequences. Despite brave talk of "unity and stability," the political situation inside China remains fragile. And if the political balance within the Politburo in Peking should swing back to the left, even partially, it is not inconceivable that Chinese foreign policy could be affected. Ever since the mid-1970s there has been criticism inside China of both Peking's alignment with the United States and its policy toward the developing countries, particularly its failure to draw distinctions between "progressive" and "reactionary" regimes in the Third World. A change in political climate in Peking might produce leaders less likely to seek, or act upon, parallel interests with the United States in matters concerning the Third World. Or such a development might lead to a reassertion of Chinese differences with the United States over a broad range of issues involving international trade and development.

Chinese opposition to American policy toward the Third World could also reemerge if the United States were to undertake significantly new foreign policy directions in the 1980s. American intervention in support of conservative Third World governments facing left wing insurgencies, particularly in such areas as Latin America (where Chinese security interests are not at stake), could produce a critical response from Peking. A harder U.S. line in support of Israel, or a tougher stance on international economic issues, might also arouse Chinese opposition. And, of course, a deterioration of bilateral relations between Peking and Washington, perhaps because of disagreements over U.S. relations with Taiwan, would almost certainly affect Chinese attitudes toward American policy in the Third World.

Even if Sino-American relations remain friendly, and even if China and the United States can identify parallel interests in the Third World, we should not overestimate the assistance that China can provide in our relations with the developing countries. China's resources will remain limited, and, at least outside of Southeast Asia, its influence will remain marginal. And, paradoxically, the more closely China aligns itself with Washington, the less leverage it may enjoy in the developing world. In effect, then, the United States may already have played its "China card" in the Third World. The end of Chinese opposition to U.S. initiatives may prove to be more significant—and more helpful—than the provision of direct Chinese support for American foreign policy.

Appendixes

KEY DOCUMENTS ASSOCIATED WITH THE
NORMALIZATION OF AMERICA'S RELATIONS
WITH THE PEOPLE'S REPUBLIC OF CHINA

1. The Shanghai Communiqué (February 28, 1972)

President Richard Nixon of the United States of America visited the People's Republic of China at the invitation of Premier Chou En-lai of the People's Republic of China from February 21 to Februray 28, 1972. Accompanying the President were Mrs. Nixon, U.S. Secretary of State William Rogers, assistant to the president Dr. Henry Kissinger, and other American officials.

President Nixon met with Chairman Mao Tse-tung of the Communist Party of China on February 21. The two leaders had a serious and frank exchange of views on Sino–U.S. relations and world affairs.

During the visit, extensive, earnest and frank discussions were held between President Nixon and Premier Chou En-lai on the normalization of relations between the United States of America and the People's Republic of China, as well as on other matters of interest to both sides. In addition, Secretary of State William Rogers and Foreign Minister Chi Peng-fei held talks in the same spirit.

President Nixon and his party visited Peking and viewed cultural, industrial and agricultural sites, and they also toured Hangchow and Shanghai where, continuing discussions with Chinese leaders, they viewed similar places of interest.

The leaders of the People's Republic of China and the United States of America found it beneficial to have this opportunity, after so many years without contact, to present candidly to one another their views on a variety of issues. They reviewed the international situation in which important changes and great upheavals are taking place and expounded their respective positions and attitudes.

The Chinese side stated: Wherever there is oppression, there is resistance. Countries want independence, nations want liberation and the people want revolution—this has become the irresistible trend of history. All nations, big or small, should be equal; big nations should not bully the small and strong nations should not bully the weak. China will never be a superpower and it opposes hegemony and power politics of any kind.

The Chinese side stated that it firmly supports the struggles of all the oppressed people and nations for freedom and liberation and that the people of all countries have the right to choose their social systems according to their own wishes and the right to safeguard the independence, sovereignty and territorial integrity of their own countries and oppose foreign aggression, interference, control and subversion. All foreign troops should be withdrawn to their own countries.

The Chinese side expressed its firm support to the peoples of Vietnam, Laos and Cambodia in their efforts for the attainment of their goal and its firm support to the seven-point proposal of the Provisional Revolutionary Government of the Republic of South Vietnam and the elaboration of February this year on the two key problems in the proposal, and to the joint declaration of the Summit Conference of the Indochinese Peoples.

It firmly supports the eight-point program for the peaceful unification of Korea put forward by the Government of the Democratic People's Republic of Korea on April 12, 1971, and the stand for the abolition of the "U.N. Commission for the Unification and Rehabilitation of Korea."

It firmly opposes the revival and outward expansion of Japanese militarism and firmly supports the Japanese people's desire to build an independent, democratic, peaceful and neutral Japan.

It firmly maintains that India and Pakistan should, in accordance with the United Nations resolutions on the India-Pakistan question, immediately withdraw all their forces to their respective territories and to their own sides of the ceasefire line in Jammu and Kashmir and firmly supports the Pakistan Government and people in their struggle to preserve their independence and sovereignty and the people of Jammu and Kashmir in their struggle for the right of self-determination.

The U.S. side stated: Peace in Asia and peace in the world requires efforts both to reduce immediate tensions and to eliminate the basic causes of conflict. The United States will work for a just and secure peace: just, because it fulfills the aspirations of peoples and nations for freedom and progress; secure, because it removes the danger of foreign aggression. The United States supports individual freedom and social progress for all the peoples of the world, free of outside pressure or intervention. The United States believes that the effort to reduce tensions is served by improving communication between countries that have different ideologies so as to lessen the risks of confrontation through accident, miscalculation or misunderstanding. Countries should treat each other with mutual respect and be willing to compete peacefully, letting performance be the ultimate judge. No country should claim infallibility and each country should be prepared to re-examine its own attitude for the common good.

The United States stressed that the peoples of Indochina should be allowed to determine their destiny without outside intervention; its constant primary objective has been a negotiated solution; the eight-point proposal put forward by the Republic of Vietnam and the United States on January 27, 1972 represents a basis for the attainment of that objective; in the absense of a negotiated settlement the United States envisages the ultimate withdrawal of all U.S. forces from the region consistent with the aim of self-determination for each country of Indochina.

The United States will maintain its close ties with and support for the Republic of Korea; the United States will support efforts of the Republic of Korea to seek a relaxation of tension and increased communication in the Korean peninsula.

The United States places the highest value on its friendly relations with Japan; it will continue to develop the existing close bonds.

Consistent with the United Nations Security Council resolution of December 21, 1971, the United States favors the continuation of the ceasefire between India and Pakistan and the withdrawal of all military forces to within their own territories and to their own sides of the ceasefire line in Jammu and Kashmir; the United States supports the right of the peoples of South Asia to shape their own future in peace, free of military threat, and without having the area become the subject of great power rivalry.

There are essential differences between China and the United States in their social systems and foreign policies. However, the two sides agreed that countries, regardless of their social systems, should conduct their relations on the principles of respect for the sovereignty and territorial integrity of all states, non-aggression against other states, non-interference in the internal affairs of other states, equality and mutual benefit, and peaceful coexistence. International disputes should be settled on this basis, without resorting to the use or threat of force. The United States and the People's Republic of China are prepared to apply these principles to their mutual relations.

With these principles of international relations in mind the two sides stated that:

—Progress toward the normalization of relations between China and the United States is in the interests of all countries;

—Both wish to reduce the danger of international military conflict;

—Neither should seek hegemony in the Asia-Pacific region and each is opposed to efforts by any other country or group of countries to establish such hegemony; and

—Neither is prepared to negotiate on behalf of any third party or to enter into agreements or understandings with the other directed at other states.

Both sides are of the view that it would be against the interests of the peoples of the world for any major country to collude with another against other countries, or for major countries to divide up the world into spheres of interest.

The two sides reviewed the long-standing serious disputes between China and the United States. The Chinese side reaffirmed its position: the Taiwan question is the crucial question obstructing the normalization of relations between China and the United States; the Government of the People's Republic of China is the sole legal government of China; Taiwan is a province of China which has long been returned to the motherland; the liberation of Taiwan is China's internal affair in which no other country has the right to interfere; and all U.S. forces and military installations must be withdrawn from Taiwan. The Chinese Government firmly opposes any activities which aim at the creation of "one China, one Taiwan," "one China, two governments," "two Chinas," an "independent Taiwan" or advocate that "the status of Taiwan remains to be determined."

The U.S. side declared: the United States acknowledges that all Chinese on either side of the Taiwan Strait maintain there is but one China and that Taiwan is a part of China. The United States Government does not challenge that position. It reaffirms its interest in a peaceful settlement of the Taiwan question by the Chinese themselves. With this prospect in mind, it affirms the ultimate objective of the withdrawal of all U.S. forces and military installations from Taiwan. In the meantime, it will progressively reduce its forces and military installations on Taiwan as the tension in the area diminishes.

The two sides agreed that it is desirable to broaden the understanding between the two peoples. To this end, they discussed specific areas in such fields as science, technology, culture, sports and journalism, in which people-to-people contacts and exchanges would be mutually beneficial. Each side undertakes to facilitate the further development of such contacts and exchanges.

Both sides view bilateral trade as another area from which mutual benefit can be derived, and agreed that economic relations based on equality and mutual benefit are in the interest of the peoples of the two countries. They agree to facilitate the progressive development of trade between their two countries.

The two sides agreed that they will stay in contact through various channels, including the sending of a senior U.S. representative to Peking from time to time for concrete consultations to further the normalization of relations between the two countries and continue to exchange views on issues of common interest.

The two sides expressed the hope that the gains achieved during this visit would open up new prospects for the relations between the two countries. They believe that the normalization of relations between the two countries is not only in the interest of the Chinese and American peoples but also contributes to the relaxation of tension in Asia and the world.

President Nixon, Mrs. Nixon and the American party expressed their appreciation for the gracious hospitality shown them by the Government and people of the People's Republic of China.

2. Joint Communiqué on the Establishment of Diplomatic Relations between the United States of America and the People's Republic of China (President Carter's Address to the Nation December 15, 1978)

Good evening, I would like to read a joint communiqué which is being issued simultaneously in Peking at this moment by the leaders of the People's Republic of China:

"Joint Communiqué on the Establishment of Diplomatic Relations Between the United States of America and the People's Republic of China. Jan. 1, 1979.

"The United States of America and the People's Republic of China have agreed to recognize each other and to establish diplomatic relations as of Jan. 1, 1979.

"The United States of America recognizes the Government of the People's Republic of China as the sole legal Government of China. Within this context, the people of the United States will maintain cultural, commercial and other unofficial relations with the people of Taiwan.

"The United States of America and the People's Republic of China reaffirm the principles agreed on by the two sides in the Shanghai Communiqué and emphasize once again that:

"¶Both wish to reduce the danger of international military conflict.

"¶Neither should seek hegemony in the Asia-Pacific region or in any other region of the world and each is opposed to efforts by any other country or group of countries to establish such hegemony.

"¶Neither is prepared to negotiate on behalf of any third party or to enter into agreements or understandings with the other directed at other states.

"The United States of America acknowledges the Chinese position that there is but one China and Taiwan is part of China.

"¶Both believe that normalization of Sino-American relations is not only in the interest of the Chinese and American peoples but also contributes to the cause of peace in Asia and the world.

"The United States of America and the People's Republic of China will exchange ambassadors and establish embassies on March 1, 1979."

Yesterday, the United States of America and the People's Republic of China reached this final historic agreement.

On Jan. 1, 1979, our two Governments will implement full normalization of diplomatic relations.

As a nation of gifted people who comprise one-fourth of the population of the earth, China already plays an important role in world affairs—a role that can only grow more important in the years ahead.

We do not undertake this important step for transient tactical or expedient reasons. In recognizing that the Government of the People's Republic is the single Government of China, we are recognizing simple reality. But far more is involved in this decision than a recognition of reality.

Before the estrangement of recent decades, the American and Chinese people had a long history of friendship. We have already begun to rebuild some of those previous ties. Now, our rapidly expanding relationship requires the kind of structure that only full diplomatic relations will make possible.

The change I am announcing tonight will be of great long-term benefit to the peoples of both the United States and China—and, I believe, to all the peoples of the world.

Normalization—and the expanded commercial and cultural relations it will bring with it—will contribute to the well-being of our own nation, to our own national interest, and it will also enhance stability in Asia.

These more positive relations with China can beneficially affect the world in which we and our children will live.

We have already begun to inform our allies and the Congress of the details of our intended action. But I wish also to convey a special message to the people of Taiwan, with whom the American people have had and will have extensive, close, and friendly relations.

As the United States asserted in the Shanghai Communiqué in 1972, on President Nixon's historic visit, we will continue to have an interest in the peaceful resolution of the Taiwan issue.

I have paid special attention to insuring that normalization of relations between the United States and the People's Republic will not jeopardize the well-being of the people of Taiwan.

The people of the United States will maintain our current commercial, cultural, trade and other relations with Taiwan through nongovernmental means. Many other countries are already successfully doing so.

These decisions and actions open a new and important chapter in our country's history and also in world affairs.

To strengthen and to expedite the benefits of this new relationship between the People's Republic of China and the United States, I am pleased to announce that Vice Premier Teng has accepted my invitation to visit Washington at the end of January. His visit will give our Governments the opportunity to consult with each other on global issues and to begin working together to enhance the cause of world peace.

These events are the result of long and serious negotiations begun by President Nixon in 1972, and continued by President Ford. The results bear witness to the steady, determined bipartisan effort of our own country to build a world in which peace will be the goal and the responsibility of all nations.

The normalization of relations between the United States and China has no other purpose than this—the advancement of peace

It is in this spirit, at this season of peace, that I take special pride in sharing this news with you tonight.

3. Unilateral Statements by the Governments of the United States of America and the People's Republic of China at the Time of Normalization (December 15, 1978)

As of January 1, 1979, the United States of America recognizes the People's Republic of China as the sole legal government of China. On the same date, the People's Republic of China accords similar recognition to the United States of America. The United States thereby establishes diplomatic relations with the People's Republic of China.

On that same date, January 1, 1979, the United States of America will notify Taiwan that it is terminating diplomatic relations and that the Mutual Defense Treaty between the U.S. and the Republic of China is being terminated in accordance with the provisions of the treaty. The United States also states that it will be withdrawing its remaining military personnel from Taiwan within four months.

In the future, the American people and the people of Taiwan will maintain commercial, cultural, and other relations without official government representation and without diplomatic relations.

The Administration will seek adjustments to our laws and regulations to permit the maintenance of commercial, cultural and other nongovernmental relationships in the new circumstances that will exist after normalization.

The United States is confident that the people of Taiwan face a peaceful and prosperous future. The United States continues to have an interest in the peaceful resolution of the Taiwan issue and expects that the Taiwan issue will be settled peacefully by the Chinese themselves.

The United States believes that the establishment of diplomatic relations with the People's Republic will contribute to the welfare of the American people, to the stability of Asia where the United States has major security and economic interest, and to the peace of the entire world.

Text of the Unilateral Statement
by the Government of the People's Republic of China

As of January 1, 1979, the People's Republic of China and the United States of America recognize each other and establish diplomatic relations, thereby ending the prolonged abnormal relationship between them. This is a historic event in Sino-U.S. relations.

As is known to all, the Government of the People's Republic of China is the sole legal Government of China and Taiwan is a part of China. The question of Taiwan was the crucial issue obstructing the normalization of relations between China and the United States. It has now been resolved between the two countries in the spirit of the Shanghai Communiqué and through their joint efforts, thus enabling the normalization of relations so ardently desired by the people of the two countries. As for the way of bringing Taiwan back to the embrace of the motherland and reunifying the country, it is entirely China's internal affair.

At the invitation of the U.S. Government, Teng Hsiao-ping, Vice-Premier of the State Council of the People's Republic of China, will pay an official visit to the United States in January 1979, with a view to further promoting the friendship between the two peoples and good relations between the two countries.

4. The Taiwan Relations Act (April 10, 1979)

TEXT OF THE TAIWAN LEGISLATION ADOPTED BY THE CONGRESS, AND SIGNED INTO LAW BY PRESIDENT CARTER ON APRIL 10, 1979

TAIWAN RELATIONS ACT

[Public Law 96–8, Apr. 10, 1979, 93 Stat. 14]

An Act To help maintain peace, security, and stability in the Western Pacific and to promote the foreign policy of the United States by authorizing the continuation of commercial, cultural, and other relations between the people of the United States and the people of Taiwan, and for other purposes.

Be it enacted by the Senate and House of Representatives of the United States of America in Congress assembled,

SECTION 1. This Act may be cited as the "Taiwan Relations Act."

FINDINGS AND DECLARATION OF POLICY

SEC. 2. (a) The President having terminated governmental relations between the United States and the governing authorities on Taiwan recognized by the United States as the Republic of China prior to January 1, 1979, the Congress finds that the enactment of this Act is necessary—

(1) to help maintain peace, security, and stability in the Western Pacific; and

(2) to promote the foreign policy of the United States by authorizing the continuation of commercial, cultural, and other relations between the people of the United States and the people on Taiwan.

(b) It is the policy of the United States—

(1) to preserve and promote extensive, close, and friendly commercial, cultural, and other relations between the people of the United States and the people on Taiwan, as well as the people on the China mainland and all other peoples of the Western Pacific area;

(2) to declare that peace and stability in the area are in the political, security, and economic interests of the United States, and are matters of international concern;

(3) to make clear that the United States decision to establish diplomatic relations with the People's Republic of China rests upon the expectation that the future of Taiwan will be determined by peaceful means;

(4) to consider any effort to determine the future of Taiwan by other than peaceful means, including by boycotts or embargoes, a threat to the peace and security of the Western Pacific area and of grave concern to the United States;

(5) to provide Taiwan with arms of a defensive character; and

(6) to maintain the capacity of the United States to resist any resort to force or other forms of coercion that would jeopardize the security, or the social or economic system, of the people on Taiwan.

(c) Nothing contained in this Act shall contravene the interest of the United States in human rights, especially with respect to the human rights of all the approximately eighteen million inhabitants of Taiwan. The preservation and enhancement of the human rights of all the people on Taiwan are hereby reaffirmed as objectives of the United States.

IMPLEMENTATION OF UNITED STATES POLICY WITH REGARD TO TAIWAN

SEC. 3. (a) In furtherance of the policy set forth in section 2 of this Act, the United States will make available to Taiwan such defense articles and defense services in such quantity as may be necessary to enable Taiwan to maintain a sufficient self-defense capability.

(b) The President and the Congress shall determine the nature and quantity of such defense articles and services based solely upon their judgment of the needs of Taiwan, in accordance with procedures established by law. Such determination of Taiwan's defense needs shall include review by United States military authorities in connection with recommendation to the President and the Congress.

(c) The President is directed to inform the Congress promptly of any threat to the security or the social or economic system of the people on Taiwan and any danger to the interests of the United States arising therefrom. The President and the Congress shall determine, in accordance with constitutional processes, appropriate action by the United States to any such danger.

APPLICATION OF LAWS; INTERNATIONAL AGREEMENTS

SEC. 4. (a) The absence of diplomatic relations or recognition shall not affect the application of the laws of the United States with respect to Taiwan, and the laws of the United States shall apply with respect to Taiwan in the manner that the laws of the United States applied with respect to Taiwan prior to January 1, 1979.

(b) The application of subsection (a) of this section shall include, but shall not be limited to, the following:

(1) Whenever the laws of the United States refer or relate to foreign countries, nations, states, governments, or similar entities, such terms shall include and such laws shall apply with respect to Taiwan.

(2) Whenever authorized by or pursuant to the laws of the United States to conduct or carry out programs, transactions, or other relations with respect to foreign countries, nations, states, governments, or similar entities, the President or any

agency of the United States Government is authorized to conduct and carry out, in accordance with section 6 of this Act, such programs, transactions, and other relations with respect to Taiwan (including, but not limited to, the performance of services for the United States through contracts with commercial entities on Taiwan), in accordance with the applicable laws of the United States.

(3) (A) The absence of diplomatic relations and recognition with respect to Taiwan shall not abrogate, infringe, modify, deny, or otherwise affect in any way any rights or obligations (including but not limited to those involving contracts, debts, or property interests of any kind) under the laws of the United States heretofore or hereafter acquired by or with respect to Taiwan.

(B) For all purposes under the laws of the United States, including actions in any court in the United States, recognition of the People's Republic of China shall not affect in any way the ownership of or other rights or interests in properties, tangible and intangible, and other things of value, owned or held on or prior to December 31, 1978, or thereafter acquired or earned by the governing authorities on Taiwan.

(4) Whenever the application of the laws of the United States depends upon the law that is or was applicable on Taiwan or compliance therewith, the law applied by the people on Taiwan shall be considered the applicable law for that purpose.

(5) Nothing in this Act, nor the facts of the President's action in extending diplomatic recognition to the People's Republic of China, the absence of diplomatic relations between the people on Taiwan and the United States, or the lack of recognition by the United States, and attendant circumstances thereto, shall be construed in any administrative or judicial proceeding as a basis for any United States Government agency, commission, or department to make a finding of fact or determination of law, under the Atomic Energy Act of 1954 and the Nuclear Non-Proliferation Act of 1978, to deny an export license application or to revoke an existing export license for nuclear exports to Taiwan.

(6) For purposes of the Immigration and Nationality Act, Taiwan may be treated in the manner specified in the first sentence of section 202(b) of that Act.

(7) The capacity of Taiwan to sue and be sued in courts in the United States, in accordance with the laws of the United States, shall not be abrogated, infringed, modified, denied, or

otherwise affected in any way by the absence of diplomatic relations or recognition.

(8) No requirement, whether expressed or implied, under the laws of the United States with respect to maintenance of diplomatic relations or recognition shall be applicable with respect to Taiwan.

(c) For all purposes, including actions in any court in the United States, the Congress approves the continuation in force of all treaties and other international agreements, including multilateral conventions, entered in to by the United States and the governing authorities on Taiwan recognized by the United States as the Republic of China prior to January 1, 1979, and in force between them on December 31, 1978, unless and until terminated in accordance with law.

(d) Nothing in this Act may be construed as a basis for supporting the exclusion or expulsion of Taiwan from continued membership in any international financial institution or any other international organization.

OVERSEAS PRIVATE INVESTMENT CORPORATION

SEC. 5. (a) During the three-year period beginning on the date of enactment of this Act, the $1,000 per capita income restriction in clause (2) of the second undesignated paragraph of section 231 of the Foreign Assistance Act of 1961 shall not restrict the activities of the Overseas Private Investment Corporation in determining whether to provide any insurance, reinsurance, loans, or guaranties with respect to investment projects on Taiwan.

(b) Except as provided in subsection (a) of this section, in issuing insurance, reinsurance, loans, or guaranties with respect to investment projects on Taiwan, the Overseas Private Insurance Corporation shall apply the same criteria as those applicable in other parts of the world.

THE AMERICAN INSTITUTE IN TAIWAN

SEC. 6. (a) Programs, transactions, and other relations conducted or carried out by the President or any agency of the United States Government with respect to Taiwan shall, in the manner and to the extent directed by the President, be conducted and carried out by or through—

(1) The American Institute in Taiwan, a nonprofit corporation incorporated under the laws of the District of Columbia,

or (2) such comparable successor nongovernmental entity as the President may designate,
(hereafter in this Act referred to as "the Institute").

(b) Whenever the President or any agency of the United States Government is authorized or required by or pursuant to the laws of the United States to enter into, perform, enforce, or have in force an agreement or transaction relative to Taiwan, such agreement or transaction shall be entered into, performed, and enforced, in the manner and to the extent directed by the President, by or through the Institute.

(c) To the extent that any law, rule, regulation, or ordinance of the District of Columbia, or any State or political subdivision thereof in which the Institute is incorporated or doing business, impedes or otherwise interferes with the performance of the functions of the Institute pursuant to this Act, such law, rule, regulation, or ordinance shall be deemed to be preempted by this Act.

SERVICES BY THE INSTITUTE TO UNITED STATES CITIZENS ON TAIWAN

SEC. 7. (a) The Institute may authorize any of its employees on Taiwan—

(1) to administer to or take from any person an oath, affirmation, affidavit, or deposition, and to perform any notarial act which any notary public is required or authorized by law to perform within the United States;

(2) To act as provisional conservator of the personal estates of deceased United States citizens; and

(3) to assist and protect the interests of United States persons by performing other acts such as are authorized to be performed outside the United States for consular purposes by such laws of the United States as the President may specify.

(b) Acts performed by authorized employees of the Institute under this section shall be valid, and of like force and effect within the United States, as if performed by any other person authorized under the laws of the United States to perform such acts.

TAX EXEMPT STATUS OF THE INSTITUTE

SEC. 8. (a) The Institute, its property, and its income are exempt from all taxation now or hereafter imposed by the United States (except to the extent that section 11(a) (3) of this Act requires the imposition of taxes imposed under chapter 21 of the Internal Revenue Code of 1954, relating to the Federal Insurance Contributions Act) or by any state or local taxing authority of the United States.

(b) For purposes of the Internal Revenue Code of 1954, the Institute shall be treated as an organization described in sections 170(b) (1) (A), 170(c), 2055(a), 2106(a) (2) (A), 2522(a), and 2522(b).

FURNISHING PROPERTY AND SERVICES TO AND OBTAINING SERVICES FROM THE INSTITUTE

SEC. 9. (a) Any agency of the United States Government is authorized to sell, loan, or lease property (including interests therein) to, and to perform administrative and technical support functions and services for the operations of, the Institute upon such terms and conditions as the President may direct. Reimbursements to agencies under this subsection shall be credited to the current applicable appropriation of the agency concerned.

(b) Any agency of the United States Government is authorized to acquire and accept services from the Institute upon such terms and conditions as the President may direct. Whenever the President determines it to be in furtherance of the purposes of this Act, the procurement of services by such agencies from the Institute may be effected without regard to such laws of the United States normally applicable to the acquisition of services by such agencies as the President may specify by Executive order.

(c) Any agency of the United States Government making funds available to the Institute in accordance with this Act shall make arrangements with the Institute for the Comptroller General of the United States to have access to the books and records of the Institute and the opportunity to audit the operations of the Institute.

TAIWAN INSTRUMENTALITY

SEC. 10. (a) Whenever the President or any agency of the United States Government is authorized or required by or pursuant to the laws of the United States to render or provide to or to receive or accept from Taiwan, any performance, communication, assurance, undertaking, or other action, such action shall, in the manner and to the extent directed by the President, be rendered or provided to, or received or accepted from, an instrumentality established by Taiwan which the President determines has the necessary authority under the laws applied by the people on Taiwan to provide assurances and take other actions on behalf of Taiwan in accordance with this Act.

(b) The President is requested to extend to the instrumentality established by Taiwan the same number of offices and complement of personnel as were previously operated in the United States by the governing authorities on Taiwan recognized as the Republic of China prior to January 1, 1979.

(c) Upon the granting by Taiwan of comparable privileges and immunities with respect to the Institute and its appropriate personnel, the President is authorized to extend with respect to the Taiwan instrumentality and its appropriate personnel, such privileges and immunities (subject to appropriate conditions and obligations) as may be necessary for the effective performance of their functions.

SEPARATION OF GOVERNMENT PERSONNEL FOR EMPLOYMENT WITH THE INSTITUTE

SEC. 11. (a) (1) Under such terms and conditions as the President many direct, any agency of the United States Government may separate from Government service for a specified period any officer or employee of that agency who accepts employment with the Institute.

(2) An officer or employee separated by an agency under paragraph (1) of this subsection for employment with the Institute shall be entitled upon termination of such employment to reemployment or reinstatement with such agency (or a successor agency) in an appropriate position with the attendant rights, privileges, and benefits which the officer or employee would have had or acquired had he or she not been so separated, subject to such time period and other conditions as the President may prescribe.

(3) An officer or employee entitled to reemployment or reinstatement rights under paragraph (2) of this subsection shall, while continuously employed by the Institute with no break in continuity of service, continue to participate in any benefit program in which such officer or employee was participating prior to employment by the Institute, including programs for compensation for job-related death, injury, or illness; programs for health and life insurance; programs for annual, sick, and other statutory leave; and programs for retirement under any system established by the laws of the United States; except that employment with the Institute shall be the basis for participation in such programs only to the extent that employee deductions and employer contributions, as required, in payment for such participation for the period of employment with the Institute, are currently deposited in the program's or system's fund or depository. Death or retirement of any such officer or employee during approved service with the Institute and prior to

reemployment or reinstatement shall be considered a death in or retirement from Government service for purposes of any employee or survivor benefits acquired by reason of service with an agency of the United States Government.

(4) Any officer or employee of an agency of the United States Government who entered into service with the Institute on approved leave of absence without pay prior to the enactment of this Act shall receive the benefits of this section for the period of such service.

(b) Any agency of the United States Government employing alien personnel on Taiwan may transfer such personnel, with accrued allowances, benefits, and rights, to the Institute without a break in service for purposes of retirement and other benefits, including continued participation in any system established by the laws of the United States for the retirement of employees in which the alien was participating prior to the transfer to the Institute, except that employment with the Institute shall be creditable for retirement purposes only to the extent that employee deductions and employer contributions, as required, in payment for such participation for the period of employment with the Institute, are currently deposited in the system's fund or depository.

(c) Employees of the Institute shall not be employees of the United States and, in representing the Institute, shall be exempt from section 207 of title 18, United States Code.

(d) (1) For purposes of sections 911 and 913 of the Internal Revenue Code of 1954, amounts paid by the Institute to its employees shall not be treated as earned income. Amounts received by employees of the Institute shall not be included in gross income, and shall be exempt from taxation, to the extent that they are equivalent to amounts received by civilian officers and employees of the Government of the United States as allowances and benefits which are exempt from taxation under section 912 of such Code.

(2) Except to the extent required by subsection (a) (3) of this section, service performed in the employ of the Institute shall not constitute employment for purposes of chapter 21 of such Code and title II of the Social Security Act.

REPORTING REQUIREMENT

SEC. 12. (a) The Secretary of State shall transmit to the Congress the text of any agreement to which the Institute is a party. However, any such agreement the immediate public disclosure of which would, in the opinion of the President, be prejudicial to the national security of the United States shall not be so transmitted to the Congress but shall be transmitted to the Committee on Foreign Relations of the Senate and the Committee on Foreign Affairs of the House of Representatives under an appropriate injunction of secrecy to be removed only upon due notice from the President.

(b) For purposes of subsection (a), the term "agreement" includes—

(1) any agreement entered into between the Institute and the governing authorities on Taiwan or the instrumentality established by Taiwan; and

(2) any agreement entered into between the Institute and an agency of the United States Government.

(c) Agreements and transactions made or to be made by or through the Institute shall be subject to the same congressional notification, review, and approval requirements and procedures as if such agreements and transactions were made by or through the agency of the United States Government on behalf of which the Institute is acting.

(d) During the two-year period beginning on the effective date of this Act, the Secretary of State shall transmit to the Speaker of the House of Representatives and the Committee on Foreign Relations of the Senate, every six months, a report describing and reviewing economic relations between the United States and Taiwan, noting any interference with normal commercial relations.

RULES AND REGULATIONS

SEC. 13. The President is authorized to prescribe such rules and regulations as he may deem appropriate to carry out the purposes of this Act. During the three-year period beginning on the effective date of this Act, such rules and regulations shall be transmitted promptly to the Speaker of the House of Representatives and to the Committee on Foreign Relations of the Senate. Such action shall not, however, relieve the Institute of the responsibilities placed upon it by this Act.

CONGRESSIONAL OVERSIGHT

SEC. 14. (a) The Committee on Foreign Affairs of the House of Representatives, the Committee on Foreign Relations of the Senate, and other appropriate committees of the Congress shall monitor—

(1) the implementation of the provisions of this Act;

(2) the operation and procedures of the Institute;

(3) the legal and technical aspects of the continuing relationship between the United States and Taiwan; and

(4) the implementation of the policies of the United States concerning security and cooperation in East Asia.

(b) Such committees shall report, as appropriate, to their respective Houses on the results of their monitoring.

DEFINITIONS

SEC. 15. For purposes of this Act—

(1) the term "laws of the United States" includes any statute, rule, regulation, ordinance, order, or judicial rule of decision of the United States or any political subdivision thereof; and

(2) the term "Taiwan" includes, as the context may require, the islands of Taiwan and the Pescadores, the people on those islands, corporations and other entities and associations created or organized under the laws applied on those islands, and the governing authorities on Taiwan recognized by the United States as the Republic of China prior to January 1, 1979, and any successor governing authorities (including political subdivisions, agencies, and instrumentalities thereof).

AUTHORIZATION OF APPROPRIATIONS

SEC. 16. In addition to funds otherwise available to carry out the provisions of this Act, there are authorized to be appropriated to the Secretary of State for the fiscal year 1980 such funds as may be necessary to carry out such provisions. Such funds are authorized to remain available until expended.

SEVERABILITY OF PROVISIONS

SEC. 17. If any provision of this Act or the application thereof to any person or circumstance is held invalid, the remainder of the Act and the application of such provision to any other person or circumstance shall not be affected thereby.

EFFECTIVE DATE

SEC. 18. This Act shall be effective as of January 1, 1979.
Approved April 10, 1979.

5. Reference List
of Other Important Documentary Materials

1. Joint Announcement of the Chinese Government's Invitation to President Richard M. Nixon to Visit the People's Republic of China (July 15, 1971). Text in Henry A. Kissinger, *White House Years* (Boston: Little, Brown, 1979), pp. 759-760.
2. Joint Communiqué Announcing the Establishment of Liaison Offices (February 22, 1973). Text in Foreign Broadcast Information Service, *People's Republic of China*, February 23, 1973, p. A-1.
3. President Carter's Remarks to the Press after the Announcement of the Intention to Establish Diplomatic Relations with the People's Republic of China (December 15, 1978). Text in *Department of State Bulletin*, January 1979, pp. 25-26.
4. Chairman Hua Guofeng's Remarks to the Press after the Announcement of the Intention to Establish Diplomatic Relations with the United States of America (December 16, 1978). Text in *Peking Review*, No. 51 (December 22, 1978), pp. 9-11.
5. Vice Premier Deng Xiaoping's Remarks to American Senators that Taiwan Can Remain Autonomous after Reunification (January 9, 1979). The New York *Times*, January 9, 1979.
6. Congressional Hearings on the Taiwan Relations Act:
   Implementation of the Taiwan Relations Act: Issues and Concerns (Hearings Before the Subcommittee on Asian and Pacific Affairs of the Committee on Foreign Affairs, House of Representatives, Ninety-Sixth Congress, February 14-15, 1979).
   Taiwan Enabling Act (Report of the Committee on Foreign Relations, United States Senate, Ninety-Sixth Congress, March 1, 1979, Report No. 96-7).
   Taiwan Relations Act (Joint House-Senate Conference Report, House of Representatives, Ninety-Sixth Congress, March 24, 1979, Report No. 96-71).
7. Vice President Mondale's Speech at Peking University (August 27, 1979). Excerpts in the New York *Times*, August 27, 1979.
8. Remarks by Secretary of Defense Harold Brown at a Press Con-

ference in Peking (January 9, 1980). Reported in the New York *Times,* January 10, 1980.

9. Address by Assistant Secretary of State for East Asia and the Pacific Richard Holbrooke, "China and the United States: Into the 1980s" (June 4, 1980). Text in *Department of State Bulletin,* August 1980, pp. 49-51.

10. Republican Presidential Candidate Ronald Reagan's Statement to the Press on America's Diplomatic Relations with China and Taiwan. Excerpts in the New York *Times,* August 26, 1980.

Index

About The American Assembly

The American Assembly was established by Dwight D. Eisenhower at Columbia University in 1950. It holds nonpartisan meetings and publishes authoritative books to illuminate issues of United States policy.

An affiliate of Columbia, with offices in the Graduate School of Business, the Assembly is a national educational institution incorporated in the State of New York.

The Assembly seeks to provide information, stimulate discussion, and evoke independent conclusions in matters of vital public interest.

AMERICAN ASSEMBLY SESSIONS

At least two national programs are initiated each year. Authorities are retained to write background papers presenting essential data and defining the main issues in each subject.

A group of men and women representing a broad range of experience, competence, and American leadership meet for several days to discuss the Assembly topic and consider alternatives for national policy.

All Assemblies follow the same procedure. The background papers are sent to participants in advance of the Assembly. The Assembly meets in small groups for four or five lengthy periods. All groups use the same agenda. At the close of these informal sessions participants adopt in plenary session a final report of findings and recommendations.

Regional, state, and local Assemblies are held following the national session at Arden House. Assemblies have also been held in England, Switzerland, Malaysia, Canada, the Caribbean, South America, Central America, the Philippines, and Japan. Over one hundred thirty institutions have co-sponsored one or more Assemblies.

ARDEN HOUSE

Home of the American Assembly and scene of the national sessions is Arden House which was given to Columbia University in 1950 by W. Averell Harriman. E. Roland Harriman joined his brother in contributing toward adaptation of the property for conference purposes. The buildings and surrounding land, known as the Harriman Campus of Columbia University, are 50 miles north of New York City.

Arden House is a distinguished conference center. It is self-supporting and operates throughout the year for use by organizations with educational objectives.

Council on Foreign Relations inc.

About the Council on Foreign Relations

The Council on Foreign Relations is an educational institution, a research institute, and a unique forum bringing together leaders from the academic, public, and private worlds.

The purposes of the Council are several and overlapping: to break new ground in the consideration of international issues; to help shape American foreign policy in a constructive, nonpartisan manner; to provide continuing leadership for the conduct of our foreign relations; and to inform and stimulate the Council's membership, as well as to reach a wider audience, through publications and other means. The Council is private, and nonpartisan, and takes no positions as an organization.

The Council conducts meetings that give its members an opportunity to talk with invited guests from the United States and abroad who have special experience and expertise in international affairs. Its study program explores foreign policy questions through research by the Council's professional staff, visiting Fellows, and others, and through study groups and conferences. The Council also publishes the journal, *Foreign Affairs,* in addition to books and monographs. It is affiliated with thirty-seven Committees on Foreign Relations located around the country and maintains a Corporation Service Program that provides meetings and other services for its almost 200 corporate subscribers.

The Council's headquarters, staff, and library are located in New York City where most meetings are held. Some meetings are held in Washington and occasionally in other cities. The Council's basic constituency is its members, but it also reaches out to the broader public so as to contribute to the national dialogue on foreign policy.